THE DECLINE
OF AMERICAN
POWER

Also by Immanuel Wallerstein

The Modern World-System (3-vol.)

After Liberalism

Historical Capitalism, with Capitalist Civilization

Utopistics: Or, Historical Choices of the Twenty-first Century

The Essential Wallerstein

The End of the World As We Know It:
Social Science for the Twenty-first Century

THE DECLINE OF AMERICAN POWER

The U.S. in a Chaotic World

IMMANUEL WALLERSTEIN

THE NEW PRESS

NEW YORK
LONDON

Published in the United States by The New Press, New York, 2003
Distributed by W. W. Norton & Company, Inc., New York

Page 295 constitutes an extension of this copyright page.

ISBN 1-56584-799-7(pbk.)
ISBN 1-56584-831-4(hc.)
CIP data available

The New Press was established in 1990 as a not-for-profit alternative to the large,
commercial publishing houses currently dominating the book publishing industry.
The New Press operates in the public interest rather than for private gain, and is
committed to publishing, in innovative ways, works of educational, cultural, and
community value that are often deemed insufficiently profitable.

The New Press
38 Greene Street, 4th floor
New York, NY 10013
www.thenewpress.com

In the United Kingdom:
6 Salem Road
London W2 4BU

Composition by dix!

Printed in Canada

10   9   8   7   6   5   4   3   2

To William H. McNeill

who will not agree with everything,
but whose persistent large-scale vision
has been and will remain an inspiration
to all those who study the human condition

CONTENTS

[ix]

INTRODUCTION

The American Dream Between Yesterday and Tomorrow

September 11, 2001, was a dramatic and shocking moment in American history. It was not, however, a defining moment. It was merely one important event within a trajectory that began much earlier, and will go on for several more decades, a long period which we may call that of the decline of U.S. hegemony in a chaotic world. Stated in this fashion, September 11 constituted a shock into awareness, to which too many have responded with denial and with anger. Americans need to respond with as much clarity and sobriety as they can command. We need to try to preserve our best values and maximize our security amidst fundamental transformations of the world-system—transformations that we may affect but that we cannot control. We need to join with others elsewhere in the construction, in the reconstruction, of the kind of world in which we want to live.

American politicians like to refer to the American dream. The American dream does exist, and is internalized in most of our psyches. It is a good dream, so good that many others across the world wish the same dream for themselves. What is this dream? The American dream is the dream of human possibility, of a society in which all persons may be encouraged to do their best, to achieve their most, and to have the reward of a comfortable life. It is the dream that there will be no artificial obstacles in the way of such individual fulfillment. It is the dream that the sum of such individual achievements is a great social good—a society of freedom, equality, and mutual solidarity. It is the dream that we are a beacon to a world that suffers from not being able to realize such a dream.

Of course it is a dream, and like all dreams, it is not an exact representation of reality. But it represents our subconscious longings and our underlying values. Dreams are not scientific analyses. Rather they offer us insights. However, to understand the world in which we live, we have to go beyond our dreams to a careful look at our history—the history of the United States, the history of the modern world-system, the history of the United States in the world-system. Not everyone wants to do that. Sometimes we fear reality will be grim or at least less beautiful than our dreams. Some of us prefer to see the world, as they say, through rose-colored glasses.

One would have thought that the events of September 11 would have shattered the illusions. And no doubt they did so for many. But the Bush administration has been working hard to prevent us from looking soberly at what happened in order to pursue an agenda that predates those events and to use them as an excuse to ram through this agenda. So I propose here to describe briefly two things: what I think is the meaning of September 11 in the light of previous history; and what I think is the agenda of the Bush administration. I believe September 11 brought to the forefront of our attention five realities about the United States: the limits of its military power; the depth of anti-American feeling in the rest of the world; the hangover from the economic binge of the 1990s; the contradictory pressures of American nationalism; and the frailty of our civil liberties tradition. None of these is consonant with the American dream as we have imagined it. And the policies of the Bush administration are exacerbating the contradictions.

Let us start with the military situation. The United States—everyone says, and correctly—is the strongest military power in the world today, and by far! Yet the fact is that a miscellaneous band of fanatic believers, with rather little money and even less military hardware, was able to launch a serious attack on the homeland of the United States, kill several thousand people, and destroy and damage major buildings in New York City and the Washington area. The attack was audacious and efficacious. It is all very well to give these people a label, that of "terrorists," and then to launch a "war on terrorism." But we should start by realizing that, from a military point of view, 9/11 should never have happened. One year later, the perpetrators have not been caught. And our major military response has been to invade Iraq, a country that had nothing to do with the September 11 attack.

Anti-American sentiment is nothing new. It is pervasive, and has been, ever since the United States became the world-system's hegemonic power after 1945. It is a reaction to those with great power and to the arrogance that seems almost inevitably to become natural to those who hold such power. Such anti-American sentiment is sometimes understandable, sometimes irrational and unjustified. The latter goes with the territory. When all is said and done, such sentiment did not impede the United States significantly for a long while. For one thing, it was balanced by the sentiment of significant groups of people, especially in the countries the United States considered allies, that the United States was playing a necessary role of leadership and defense of their values in the world-system. For these people, American power was legitimate because it served the needs of the world-system as a whole. Even in those parts of the world that are poor and oppressed, there was often some sense that, despite what they thought were the negatives of American power, it had a worthy side implementing some universalistic values.

September 11 demonstrated that in spite of these sentiments, the depth of anger may have been greater than the United States has ever acknowledged. To be sure, the immediate reaction of many throughout the world was to express sympathy and solidarity with the United States, but one year later that sympathy and solidarity seems to be evaporating, while those expressing the anger have not at all muted the expression of their sentiments.

The United States had seemed to do exceptionally well economically in the 1990s—high productivity, a booming stock market, low unemployment, low inflation, and a liquidation of an enormous U.S. governmental debt, creating a quite remarkable surplus. In general, Americans took this as a validation of their dream, of their leaders' economic policies, and the promise of an unendingly glorious future. It is quite clear now that this was not a dream but an illusion, and a dangerous one.

September 11 was not the primary cause of the subsequent economic difficulties of the United States, although no doubt it exacerbated them. What is causing the downturn in American economic perspectives is that the prosperity of the 1990s (actually, primarily the late 1990s) was in many ways just a bubble, sustained very artificially, as all the revelations of corporate greed have made clear. In fact, however, the cause of the downturn lies deeper. The world-economy has been in a long relative economic stagnation since the 1970s. One of the things that happened in this period, as in any such period, is that the three areas with powerful economic loci—the United States, Western Europe, and Japan—tried to shift the losses to each other. In the 1970s, Europe did relatively well. In the 1980s, Japan did well, and in the 1990s, the United States did well. But the world-economy as a whole did not do well in any of these periods. And the economic pain across the world has been stupendous. We are now in the final stage of this long downward spiral, and once the bankruptcies are rampant, the world-economy may start to turn up again. It is not all clear, or even too likely, that the United States will outshine western Europe and East Asia in the eventual upturn. A below-the-surface set of fears about this less-than-sterling economic future is shaping American politics today.

The fourth problem is the historical nature of American nationalism. The United States is no more and no less nationalist than most other countries. But because it has been the hegemonic power, the instabilities of American nationalism can cause more havoc than that of most other nations. American nationalism has taken two different forms. One is withdrawal, crawling into Fortress America, what we usually call isolationism.

But the United States has always been an expansionist power as well—first across the continent, then across the Caribbean and the Pacific. And expansion involves military conquest—whether of Native Americans, Mexicans, or Filipinos. The United States has had its fair share of victories (the Mexican War, the Second World War, most of the Indian campaigns) and its fair share of defeats or at least ambiguous results (the War of 1812, Vietnam). Our record in this regard is not much worse than that of other major military powers. Of course, no country likes to talk about its defeats, if it isn't unavoidable. Defeats tend to be redefined as the weakness of wimpy leaders. This "stab-in-the-back" thesis underlies the macho militarist side of American nationalism, which commands considerable support among the populace.

Isolationism and macho militarism are on the surface quite different. But they share the same fundamental attitude towards the rest of the world, the "others"—fear and disdain, combined with the assumption that our way of life is pure and should not be defiled by involvement in the miserable quarrels of others, unless we are in a position to impose on them "our way of life." It is not hard therefore for nationalists to move back and forth from isolationism to macho militarism, even if the immediate policy implications of each can be quite different in particular situations. September 11 seems to have reinforced both sides of this contradictory stance. And of course, as happens whenever the country seems to be under attack, September 11 has made other voices by and large quite timid.

Finally, there is our civil liberties tradition. It is quite glorious in concept, and quite frail in practice. The wisdom of enacting the Bill of Rights as amendments to the Constitution was that it made them more resistant to passing majorities that would ignore them or violate them egregiously. Even so, they have been violated endlessly—blatantly, as in Lincoln's suspension of habeas corpus, the Palmer raids, or Roosevelt's internment of Japanese-Americans; less obviously but no less importantly by the repeated illegal actions by federal agencies (the Department of Justice, the FBI, the CIA), not to speak of local agencies. The Supreme Court is supposed to serve as a bulwark of these constitutional rights, but it has been an exceedingly erratic one, and not at all reliable.

For the Bush administration, September 11 was a bonanza for its preexisting agenda on all five issues. I am not making paranoiac accusations of a conspiracy. I merely note that they jumped in immediately to take advantage of the situation in order to pursue the agenda that was in their minds and hearts before September 11. They have dealt with military decline by an incredible escalation of military expenditures. Whether this will turn out to be a gigantic waste—or, worse, counterproductive militarily—is yet to be seen. What is certain is that this expansion was not the result of reasoned analysis and careful national political judgment.

Our expanded military hardware is receiving its first major use in the invasion of Iraq. I believe that such an invasion, far from validating and increasing the military power of the United States, will undermine it grievously in the short, middle, and long run. But the current Bush administration is not really open to discussion on these matters. They merely express openly their disdain for the "McGovernites" resurgent and the "old Bushies" (that is, the president's father, and all his close advisers—Brent Scowcroft, James Baker, Lawrence Eagleburger). Full speed ahead is the motto of the present administration because a slowdown would make them look foolish, and a crash later is less harmful politically than a crash now.

The way the Bush administration is dealing with anti-American sentiment in the world is, one must admit, original. Its policies increase it, and spread it to all those groups that have been hitherto resistant to it—our friends and allies, whom we may soon be calling our former friends and allies. Great powers seldom really consult, but at least they usually make a pretense of it. For the Bush administration, consultation seems to entail announcing: here's what we are going to do; are you with us, or are you against us? And to any answer that raises questions about the wisdom or advisability of a specific proposal, the Bush administration seems to say: May we twist your arm a little more?

On the economic front, Bush and his advisers preach pollyanna optimism, governmental inaction, and the argument that any economic binge was Clinton's fault. They seem to think that September 11 reinforces this stance. They seem not the least interested in a cold appraisal of current economic realities, even less at a longer-term historical perspective. The one thing they have offered the economic conservative part of their coalition is the tax reductions and the undoing of environmental protections. These actions are now sacred cows, since the economic conservatives are by and large "old Bushies" and are otherwise quite unhappy with the present Bush administration. They must not be antagonized further. But of course, the tax reductions make impossible the kind of New Deal measures that will be needed to pull the United States out of the deep deflation into which it is speedily heading.

The Bush administration clearly hopes that its macho militarism will compensate with the voters for the sad state of the U.S. economy. So, in addition to all the other reasons why Bush and his advisers believe the United States should take on the whole "axis of evil," there is the crassly political side: a wartime president gets votes, for himself and for his party. This did not escape the notice of Bush's top political adviser, Karl Rove. We may expect these political considerations to remain high in the decision-making process.

As for civil liberties, we have not seen such an outright, unashamed assault on civil liberties from an attorney general since that of the infamous A. Mitchell Palmer in the Harding administration. Furthermore, they seem determined not to be restrained in any way by the courts. Even if the Supreme Court were to rule against them 9–0, which is highly improbable, they would find ways to ignore and defy such restraints. We are in for a bad period.

This book is organized in a simple way. It has three parts.

Part I presents the thesis: that the United States is a declining hegemonic power, and that September 11 is a further evidence of this. It was written and originally published in 2002. Part II is a series of essays that discuss the difference between the rhetoric and the reality surrounding the major buzzwords of our contemporary political discourse: *the twentieth century, globalization, racism, Islam, the "others," democracy,* and *intellectuals.* These essays were all written before 9/11, most of them as talks or conference papers. I would not however change a word of them because of it. There is one further essay, written after the events, concerning how the United States views the world. It is a call to reflection about how we view the world.

Finally, part III addresses what we can do about the difficult world in which we find ourselves. The first two essays, both written before 9/11, discuss the agenda I think the left should put forward today, in the United States and the world. The last two, written after 9/11, address what are to me the central contemporary questions from a political point of view: What does it mean to be antisystemic today? And what future for humanity?

I am following in this book my view that we are all engaged in a triple task: the intellectual task of analyzing reality critically and soberly; the moral task of deciding what values to which we should give priority today are; and the political task of deciding how we might contribute immediately to the likelihood that the world emerges from the present chaotic structural crisis of our capitalist world-system into a different world-system that would be appreciably better rather than appreciably worse than the present one.

February 2003

PART ONE

THE THESIS

CHAPTER ONE

Decline of the U.S.:
The Eagle Has Crash Landed

The United States in decline? Few people today would believe this assertion. The only ones who do are the U.S. hawks, who argue vociferously for policies to reverse the decline. This belief that the end of U.S. hegemony has already begun does not follow from the vulnerability that became apparent to all on September 11, 2001. In fact, the United States has been fading as a global power since the 1970s, and the U.S. response to the terrorist attacks has merely accelerated this decline. To understand why the so-called Pax Americana is on the wane requires examining the geopolitics of the twentieth century, particularly of the century's final three decades. This exercise uncovers a simple and inescapable conclusion: The economic, political, and military factors that contributed to U.S. hegemony are the same factors that will inexorably produce the coming U.S. decline.

The rise of the United States to global hegemony was a long process that began in earnest with the world recession of 1873. At that time, the United States and Germany began to acquire an increasing share of global markets, mainly at the expense of the steadily receding British economy. Both nations had recently acquired a stable political base—the United States by successfully terminating the Civil War and Germany by achieving unification and defeating France in the Franco-Prussian War. From 1873 to 1914, the United States and Germany became the principal producers in certain leading sectors: steel and later automobiles for the United States and industrial chemicals for Germany.

The history books record that World War I broke out in 1914 and ended in 1918 and that World War II lasted from 1939 to 1945. However, it makes more sense to consider the two as a single, continuous "thirty years' war" between the United States and Germany, with truces and local conflicts scattered in between. The competition for hegemonic succession took an ideological turn in 1933, when the Nazis came to power in Germany and began their quest to transcend the global system altogether, seeking not hegemony within the current system but rather a form of global empire. Recall the Nazi slogan *"ein tausendjähriges Reich"* (a thousand-year empire). In turn, the United States assumed the role of advocate of centrist world liberalism—recall former U.S. President Franklin D. Roosevelt's "four freedoms" (freedom of speech, of worship, from want, and from fear)—and entered into a strategic alliance with the Soviet Union, making possible the defeat of Germany and its allies.

World War II resulted in enormous destruction of infrastructure and populations throughout Eurasia, from the Atlantic to the Pacific oceans, with almost no country left unscathed. The only major industrial power in the world to emerge intact—and even greatly strengthened, from an economic perspective—was the United States, which moved swiftly to consolidate its position.

But the aspiring hegemon faced some practical political obstacles. During the war, the Allied powers had agreed on the establishment of the United Nations, composed primarily of countries that had been in the coalition against the Axis powers. The organization's critical feature was the Security Council, the only structure that could authorize the use of force. The U.N. Charter gave the right of veto on the Security Council to five powers, including the United States and the Soviet Union, and this rendered the council largely toothless in practice. So it was not the founding of the United Nations in April 1945 that determined the geopolitical constraints of the second half of the twentieth century but rather the Yalta meeting between Roosevelt, Great Britain's Prime Minister Winston Churchill, and the Soviet leader, Joseph Stalin, two months earlier.

The formal accords at Yalta were less important than the informal, unspoken agreements, which one can only assess by observing the behavior of the United States and the Soviet Union in the years that followed. When the war ended in Europe on May 8, 1945, Soviet and Western (that is, U.S., British, and French) troops were located in particular places—essentially, along a north–south line in the center of Europe, the Elbe river, Germany's historic dividing line. Aside from a few minor adjustments, they stayed there. In hindsight, Yalta signified the agreement of both sides that they could stay there and that neither side would use force to push the other out. This tacit accord applied to Asia as well, as evinced by U.S. occupation of Japan and the division of Korea. Politically, therefore, Yalta was an agreement on the status quo in which the Soviet Union controlled about one-third of the world and the United States the rest.

Washington also faced more serious military challenges. The Soviet Union had the world's largest land forces, while the U.S. government was under domestic pressure to downsize its army, particularly by ending the draft. The United States therefore decided to assert its military strength not via land forces but through a monopoly of nuclear weapons (plus an air force capable of deploying them). This monopoly soon disappeared: by 1949 the Soviet Union had developed nuclear weapons as well. Ever since, the United States has been reduced to trying to prevent the acquisition of nuclear weapons (and chemical and biological weapons) by additional powers, an effort that, by the twenty-first century, does not seem to have been terribly successful.

Until 1991, the United States and the Soviet Union coexisted in the "balance of terror" of the Cold War. This status quo was tested seriously only three times: the Berlin blockade of 1948–49, the Korean War, from 1950 to 1953, and the Cuban missile crisis of 1962. The result in each case was restoration of the status quo. Moreover, note how each time the Soviet Union faced a political crisis among its satellite regimes—East Germany in 1953, Hungary in 1956, Czechoslovakia in 1968, and Poland in 1981—the United States engaged in little more than propaganda exercises, allowing the Soviet Union to proceed largely as it deemed fit.

Of course, this passivity did not extend to the economic arena. The United States capitalized on the Cold War ambiance to launch massive economic reconstruction efforts, first in western Europe and then in Japan, as well as in South Korea and Taiwan. The rationale was obvious: What was the point of having such overwhelming productive superiority if the rest of the world could not muster effective demand? Furthermore, economic reconstruction helped create clientelistic obligations on the part of the nations receiving U.S. aid; this sense of obligation fostered willingness to enter into military alliances and, even more important, into political subservience.

Finally, one should not underestimate the ideological and cultural component of U.S. hegemony. The immediate post-1945 period may have been the historical high point for the popularity of Communist ideology. We easily forget today the large votes for Communist parties in free elections in countries such as Belgium, France, Italy, Czechoslovakia, and Finland, not to mention the support Communist parties gathered in Asia—in Vietnam, India, and Japan—and throughout Latin America. And that still leaves out areas such as China, Greece, and Iran, where free elections remained absent or constrained but where Communist parties enjoyed widespread appeal. In response, the United States sustained a massive anti-Communist ideological offensive. In retrospect, this initiative appears largely successful: Washington brandished its role as the leader of the "free world" at least as effectively as the Soviet Union brandished its position as the leader of the "progressive" and "anti-imperialist" camp.

The United States' success as a hegemonic power in the postwar period created the conditions of the nation's hegemonic demise. This process is captured in four symbols: the war in Vietnam, the revolutions of 1968, the fall of the Berlin Wall in 1989, and the terrorist attacks of September 2001. Each symbol built upon the prior one, culminating in the situation in which the United States currently finds itself—a lone superpower that lacks true power, a world leader nobody follows and few respect, and a nation drifting dangerously amidst a global chaos it cannot control.

What was the Vietnam War? First and foremost, it was the effort of the Vietnamese people to end colonial rule and establish their own state. The Vietnamese fought the French, the Japanese, and the Americans, and in the end the Vietnamese won—quite an achievement, actually. Geopolitically, however, the war represented a rejection of the Yalta status quo by populations then labeled Third World. Vietnam became such a powerful symbol because Washington was foolish enough to invest its full military might in the struggle, but the United States still lost. True, the United States didn't deploy nuclear weapons (a decision certain myopic groups on the right have long reproached), but such use would have shattered the Yalta accords and might have produced a nuclear holocaust—an outcome the United States simply could not risk.

But Vietnam was not merely a military defeat or a blight on U.S. prestige. The war dealt a major blow to the United States' ability to remain the world's dominant economic power. The conflict was extremely expensive and more or less used up the U.S. gold reserves that had been so plentiful since 1945. Moreover, the United States incurred these costs just as western Europe and Japan experienced major economic upswings. These conditions ended U.S. preeminence in the global economy. Since the late 1960s, members of this triad have been nearly economic equals, each doing better than the others for certain periods but none moving far ahead. When the revolutions of 1968 broke out around the world, support for the Vietnamese became a major rhetorical component. "One, two, many Vietnams" and "Ho, Ho, Ho Chi Minh" were chanted in many a street, not least in the United States. But the 1968ers did not merely condemn U.S. hegemony. They condemned Soviet collusion with the United States, they condemned Yalta, and they used or adapted the language of the Chinese cultural revolutionaries, who divided the world into two camps—the two superpowers and the rest of the world.

The denunciation of Soviet collusion led logically to the denunciation of those national forces closely allied with the Soviet Union, which meant in most cases the traditional Communist parties. But the 1968 revolutionaries also lashed out against other components of the Old Left—national liberation movements in the Third World, social democratic movements in western Europe, and New Deal Democrats in the United States—accusing them, too, of collusion with what the revolutionaries generically termed "U.S. imperialism."

The attack on Soviet collusion with Washington plus the attack on the Old Left further weakened the legitimacy of the

Yalta arrangements on which the United States had fashioned the world order. It also undermined the position of centrist liberalism as the lone, legitimate global ideology. The direct political consequences of the world revolutions of 1968 were minimal, but the geopolitical and intellectual repercussions were enormous and irrevocable. Centrist liberalism tumbled from the throne that it had occupied since the European revolutions of 1848 and that had enabled it to co-opt conservatives and radicals alike. These ideologies returned and once again represented a real gamut of choices. Conservatives would again become conservatives, and radicals, radicals. The centrist liberals did not disappear, but they were cut down to size. And in the process, the official U.S. ideological position—antifascist, anticommunist, anticolonialist—came to seem thin and unconvincing to a growing portion of the world's populations.

The onset of international economic stagnation in the 1970s had two important consequences for U.S. power. First, stagnation resulted in the collapse of "developmentalism"—the notion that every nation could catch up economically if the state took appropriate action—which was the principal ideological claim of the Old Left movements then in power. One after another, these regimes faced internal disorder, declining standards of living, increasing debt dependency on international financial institutions, and eroding credibility. What had seemed in the 1960s to be the successful navigation of Third World decolonization by the United States—minimizing disruption and maximizing the smooth transfer of power to regimes that were developmentalist but scarcely revolutionary—gave way to disintegrating order, simmering discontents, and unchanneled radical temperaments. When the United States tried to intervene, it failed. In 1983, U.S. President Ronald Reagan sent troops to Lebanon to restore order. The troops were in effect forced out. He compensated by invading Grenada, a country without troops. President George

H.W. Bush invaded Panama, another country without troops. But after he intervened in Somalia to restore order, the United States was in effect forced out, somewhat ignominiously. Since there was little the U.S. government could actually do to reverse the trend of declining hegemony, it chose simply to ignore this trend—a policy that prevailed from the withdrawal from Vietnam until September 11, 2001.

Meanwhile, true conservatives began to assume control of key states and interstate institutions. The neoliberal offensive of the 1980s was marked by the Thatcher and Reagan regimes and the emergence of the International Monetary Fund (IMF) as a key actor on the world scene. Where once (for more than a century) conservative forces had attempted to portray themselves as wiser liberals, now centrist liberals were compelled to argue that they were more effective conservatives. The conservative programs were clear. Domestically, conservatives tried to enact policies that would reduce the cost of labor, minimize environmental constraints on producers, and cut back on state welfare benefits. Actual successes were modest, so conservatives then moved vigorously into the international arena. The gatherings of the World Economic Forum in Davos provided a meeting ground for elites and the media. The IMF provided a club for finance ministers and central bankers. And the United States pushed for the creation of the World Trade Organization to enforce free commercial flows across the world's frontiers.

While the United States wasn't watching, the Soviet Union was collapsing. Yes, Ronald Reagan had dubbed the Soviet Union an "evil empire" and had used the rhetorical bombast of calling for the destruction of the Berlin Wall, but the United States didn't really mean it and certainly was not responsible for the Soviet Union's downfall. In truth, the Soviet Union and its Eastern European imperial zone collapsed because of popular disillusionment with the Old Left in combination with Soviet

leader Mikhail Gorbachev's efforts to save his regime by liquidating Yalta and instituting internal liberalization (*perestroika*
plus *glasnost*). Gorbachev succeeded in liquidating Yalta but not
in saving the Soviet Union (although he almost did, be it said).

The United States was stunned and puzzled by the sudden
collapse, uncertain how to handle the consequences. The collapse of Communism in effect signified the collapse of liberalism
by removing the only ideological justification behind U.S. hegemony, a justification tacitly supported by liberalism's ostensible
ideological opponent. This loss of legitimacy led directly to the
Iraqi invasion of Kuwait, which Iraqi leader Saddam Hussein
would never have dared had the Yalta arrangements remained
in place. In retrospect, U.S. efforts in the Gulf War accomplished
a truce at basically the same line of departure. But can a hegemonic power be satisfied with a tie in a war with a middling regional power? Saddam demonstrated that one could pick a fight
with the United States and get away with it. Even more than the
defeat in Vietnam, Saddam's brash challenge has eaten at the in-
nards of the U.S. right, in particular those known as the hawks,
which explains the fervor of their current desire to invade Iraq
and destroy its regime.

Between the Gulf War and September 11, 2001, the two
major arenas of world conflict were the Balkans and the Middle
East. The United States has played a major diplomatic role in
both regions. Looking back, how different would the results
have been had the United States assumed a completely isolationist position? In the Balkans, an economically successful
multinational state, Yugoslavia, broke down, essentially into its
component parts. Over ten years, most of the resulting states
have engaged in a process of ethnification, experiencing fairly
brutal violence, widespread human rights violations, and outright wars. Outside intervention—in which the United States
figured most prominently—brought about a truce and ended

the most egregious violence, but this intervention in no way reversed the ethnification, which is now consolidated and somewhat legitimated. Would these conflicts have ended differently without U.S. involvement? The violence might have continued longer, but the basic results would probably not have been too different. The picture is even grimmer in the Middle East, where, if anything, U.S. engagement has been deeper and its failures more spectacular. In the Balkans and the Middle East alike, the United States has failed to exert its hegemonic clout effectively, not for want of will or effort but for want of real power.

Then came September 11—the shock and the reaction. Under fire from U.S. legislators, the Central Intelligence Agency (CIA) now claims it had warned the Bush administration of possible threats. But despite the CIA's focus on Al Qaeda and the agency's intelligence expertise, it could not foresee (and therefore prevent) the execution of the terrorist strikes. Or so CIA Director George Tenet argued. This testimony can hardly comfort the U.S. government or the American people. Whatever else historians may decide, the attacks of September 11, 2001, posed a major challenge to U.S. power. The persons responsible did not represent a major military power. They were members of a nonstate force, with a high degree of determination, some money, a band of dedicated followers, and a strong base in one weak state. In short, militarily, they were nothing. Yet they succeeded in a bold attack on U.S. soil.

George W. Bush came to power very critical of the Clinton administration's handling of world affairs. Bush and his advisers did not admit—but were undoubtedly aware—that Clinton's path had been the path of every U.S. president since Gerald Ford, including that of Ronald Reagan and George H.W. Bush. It had even been the path of the current Bush administration before September 11. One only needs to look at how Bush handled the downing of a U.S. plane off China in April 2001 to see that prudence had been the name of the game.

Following the terrorist attacks, Bush changed course, declaring war on terrorism, assuring the American people that "the outcome is certain," and informing the world that "you are either with us or against us." Long frustrated by even the most conservative U.S. administrations, the hawks finally came to dominate American policy. Their position is clear: The United States wields overwhelming military power, and even though countless foreign leaders consider it unwise for Washington to flex its military muscles, these same leaders cannot and will not do anything if the United States simply imposes its will on the rest. The hawks believe the United States should act as an imperial power for two reasons: First, the United States can get away with it. And second, if Washington doesn't exert its force, the United States will become increasingly marginalized.

Today, this hawkish position has three expressions: the military assault in Afghanistan, the de facto support for the Israeli attempt to liquidate the Palestinian Authority, and the invasion of Iraq. One year after the September 2001 terrorist attacks, it is perhaps too early to assess what such strategies will accomplish. Thus far, these schemes have led to the overthrow of the Taliban in Afghanistan (without the complete dismantling of Al Qaeda or the capture of its top leadership); enormous destruction in Palestine (without rendering Palestinian leader Yasir Arafat "irrelevant," as Israeli Prime Minister Ariel Sharon said he is); and heavy opposition from U.S. allies in Europe and the Middle East to plans for an invasion of Iraq.

The hawks' reading of recent events emphasizes that opposition to U.S. actions, while serious, has remained largely verbal. Neither Western Europe nor Russia nor China nor Saudi Arabia has seemed ready to break ties in serious ways with the United

States. In other words, hawks believe, Washington has indeed gotten away with it. The hawks assume a similar outcome will occur when the U.S. military actually invades Iraq and after that, when the United States exercises its authority elsewhere in the world, be it in Iran, North Korea, Colombia, or perhaps Indonesia. Ironically, the hawk reading has largely become the reading of the international left, which has been screaming about U.S. policies—mainly because they fear that the chances of U.S. success are high.

But hawk interpretations are wrong and will only contribute to the United States' decline, transforming a gradual descent into a much more rapid and turbulent fall. Specifically, hawk approaches will fail for military, economic, and ideological reasons.

Undoubtedly, the military remains the United States' strongest card; in fact, it is the only card. Today, the United States wields the most formidable military apparatus in the world. And if claims of new, unmatched military technologies are to be believed, the U.S. military edge over the rest of the world is considerably greater today than it was just a decade ago. But does that mean, then, that the United States can invade Iraq, conquer it rapidly, and install a friendly and stable regime? Unlikely. Bear in mind that of the three serious wars the U.S. military has fought since 1945 (Korea, Vietnam, and the Gulf War), one ended in defeat and two in draws—not exactly a glorious record.

Saddam Hussein's army is not that of the Taliban, and his internal military control is far more coherent. A U.S. invasion would necessarily involve a serious land force, one that would have to fight its way to Baghdad and would likely suffer significant casualties. Such a force would also need staging grounds, and Saudi Arabia has made clear that it does not wish to serve in this capacity. Would Kuwait or Turkey help out? Perhaps, if Washington calls in all its chips. Meanwhile, Saddam can be expected to deploy all weapons at his disposal, and it is precisely the

U.S. government that keeps fretting over how nasty those weapons might be. The United States may twist the arms of regimes in the region, but popular sentiment there clearly views the whole affair as reflecting a deep anti-Arab bias in the United States. Can such a conflict be won? The British general staff has apparently already informed Prime Minister Tony Blair that it does not believe so.

And there is always the matter of "second fronts." Following the Gulf War, U.S. armed forces sought to prepare for the possibility of fighting two simultaneous regional wars. After a while, the Pentagon quietly abandoned the idea as impractical and costly. But who can be sure that no potential U.S. enemies would strike when the United States appears to be bogged down in Iraq? Consider, too, the question of U.S. popular tolerance of nonvictories. Americans hover between a patriotic fervor that lends support to all wartime presidents and a deep isolationist urge. Since 1945, patriotism has hit a wall whenever the death toll has risen. Why should today's reaction differ? And even if the hawks (who are almost all civilians) feel impervious to public opinion, U.S. Army generals, burned by Vietnam, do not.

And what about the economic front? In the 1980s, countless American analysts became hysterical over the Japanese economic miracle. They calmed down in the 1990s, given Japan's well-publicized financial difficulties. Yet after overstating how quickly Japan was moving forward in the 1980s, U.S. authorities now seem to be complacent, confident that Japan lags far behind. These days, Washington seems more inclined to lecture Japanese policymakers about what they are doing wrong.

Such triumphalism hardly appears warranted. Consider the following April 20, 2002, *New York Times* report: "A Japanese laboratory has built the world's fastest computer, a machine so powerful that it matches the raw processing power of the 20 fastest American computers combined and far outstrips the previous leader, an I.B.M.-built machine. The achievement . . . is evidence that a technology race that most American engineers thought they were winning handily is far from over." The analysis goes on to note that there are "contrasting scientific and technological priorities" in the two countries. The Japanese machine is built to analyze climatic change, but U.S. machines are designed to simulate weapons. This contrast embodies the oldest story in the history of hegemonic powers. The dominant power concentrates (to its detriment) on the military; the candidate for successor concentrates on the economy. The latter has always paid off, handsomely. It did for the United States. Why should it not pay off for Japan as well, perhaps in alliance with China?

Finally, there is the ideological sphere. Right now, the U.S. economy seems relatively weak, even more so considering the exorbitant military expenses associated with hawk strategies. Moreover, Washington remains politically isolated; virtually no one (save Israel) thinks the hawk position makes sense or is worth encouraging. Other nations are afraid or unwilling to stand up to Washington directly, but even their foot dragging is hurting the United States. Yet the U.S. response amounts to little more than arrogant arm twisting. Arrogance has its own negatives. Calling in chips means leaving fewer chips for next time, and surly acquiescence breeds increasing resentment. Over the two hundred years, the United States acquired a considerable amount of ideological credit. But these days, the United States is running through this credit even faster than it ran through its gold surplus in the 1960s.

The United States faces two possibilities during the next ten years: it can follow the hawks' path, with negative consequences for all, but especially for itself, or it can realize that the negatives are too great. Simon Tisdall of *The Guardian* recently argued that even disregarding international public opinion, "The U.S. is not able to fight a successful Iraqi war by itself without incurring immense damage, not least in terms of its economic interests and its energy supply. Mr. Bush is reduced to talking tough and looking ineffectual." And if the United States still invades Iraq and is then forced to withdraw, it will look even more ineffectual.

President Bush's options appear extremely limited, and there is little doubt that the United States will continue to decline as a decisive force in world affairs over the next decade. The real question is not whether U.S. hegemony is waning but whether the United States can devise a way to descend gracefully, with minimum damage to the world, and to itself.

PART TWO

MULTIPLE RHETORICS AND REALITIES

Chapter Two

The Twentieth Century:
Darkness at Noon?

I n the middle of the twentieth century, Arthur Koestler
wrote a novel about the Soviet regime and its show trials
that he entitled *Darkness at Noon*. I would like to take this as
my metaphor for the entire twentieth century, not just the Soviet
regime. But at the same time, the century was in many ways also
"Bright Sun at Midnight." Indeed, the way we think about this
century, which is so difficult to assess, has depended very much
on the place from which and the moment at which we were observing it. We have been on something of a roller-coaster ride.
We should remember that roller-coaster rides end in one of two
ways. Usually, they return to their starting point, more or less, although the riders may have been either exhilarated or very
frightened. But sometimes, they derail.

Henry Luce called the twentieth century "the American century." He was unquestionably right, although this is only part of
the story. The rise of the United States to hegemony in the
world-system started circa 1870 in the wake of the beginning of
the decline of the United Kingdom from its erstwhile heights.
The United States and Germany competed with each other as
contenders for the succession to Great Britain. What happened is

well known and straightforward. Both the United States and Germany greatly expanded their industrial base between 1870 and 1914, both surpassing Great Britain. One, however, was a sea and air power and the other a land power. Their lines of economic expansion were correspondingly different, as was the nature of their military investment. The United States was allied economically and politically with the declining erstwhile hegemonic power, Great Britain. Eventually, there were the two world wars, which one can best think of as a single "thirty years' war," one essentially between the U.S. and Germany, to determine hegemony in the world-system.

Germany tried the path of transforming the world-system into a world-empire, what they called their *tausendjähriges Reich*. The path of imperial conquest has never worked as a viable path to dominance within the framework of the capitalist world-economy, as Napoleon had previously learned. The world-imperial thrust has the short-term advantage of military vigor and precipitateness. It has the middle-term disadvantage of being very expensive and of uniting all the opposition forces. As the constitutional and quasi-liberal monarchy of Great Britain had rallied autocratic, Tsarist Russia again Napoleon, so the quasi-liberal representative republic of the United States rallied the Stalinist Soviet Union against Hitler—or, rather, both Napoleon and Hitler did good jobs in uniting the powers at the two ends of the European land mass against a voracious power structure located between them.

But how shall we assess the consequences of this struggle? Let us start with the material outcome. In 1945, after what was incredibly destructive warfare everywhere on the European continent and similarly destructive warfare in East Asia—destructive in terms both of lives and of infrastructure—the United States was the only major industrial power to emerge unscathed economically, even strengthened, as the result of wartime buildup.

For several years after 1945, there was actual hunger in all the other previously economically advanced regions, and in any case there was a difficult process of basic reconstruction of these zones.

It was quite easy in such a situation for United States industries to dominate the world market. Their major problem initially was not too many competitive sellers but too little effective demand, two few buyers worldwide because of the decline of purchasing power in western Europe and East Asia. This required more than relief; it required reconstruction. However profitable such reconstruction would be for U.S. industry, it was costly for U.S. taxpayers. Meeting the short-run costs posed an internal political problem for the U.S. government.

Meanwhile, there seemed to be a political-military problem as well. The U.S.S.R., despite the destruction, loomed large as a military power, occupying half of Europe. It proclaimed itself a socialist state with a theoretical mission to lead the whole world to socialism (and then, in theory again, to Communism). Between 1945 and 1948, so-called popular democracies, under the aegis of the Communist Party, were put into place one by one in the zones where the Red Army was to be found at the end of the Second World War. By 1946, Winston Churchill would speak of an "iron curtain" that had fallen on Europe, from Stettin to Trieste.

In addition, in the immediate post-1945 years, Communist parties showed themselves to be extremely strong in a large number of European countries. Communist parties won 25 to 40 percent of the vote in the early postwar elections in France, Italy, Belgium, Finland, and Czechoslovakia—the result both of their previous strength in the interwar years and of their wartime role in animating a good part of the resistance against Nazism and fascism. The same was true in Asia. In China, the Communist Party was marching on Shanghai against a Nationalist government that had lost its legitimacy. Communist parties and/or guerilla forces were remarkably strong as well in Japan, the Philippines, Indochina, and the Dutch East Indies, and were not negligible elsewhere.

Communist movements had the wind in their sails. They claimed that history was on their side, and they acted as though they believed it. So did a lot of others, ranging from conservative movements to center-left movements, and most particularly the majority of the social democrats. These others were afraid that, in a few years, their countries too would become popular democracies. And they didn't wish this to happen. More emphatically, they were ready to resist actively what now was rhetorically called the Communist menace to the free world.

In the last thirty years, a large amount of revisionist historiography has come from both the left and the right. The left-wing revisionists have tended to claim that the so-called Communist menace was a bogeyman, erected by the U.S. government and world right forces, both to ensure U.S. hegemony in the world-system and to put down (or at least limit) the strength of left and workers' movements in the Western liberal states. The right-wing revisionists have tended to claim, especially since the availability of Soviet documents after 1989, that there was indeed a worldwide network of spies for the Soviet Union, which did indeed have every intention of subverting non-Communist states and transforming them into popular democracies.

The fact is that both the left and the right historiographical revisionists are probably largely right in their empirical assertions and fundamentally wrong in their historical interpretations. No doubt, both sides asserted both publicly and even more in private what the revisionists said they had asserted. Probably, most individuals in the key agencies of each side believed the rhetoric, or at least believed much of it. No doubt, too, both sides engaged in actions that went in the direction of carrying out the expansionist rhetoric. And no doubt, finally, both sides would have been delighted to see the other side collapse, and were for the most part even hoping for it.

Still, we need a little sangfroid, and a little *Realpolitik* in our appreciation of what really went on. It seems clear, in retrospect, that the Cold War was a highly restrained, carefully constructed and monitored exercise that never got out of hand and never led to the world war of which everyone was afraid. I have called it a minuet. Furthermore, in retrospect, nothing much happened, in the sense that the boundary lines as of 1989 were pretty much the boundary lines as of 1945, and there was in the end neither Soviet aggression in western Europe nor U.S. "rollback" (that is, ending Communist regimes) in eastern Europe. Furthermore, there were many points at which each side showed restraint above and beyond the call of rhetoric. Of course, we can say none of this was the intent, merely the result of a stalemate, and to some extent that may be true. Still, stalemates are abetted by lassitudes that result from tacit intents.

Such a historical scenario calls for caution in assessing the motives and the priorities of each side. Let us look at two codewords: Yalta and containment. Yalta ostensibly fixed the boundaries of the prospective postwar garrisoning of troops and therefore of geopolitical influence, as well as the modalities of constituting governments in liberated countries. Containment was a doctrine invented by George Kennan a few years later. Kennan, speaking for himself but indirectly for the U.S. establishment, advocated just that, containment by the U.S. of the Soviet Union—not, however, containment in place of welcome but containment in place of rollback, a Cold War that would not and should not become a hot one. Before John Foster Dulles became secretary of state under Eisenhower in 1953, he had advocated, against Kennan, rollback. But once in power, Dulles in fact practiced containment (most notably in 1956 in relation to the Hungarian Revolution), and rollback was relegated to the discourse of marginal politicians.

What Yalta and containment achieved—who will ever know the inner motives of all the actors?—is quite clear. The Soviet Union had a zone under its absolute control (most of what we call eastern and central Europe). The United States claimed all the rest of the world. The United States never interfered in the Soviet zone (except by means of propaganda). On the other hand, the U.S.S.R. never really interfered in any zone outside its sphere with more than political propaganda and a little money, with the sole serious exception of Afghanistan (a big mistake, as they were to learn). To be sure, some countries ignored this nice bilateral U.S.-Soviet arrangement, and we will come to that.

What had Yalta to do with the issue of U.S. world economic priorities in the immediate postwar period? As we have said, the United States needed to create world effective demand; however, the U.S. did not have unlimited money with which to do that. In the allocation of its resources, the United States gave priority to western Europe, for both economic and political reasons. The result was the Marshall Plan. The Marshall Plan, let us nonetheless remember, was offered by Marshall to *all* the allies. Did the U.S. really want the Soviet Union to accept? I doubt it very much, and remember hearing a State Department spokesman admit as much publicly at the time.

In any case, the Soviet Union declined to be part of the proposal, and made sure none of the countries in its zone responded favorably. This was a bonanza for the U.S. government, for two reasons. Had the Soviet Union come in on the plan, it would have become too expensive, and in addition the U.S. Congress would never have voted for it. The main argument that made possible bipartisan congressional support for the Marshall Plan was the need to contain Communism. So what in fact was happening? Marshall Plan aid was the other side of the Yalta arrangements. The Soviet Union was free to establish a mercantilist bloc within the world-economy, but then it would receive no economic aid in its reconstruction. No interference, but no aid. The only time these nice arrangements seemed threatened was the moment of the Berlin Blockade. But the net result of the blockade was a truce at the point where it started, giving the U.S. the excuse to launch NATO and the Soviet Union the excuse to create the Warsaw Pact. It also gave each side the excuse to spend a lot more on its military, which was actually beneficial economically in the short run, if not in the longer run.

Of course, Asia was a bit left out in these arrangements. And the Chinese Communists had no intention of being left out. So they marched on Shanghai, contra Stalin's wishes. In the United States, the right said that the U.S. lost China, but actually it was the Soviet Union that lost China, and that turned out to be more important in the long run. Then came the Korean War. Whatever the real story about who started what, and when, it seems clear, again in retrospect, that neither the United States nor the Soviet Union wanted to start such a war. And after a long and nasty involvement, in which the United States lost lives but the Soviet Union did not, the war ended with a truce more or less at the starting point, a result very similar to that of the Berlin Blockade. But once again, this war gave the needed excuse for the U.S. to bolster enormously the Japanese economy and to sign a defense pact. So East Asia, from a U.S.-Soviet viewpoint, was in on the Yalta arrangement. And after the Quemoy-Matsu imbroglio in 1955, China now de facto accepted it as well.

The American century was a geopolitical reality, one in which the other so-called superpower, the U.S.S.R., had a role, a voice, but not really the power to do anything but strut around in its cage; and then, in 1989, the cage imploded. With this implosion, however, the underlying political justification for U.S. hegemony disappeared as well, and the geopolitics of the world-system would now change, a subject to which we shall return.

Let us turn to the second great happening of the twentieth century, the exact opposite of United States hegemony: the slow but steady pushback by the non-Western world of pan-European dominance. The height of the "expansion of Europe" was actually circa 1900, a full century ago. It was then that W.E.B. Du Bois was proclaiming that "the problem of the twentieth century was the problem of the color line." No one believed him at the time, but he was absolutely right. Even before the First World War, there were a number of so-called revolutions that should have made analysts take notice: Mexico, Afghanistan, Persia, China, and, not least, the Japanese defeat of Russia in 1905. By then there was already a pan-extra-Western world mutual cheering society such that these events were noticed far and wide and served to encourage further action against pan-European dominance.

Indeed, I believe we should think of the Russian Revolution not as a proletarian revolution—which it clearly was not—but as the most successful and spectacular of the efforts to push back pan-European dominance. To be sure, many Russians insisted they were Europeans. And the Bolsheviks were on that side of the long-standing debate in Russia between Westernizers and Slavophiles. But this only points to the central ambivalence of the movements to push back pan-European dominance. They were demanding separation and integration at the same time, both in the name of equality. In any case, the Bolsheviks realized, after the non-occurrence of the much anticipated German revolution, that their survival and world role was linked to the world anti-imperialist struggle. This was the meaning of the Baku Congress in 1920.

In the post-1945 period, decolonization became the order of

the day. This was in part an intelligent and timely withdrawal by the colonizing powers. But this wisdom on their part was very largely the result of some heroic struggles by national liberation movements across three continents. The three that had the greatest geopolitical impact were those in Vietnam, Algeria, and Cuba. It cannot be argued that any of these movements were agents of the Soviet Union. Quite the opposite. These movements essentially were defying the Yalta arrangements and imposing another set of priorities in the geopolitical arena, one to which both the Soviet Union and the United States eventually had to bend.

Now, if we compare 2000 and 1900, we see the degree to which the anti-imperialist struggle was magnificently successful and yet changed much less of the realities of the world-system than its participants had hoped, intended, and expected it to do. In 2000, there are no significant formal colonies left. We have an African secretary-general of the United Nations. And formal, avowed racism has become taboo rhetoric. On the other hand, we know the degree to which neocolonialism (in Nkrumah's now forgotten but apt phrase) is rampant. An African may be secretary-general of the U.N. but an American heads the more important World Bank, and a western European, the International Monetary Fund. And although the rhetoric of racism is taboo, the reality is as great as ever, and everyone understands the unavowed code words that permit it to operate.

Indeed, the very success of the antisystemic movements has been the major cause of their undoing. In the late nineteenth century, the various antisystemic movements, all politically weak, evolved their strategy for social transformation, the famous two-step plan: first, mobilize to achieve state power in each state; then use state power to transform society. This was the strategy adopted by the Marxists in the name of the workers' movement. This was the strategy adopted by the political nationalists. This was even the strategy adopted by the women's movements as well as movements of so-called minorities insofar as they concentrated on suffrage and other political rights. In 1900, this strategy seemed the only plausible road for these movements, and probably it was. It certainly seemed to be a difficult road. By the 1960s, the mobilizations had achieved step one all over the world. The antisystemic movements were in power, or at least partial power, almost everywhere. Step two, transforming society, could now be undertaken, and its results could be assessed. It was the militants and the masses who ultimately found the results to be so far below their expectations that they would come to vent their disillusionment upon the movements themselves and their leaders, first in the 1968 world revolution and then in the follow-up of the next three decades.

The two twentieth-century trends became conjoined in the last decades of this century. The collapse of the Communisms in 1989–1991 was the climax of the process of disillusionment that had surfaced in 1968. Also and simultaneously, however, it sounded the knell of U.S. global power, removing its political underpinnings in two ways. On the one hand, it ended the political justification for a continuing subordination to U.S. leadership of its two main economic rivals, a now revitalized western Europe and Japan. And on the other hand, it ended the constraints that the antisystemic movements had placed on mass political activity, which they had been channeling and in reality largely depoliticizing. So we can say that in 2000, by comparison with 1900, the pan-European world was actually much weaker geopolitically and culturally, but the rest of the world had spent the ammunition it had mobilized and was wallowing in economic and political distress without the certainty that these movements had once had: that history was on their side. Hence, darkness at noon for both the pan-European world and the rest of the world, after a long period (especially 1945 to 1970) of bright sun at midnight.

In this story that I am telling, I have not mentioned the Nazi/fascist onslaught in the interwar years, nor the so-called ethnic purifications we have been undergoing of late, nor the Gulag horrors of the Communist regimes (but of course also of many other regimes). Are they not important? Yes, of course, in the sense that horrendous suffering is always important and always morally repugnant. But how do we assess, first, the causes of these horrors and, second, the trajectory? The dominant centrist myth is that these horrors were caused by ideological presumption and collective social deviance from the moderate, steady path laid out for the world-system by those who have had the most power in it. Auschwitz is said to have been the result of irrational racism, Gulags the consequence of arrogant imposition (and expectation) of utopias, ethnic purification the result of atavistic, culturally ingrained xenophobias.

Even without looking at the details, this is an implausible form of analysis. Auschwitz, Gulags, and ethnic purification all occurred within the framework of a historical social system, the capitalist world-economy. We have to ask what it is about this system that produced such phenomena and allowed them to flourish in the twentieth century, in ways and to a degree that hadn't occurred before. We live in a system in which there has been a continuing class struggle. We live in a system that has involved the steady polarization of the populations—economically, politically, socially, and now even demographically. We live in a system that has built racism and sexism into its structures from the outset. And of course we live in a system that has structured the very antisystemic movements that have challenged the legitimacy and viability of the system itself.

One of the ways in which 1900 was different from 1800, a fortiori from 1700 or 1600, is that the stakes of the global casino had become much higher. Winning and losing had greater consequences for the combatants, both because the possibility of mobility (upward and downward) for individuals and collectivities was ever greater and because the gap was ever greater and growing steadily at a geometric, not arithmetic, pace. I shall not attempt here to explicate of the particulars of any of these phenomena. I wish merely to insist that the explanation must be found in the functioning of the system and not in some supposed deviance from its proper functioning. I wish also to insist that, however terrible these happenings were for all those who suffered from them, they mattered less to the historical evolution of the modern world-system than the two central realities of the twentieth century, the rise and beginning of the decline of U.S. hegemony and the spectacular political reassertion of the extra-European world, which changed less than everyone had supposed it would.

If one compares the twentieth-century capitalist world-economy with the nineteenth-century capitalist world-economy, there is really one remarkable difference. The nineteenth century was the century of progress, in which the capitalist system seemed at last to be bearing its technological fruits and its potential for capital accumulation. It was the century in which the new ascendant geoculture of liberalism seemed to sweep away the last cultural vestiges of the Ancien Régime. It was the century in which the citizen was at last enthroned as the bearer of sovereignty. It was the century of Pax Britannica in the core zones (or at least people were deluded into ignoring the occasional ruptures) and of the final imperial conquests in the extra-European zones. It was the period in which to be bourgeois, White, male, Christian, and skilled were proof of civilization, and guaranteed progress. This is why the outbreak of the First World War in 1914 was such a cultural shock within the pan-European zones.

The twentieth century, as we said at the outset, has been a roller coaster. On the one hand, the technological advances in all fields have outstripped the anticipation of the nineteenth century by far. We live amidst a Jules Verne fantasy, and we are promised far more in the next thirty years. The same can be said of capital accumulation, even if we subtract all the capital stock destroyed in the multiple conflagrations. The democratization of the world has also proceeded apace, in the sense that the demands of full citizenship have been taken up by all and sundry, and have gone far beyond the imaginations of even the most daring nineteenth-century advocates. So there we are, bright sun at midnight.

Yet, as we all know, in the twenty-first century we are surrounded by fear, confusion, desperate scrambling again by all and sundry. We are discouraged by the horrors of the twentieth century. We are discouraged even more by the failures: the failure of the United States to fulfill the promise of the world liberal utopia constantly made by their ideologists; the failure of the antisystemic movements to create the new society, *les lendemains qui chantent,* they had constantly promised, at least until very recently. It is as though the incredible and ever faster growth of the capitalist system had gotten out of hand, and created cancers that are metastasizing all over the place.

We are face to face with uncertainty. It is all very well for Ilya Prigogine to tell us that uncertainty is the central reality of the universe, and not merely of our present historical situation. We still do not like it, and we find it very hard to handle—psychologically and politically. And yet we must. We find ourselves in the terminal phase of a historical system, an "age of transition." We must turn to our intellectual, moral, and hence political duties in an age of transition. The first in line is the search for lucidity about where we are. Rosa Luxemburg said already at the beginning of the twentieth century that "the most revolutionary thing one can do is always to proclaim loudly what is happening."

But once we've done that, we must discuss with our friends, with our allies, with all those who seem to want a more democratic and egalitarian world what kinds of new structures we might want, at least in broad outline, and what kinds of strategies we might use in the very intense, but inevitably confused, struggle of a major historical transition. We have to conduct such a discussion without hierarchy, with much openness, and with a certain amount of humility, but on the other hand with some clarity about minimal standards of inclusiveness and some insistence on maintaining a long-term historical view.

This will not be easy. Such discussion is of course already going on. But not enough. We need to add our voices, both in scholarly arenas and in more public arenas. We must be serious. We must be committed. We must be cool-headed. And we must be imaginative. No small order. But as Hillel said two thousand years ago, if not I, who? If not now, when?

CHAPTER THREE

Globalization:
A Long-Term Trajectory
of the World-System

The 1990s have been deluged with a discourse about globalization. We are told by virtually everyone that we are now living, and for the first time, in an era of globalization. We are told that globalization has changed everything: the sovereignty of states has declined; everyone's ability to resist the rules of the market has disappeared; our possibility of cultural autonomy has been virtually annulled; and the stability of all our identities has come into serious question. This state of presumed globalization has been celebrated by some, and bemoaned by others.

This discourse is in fact a gigantic misreading of current reality—a deception imposed upon us by powerful groups and, even worse, one that we have imposed upon ourselves, often despairingly. It is a discourse that leads us to ignore the real issues before us, and to misunderstand the historical crisis within which we find ourselves. We do indeed stand at a moment of transformation. But this is not that of an already established newly globalized world with clear rules. Rather we are located in an age of transition, transition not merely of a few backward countries who need to catch up with the spirit of globalization, but a transition in which the entire capitalist world-system will be transformed into something else. The future, far from being inevitable, one to which there is no alternative, is being determined in this transition, which has an extremely uncertain outcome.

The processes that are usually meant when we speak of globalization are not in fact new at all. They have existed for some five hundred years. The choice we have to make today is not whether or not to submit to these processes but, rather, what to do when these processes crumble, as they are presently crumbling. One would think, reading most accounts, that "globalization" is something that came into existence in the 1990s—perhaps only upon the collapse of the Soviet Union, perhaps a few years earlier. The 1990s are not, however, a significant time marker to use if one wants to analyze what is going on. Rather, we can most fruitfully look at the present situation in two other time frameworks, the one going from 1945 to today, and the one going from circa 1450 to today.

The period 1945 to today is that of a typical Kondratieff cycle of the capitalist world-economy, which has had, as always, two parts: an A-phase, or upward swing or economic expansion, which in this case went from 1945 to 1967/1973, and a B-phase, or downward swing or economic contraction, which has been going from 1967/1973 to today and probably will continue on for several more years. The period 1450 to today, by contrast, marks the life cycle of the capitalist world-economy, which had its period of genesis, its period of normal development, and now has entered into its period of terminal crisis. In order to comprehend the present situation, we need to distinguish between these two social times, and the empirical evidence for each of them.

In many ways, the Kondratieff cycle in which we find ourselves is the easier of the two social times to understand, since it resembles all previous Kondratieff cycles, which have been much studied. The A-phase of the present Kondratieff was what the French aptly called "*les trente glorieuses,*" It coincided with the high point of United States hegemony in the world-system, and occurred within the framework of a world order that the U.S. established after 1945. The United States, as we know, emerged from the Second World War as the only major industrial power whose industries were intact and whose territories had not been badly damaged by wartime destruction. U.S. industries had of course been perfecting their efficiencies for over a century. This long-term economic development combined with the literal collapse of the economic structures of the other major loci of world production gave the United States a productivity edge that was enormous, at least for a time, and made it easy for U.S. products to dominate the world market. It made possible furthermore the largest expansion of both value and real production in the history of the capitalist world-economy, creating simultaneously great wealth and great social strain in the world social system.

As of 1945, the United States had two major problems. It needed a relatively stable world order in which to profit from its economic advantages. And it needed to reestablish some effective demand in the rest of the world, if it expected to have customers for its flourishing productive enterprises. In the period from 1945 to 1955, the United States was able to solve both these problems without too much difficulty. The problem of world order was resolved in two parts. On the one hand, there was the establishment of a set of interstate institutions—notably, the United Nations, the IMF, and the World Bank—which the United States was able to control politically and which provided the formal framework of order. And on the other hand, and more important, the United States came to an arrangement with the only other serious military power in the post-1945 world, the U.S.S.R.

The Yalta agreement, worked out in detail over a decade, basically had three clauses. First, the world was to be divided de facto into a U.S. zone (most of the world) and a Soviet zone (the rest), the dividing line to be where their respective troops were located when the Second World War ended. Second, the Soviet zone could, if it wished, reduce to a minimum trade transactions with the U.S. zone until it strengthened its own productive machinery, but this involved as a counterpart that the United States would not be expected to contribute to the economic reconstruction of this zone. And third, both sides were free, indeed encouraged, to engage in vigorous, reciprocally hostile rhetoric, whose chief function seemed to be to consolidate the political control of the United States and the U.S.S.R. over their respective zones. The Berlin Blockade and the Korean War, both of which ended in truces reaffirming the original lines of partition, were the final capstones of this global agreement.

The problem of creating enough world-effective demand for U.S. production was solved by means of the Marshall Plan for western Europe and equivalent economic assistance to Japan, the latter occurring particularly after the outbreak of the Korean War and on the excuse of the war. The U.S. took advantage of the Cold War tensions to reinforce these economic links with military ties—the North Atlantic Treaty Organization (NATO) plus the United States–Japan Security Treaty—which ensured that these zones would follow faithfully the political lead of the United States on all major issues in the international arena.

To be sure, not everyone was happy with these arrangements. There were after all those left out of the benefits of Yalta—the Third World as a whole, the least-favored groups within the Western world, and the Soviet satellite states of eastern and central Europe, who endured their yoke but did not celebrate it.

Those left out erupted with some regularity, and on occasion with particular force: China in 1945–48, Vietnam, Algeria, Hungary in 1956, Cuba, southern Africa. These successive eruptions posed problems for the U.S. world order, and indeed for the Soviet Union as well. But they were like punches to the stomach of a strong boxer; the punches could be absorbed, and they were. The big exception was the Vietnam War, which began to bleed the United States, in terms of finance and lives lost, and therefore also in terms of U.S. national morale.

But the biggest blow to the United States, the hardest to absorb, was the economic recovery and then flourishing of western Europe and Japan. By the 1960s the productivity gap between these countries and the United States had been more or less eliminated. The western European countries and Japan recovered control over their national markets and began to compete effectively with U.S. products in the markets of third countries. They even began to be competitive within the U.S. home market. The automaticity of U.S. economic advantage had thus largely disappeared by the late 1960s.

The increase in world production resulting from the recovery and expansion of western European and Japanese production led to a glut on the world market and a sharp decline in the profitability of many of the principal industrial sectors, such as steel, automobiles, and electronics. The consequent downturn in the world-economy was marked by two major events: the necessity for the United States to go off the gold standard, and the world revolution of 1968. The first was caused by the fact that the politico-military expenses of enforcing U.S. hegemony plus the lessened competitivity in world markets turned out to be quite expensive and thus drained the U.S. financial surplus. The United States had to begin to work hard politically to maintain the economic advantages it had had so easily in the A-phase, and began by pulling in its monetary belt somewhat.

The world revolution of 1968 was triggered by the discontents of all those who had been left out in the well-organized world order of U.S. hegemony. The details of the 1968 uprisings were different in the various arenas of the world-system, but such uprisings did occur everywhere: in addition to the obvious 1968 events in the Western world and Japan, usually noted, I include the cultural revolution in China beginning in 1966 and the turn to "socialism with a human face" in Czechoslovakia in 1968, as well as the diverse happenings in Mexico, Senegal, Tunisia, India, and many other countries of the Third World. In all of them, however different the local situation, there was a recurrent double theme. The first was opposition to U.S. hegemony *and* to Soviet collusion with that hegemony. And the second was disillusionment with the Old Left in all its forms. The latter disillusionment was the unpredicted consequence of the very success of these old Left movements. The fact is that, in the period of U.S. hegemony, paradoxically (or perhaps not so paradoxically) the movements of the Old Left had come to power almost everywhere: as Communist parties in the socialist countries from the Elbe to the Yalu; as social democratic parties or their equivalents in the pan-European world of western Europe, North America, and Australasia; and as national liberation movements in the Third World or, equivalently, as populist movements in Latin America. They had come to power but they had not been able to achieve the second step they had envisaged, the transformation of society, or so the revolutionaries of 1968 believed. The movements in power were seen as having failed to deliver on their historic promises.

It is just at this point that the world-economy entered into a long period of stagnation. The crucial measure of a stagnation in the world-economy is that profits from production drop considerably from their levels at which they were in the preceding period, the A-phase. This has a series of clear consequences. First, persons with capital shift their primary locus of seeking profit from the productive sphere to the financial sphere. Second, there is significantly increased unemployment worldwide. Third, there occur significant shifts of loci of production from higher-wage areas to lower-wage areas (what used to be called the phenomenon of "runaway factories"). This trio of consequences can be seen to have occurred worldwide since circa 1970. We have had endless escalation of speculative activity, which is of course very profitable for a relatively small group of people, at least until the point when the bubble bursts. We have had very large shifts of production from North America, western Europe, and even Japan to other parts of the world-system, which have consequently claimed that they were "industrializing" and therefore developing. Another way of characterizing what happened is to say that these semiperipheral countries were the recipients of what were now less profitable industries. And we have had a rise in unemployment everywhere—in most countries of the South to be sure, but in the North as well. To be sure, unemployment rates do not have to be uniform in all countries. Far from it! Indeed, one of the major activities of the governments of all states during this period has been to try to shift the unemployment burden to other states, but such shifts can be only temporarily successful.

Let us rapidly review how this scenario has been played out.

The most striking economic happening of the early 1970s, now almost forgotten but at the time one that absorbed the newspaper headlines of the entire world, was the OPEC oil price rise. All of a sudden, the major oil-producing states created in effect a serious cartel and raised the price of oil on the world market considerably. Originally this was hailed by some as an intelligent political move by Third World states against the principal states of the North. But observe right away something strange. The decision of OPEC, a decision that had been advocated for a long time by the so-called radical states such as Libya and Algeria, was only made possible now by the suddenly acquired enthusiastic support of the two closest friends of the United States in the Middle East, Saudi Arabia and Iran under the shah. How curious!

The effect of the oil-price rise was immediate. It raised prices of virtually all other products, but unevenly. It led to a reduction in production of many commodities, which was useful, given the production glut. Countries that relied on income from the export of raw materials saw their income from this source go down at the very moment that their imports went up in price; hence, they encountered acute balance-of-payments difficulties. The increased income from the sale of oil went first of all to oil-producing countries, and of course to the so-called Seven Sisters, the great transnational megastructures in the petroleum industry. The oil-producing countries suddenly had a monetary surplus. Some of it went to increased expenditures on their part, largely imports from the North, which helped restore demand in the countries of the North. But another part went into bank accounts, largely in the United States and Germany. The increased funds in the banks had to be lent to someone. These banks aggressively peddled loans to the finance ministers of poorer countries suffering from balance-of-payment difficulties, acute unemployment, and consequent internal unrest. These countries borrowed extensively, but then found it difficult to repay the loans, on which interest compounded until debt payments rose to intolerable levels by 1980. It was just at this point that the Japanese competitive advantage suddenly blossomed, although western Europe was also not doing badly, whereas the United States was suffering from so-called stagflation.

In the meantime, the U.S. sought to maintain its political hold on western Europe and Japan by erecting a pastiche of consultative structures: the Trilateral Commission and the G-7 (which, be it said, was an idea of Valéry Giscard d'Estaing, which he thought might limit U.S. power, but which turned out to do the opposite). The United States reacted politically to the Vietnam fiasco by adopting for a time a "low posture" in the Third World—becoming more flexible in zones like Angola, Nicaragua, Iran, and Cambodia. But not everyone was ready to respond to such flexibility by lowering their demands. The new revolutionary government of Iran, under Ayatollah Khomeini, refused to play by the rules of the interstate game, denouncing the United States as the Great Satan (and the Soviet Union as the number two Satan) and imprisoning U.S. diplomats. Liberal centrism and Keynesian economics suddenly went out of fashion. Margaret Thatcher launched so-called neoliberalism, which was of course really an aggressive conservatism of a type that had not been seen since 1848, and which involved an attempt to reverse welfare-state redistribution so that it went to the upper classes rather than to the lower classes.

If the 1970s thus ended with a bang, the 1980s were not far behind. The loans to the poorer states had gotten out of hand, and the debt crisis began. It began, not in 1982, as usually argued, when Mexico announced it could not repay its debt, but in 1980, when the Gierek government of Poland decided to try to meet its debt problems by squeezing its working class, a move that met spectacular resistance with the emergence of Solidarity (*Solidarność*) in Gdansk. The events in Poland marked the death knell of the Soviet satellite system in eastern and central Europe, a key linchpin in the Yalta arrangements, although it would still take a decade for the disintegration to be fully accomplished. This was the same moment that the U.S.S.R. made the crucial tactical error of going into Afghanistan. It would thus bleed itself in the same way the United States had done in Vietnam, but it had less social resilience to enable it to survive the consequences.

The 1980s can be summed up in a few code phrases. The first

was the "debt crisis," which brought down not only most of Latin America (not to speak of Africa) but also eastern and central Europe. The debt crisis revealed the degree to which the economic realities of eastern and central Europe were not essentially different from those of the Third World. The second was the "flying geese" of East Asia—Japan's amazing economic romp through the world-economy, followed by and dragging along first the four dragons (South Korea, Taiwan, Hong Kong, and Singapore), and eventually southeast Asia and mainland China as well. The third was the "military Keynesianism" of the Reagan administration, which overcame U.S. recession and high unemployment by means of enormous government borrowing, in particular from Japan, using as its excuse the buildup of military structures, whose single biggest consequence was the creation of an incredible U.S. national debt. The fourth was the flourishing on the U.S. stock exchange of "junk bonds," which essentially meant enormous borrowing on the part of large corporations in order to make short-run speculative profits at the expense of productive machinery; it caused in turn so-called downsizing, which meant forcing middle-income strata into lower-paying jobs in the economy.

In the 1980s, the whole world-economy looked in bad shape except for East Asia, although that did not prevent financial speculators from making astounding profits. And along with this, and for a time, a certain stratum of the upper middle class, the so-called yuppies, prospered, causing inflationary pressures in the luxury market and in real estate worldwide. But most of the world suffered loss of income and deflation through the collapse of currencies. In the wake of these worldwide difficulties, the Soviet Union came apart. Or rather, Gorbachev made a spectacular attempt to prevent this by throwing ballast overboard. He unilaterally disarmed, forcing U.S. reciprocity. He abandoned Afghanistan and, in effect, eastern and central Europe. And he sought cautiously to reform the internal political system. His downfall was due to the fact that he grievously underestimated the emergent forces of nationalism within the Soviet Union itself, and most of all, that of Russian nationalism.

The tensile strength of the Yalta agreements came undone, as much because of U.S. as because of Soviet weakness. Neither the United States nor Gorbachev wanted the arrangements to come apart. But the long stagnation in the world-economy had undone them. And Humpty Dumpty could not be put together again.

Since 1970 the world-economy had gone through three debt cycles, which were all attempts to maintain the spending power of the world-system: the oil-money loans to the Third World and to the socialist countries; the borrowing of the U.S. government; and the borrowing of the large corporations. Each spate of borrowing artificially raised prices in some areas beyond their market value. Each led to great difficulties about repayment, which were handled by various kinds of pseudo-bankruptcies. Finally, in 1990, the Japanese real estate bubble burst, reducing paper value enormously. The last bulwark of productive economic strength in the world-economy had come under assault. This was to be the story of the 1990s.

The U.S. political position now came under severe attack, not despite but precisely because of the collapse of the Soviet Union. Saddam Hussein decided to take advantage of the post-Yalta reality, directly challenging the United States militarily by invading Kuwait. He was able to do this because the U.S.S.R. was no longer in a position to restrain him. He did this because, in the short run, it promised to solve the problems of Iraq's heavy debts to Kuwait and to increase its oil income. And he did this because he hoped to use this invasion in the middle run as the basis for a military unification of the Arab world under his aegis, a unification he saw as a necessary step in a direct military challenge to the North in general, and to the United States in particular.

There were two possibilities for Saddam, that the United States would back down or that it would not. If the first occurred, his victory would be immediate. But he counted on the fact that, even if the second occurred, he would gain over the longer run. Thus far, history has not proved his calculation wrong. The United States of course did mobilize the necessary military force to drive the Iraqis out of Kuwait and to place Iraq under severe international constraints after that. But the price for the United States was high. The Gulf War demonstrated that the U.S. could not afford financially to conduct such operations. The entire military bill of the U.S. was borne by Saudi Arabia, Kuwait, Japan, and Germany. And the war demonstrated that the U.S. could not remove Saddam inside Iraq because it was unwilling to send troops into the interior of Iraq. The two constraints—financial and military—of the United States were both dictated by U.S. public opinion, which was ready to applaud nationalist victory, provided it cost no money and no lives. This is the basic explanation of how Saddam has been able to survive ever since and why the efforts to limit Iraq's maintenance of weapons of mass destruction have been so ineffectual.

In the 1990s, western Europe took an essential step forward in its unification with the creation of the euro and thus achieved the financial underpinning necessary to pull away from its close political links to the United States. This will no doubt lead in the coming decade to the creation of a real European army, and thereby a military disjunction from the U.S. The disintegration of the Balkan zone has demonstrated clearly the very limited effectiveness of NATO as a political force, and has managed to strain even further U.S.–western European relations.

And in the midst of all this came the so-called Asian crisis.

The financial collapse of the southeast Asian states and the four dragons was followed by the disastrous interference of the IMF, which exacerbated both the economic and political consequences of the crisis. What we should note essentially about this collapse is that deflation had at last hit East Asia and its derivative zone, followed, as we know, by Russia and Brazil. The world holds its breath, waiting for it to hit the United States. When this occurs we shall then enter into the last subphase of this Kondratieff B-phase.

After that, will we at last see a new Kondratieff A-phase? Yes, assuredly, but one within a secular deflation as in the seventeenth and nineteenth centuries, and not one within a secular inflation as in the sixteenth, eighteenth, and twentieth centuries. But we shall also see something different. We must now turn our attention away from the Kondratieff cycles and onto the long-term development of the modern world-system as an historical system.

The capitalist world-economy has long maintained itself, as any system does, by mechanisms that restore equilibrium every time its processes move away from it. The equilibrium is never restored immediately, but only after a sufficient deviation from the norm occurs, and of course it never is restored perfectly. Because it requires that deviations go a certain distance before they trigger countermovements, the result is that the capitalist world-economy, like any other system, has cyclical rhythms of multiple kinds. We have been discussing one of the principal ones it has developed, which are called Kondratieff cycles. They are not the only ones.

The equilibrium is never restored to the same point because the countermovements require some change in the underlying parameters of the system. Hence the equilibrium is always a moving equilibrium, and therefore the system has secular trends. It is this combination of cyclical rhythms and secular trends that define a system that is functioning "normally." However, secular trends cannot go on forever, because they hit asymptotes. Once this happens, it is no longer possible for the cyclical rhythms to bring the system back into equilibrium, and this is when a system gets into trouble. It then enters into its terminal crisis, and bifurcates—that is, it finds itself before two or more alternative routes to a new structure, with a new equilibrium, new cyclical rhythms, and new secular trends. But which of the two alternative routes the system will take, that is, what kind of new system will be established, is intrinsically not possible to determine in advance, since it is a function of an infinity of particular choices that are not systemically constrained. This is what is happening now in the capitalist world-economy.

To appreciate this, we must look at the three major secular trends that are approaching their asymptotes. Each of them is thereby creating limits to the accumulation of capital. Since the endless accumulation of capital is the defining feature of capitalism as an historical system, the triple pressure is tending to make unfeasible the primary motor of the system and hence is creating a structural crisis.

The first secular trend is the rise of the real wage level as a percentage of costs of production, calculated as an average throughout the whole world-economy. Obviously the lower this is, the higher the profit level, and vice versa. What determines the real wage level? Quite clearly, the answer is the *rapport de forces* between the labor force in a given zone and sector of the world-economy and the employers of such labor. This *rapport de forces* is a function primarily of the political strength of the two groups in what we call the class struggle. To speak of the market as the constraining element in determining wage levels is deceptive, since the market value of labor is a function of the multiple *rapports de force* in the various zones of the world-economy. These varying political strengths are in turn a function of the efficacy of political organization in one form or another of given workforces and the real alternatives of the employers in terms of relocating their operations. Both of these factors constantly change.

What one can say is that, over time, in any given geographical or sectoral locality, the workforce will seek to create some form of syndical organization and action that will enable its members to bargain more effectively, either directly with the employer or indirectly via their influence on the relevant political machinery. While no doubt such political strength can be set back in given localities through political counteroffensives of capitalist groups, it is also true that the long-run "democratization" of the political machineries throughout the history of the modern world-system have served to make the curve of the political strength of the working classes an upward one over the *longue durée* in virtually all states in the world-system.

The principal mechanism by which capitalists worldwide have been able to limit this political pressure has been the relocation of given sectors of production to other zones of the world-economy that are on the average lower-wage areas. This is a difficult operation politically as well as one dependent on taking skill levels into the calculations of eventual profits. Hence, it has tended to be done primarily during Kondratieff B-phases, as we suggested above. Nonetheless, it has been done repeatedly during the historical development of the modern world-system. But why are the areas into which the sectors are being relocated lower-wage areas in the first place? It solves nothing to say that this is the consequence of "historical" wage levels. Whence this history?

The primary source of truly low-wage labor has always been newly recruited migrants from rural areas, often entering the wage-labor market for the first time. They are ready to accept what are by world standards low wages for two reasons. The net income they are receiving is in fact higher than the net income they previously received in their rural activity. And they are socially uprooted, and consequently politically somewhat in disarray, and unable therefore to defend their interests very effectively. Both explanations wear out over time, certainly after, say, thirty years, and such workers begin to exert pressures on wage levels parallel to those of workers in other regions of the world-economy. In this case, the major option for capitalists is to relocate yet again.

As one can see, such a mode of conducting the class struggle is dependent on there always being new areas of the world-system into which to relocate, and this is dependent on the existence of a significant rural sector not yet engaged in the wage-labor market. But the latter is precisely what has been diminishing as a secular trend. The deruralization of the world is on a fast upward curve. It has occurred continuously over five hundred years, but has accelerated most dramatically since 1945. It is quite possible to foresee that the rural sector will have largely disappeared in another twenty-five years. Once the whole world-system is deruralized, the only option for capitalists is to pursue the class struggles where they are presently located. And here the odds are against them. Even with the increased polarization of levels of real income not only in the world-system as a whole but also within the wealthiest countries, the political and market sophistication of the lower strata continues to grow. Even where there are large numbers of persons who are technically unemployed and are deriving their income, such as it is, from the informal economy, the real alternatives available to workers located in the barrios and favelas of the world-system mean that they are in a position to demand reasonable wage levels in order to enter the formal wage economy. The net result of all of this is a serious pressure on profit levels that will increase over time.

The second secular trend disturbing to capitalists is rather different. It has to do not with the cost of wage labor but with the cost of material inputs. What is involved in the cost of inputs? It is not only the price at which they are bought from a different firm but also the cost of treating them. Now while the cost of purchase is normally borne entirely by the firm that will eventually get the profits, the costs of treating the materials is often partially borne by others. For example, if the treatment of raw materials results in toxic or cumbersome waste, part of the cost involved is getting rid of such waste, and if toxic, in a safe manner. Firms of course desire to minimize these costs of disposal. One way they can do this, a way very widely practiced, is by placing it somewhere away from the factory site after minimal detoxification, for example, by dumping chemical toxins into a stream. This is called by economists "externalizing the costs." Of course, this is not the end of the costs of disposal. To stick to the example, if toxins are dumped into a stream, this may poison the stream, and eventually (perhaps decades later) there will be damage to people or to other matter, at costs that are real, if difficult to calculate. And there may be a social decision to clean up the toxins, in which case the body that undertakes the cleanup, often the state, is bearing the cost. Another mode of reducing costs is to utilize raw materials, but not to provide for (that is, pay for) their renewal, a problem especially true of organic matter. Such externalization of costs significantly reduces the costs of raw materials to given producers and hence increases the margin of profit.

The problem here is akin to that with relocation as a solution to wage costs. It works as long as there are previously unutilized areas in which to dump waste. But eventually there are no more streams to pollute, or trees to cut down—or at least, not without serious immediate consequences for the health of the biosphere. This is the situation in which we find ourselves today after five hundred years of such practices, which is why today we have an ecology movement that has been growing rapidly throughout the world.

What can be done? Well, the governments of the world can undertake what amounts to a vast cleanup campaign and a vast campaign of organic renewal. The problem is the cost of an effective operation, which is enormous, and thus must be paid for by some form of taxes. There are only two sources: either the firms that are considered to have been the perpetrators of the waste, or the rest of us. If it is the former, the pressure on the profit margins will be impressively high. If it is the latter, the tax burdens will mount significantly, a problem to which we are coming. Furthermore, there is not much point in cleanup and organic renewal if the practices remain as at present, since it would amount to cleaning the Augean stables. Hence, the logical inference is to require the total internalization of all costs. This, however, would add still further to the pressure on the profits of individual firms. I do not see any plausible solution for this social dilemma within the framework of a capitalist world-economy, and hence I suggest that the rising cost of material inputs is the second structural pressure on the accumulation of capital.

The third pressure lies in the realm of taxation. Taxation is a payment for social services, and therefore is accepted as a reasonable cost of production, provided taxes are not too high. Now what has determined the level of taxation? To be sure, there has been the constant demand of security (the military, the police). This demand has steadily risen over the centuries because of the increasing relative costs of the means of security, the scope of military actions, and the perceived need of police actions. The second steady rise has been in the size of the civil bureaucracies of the world, a function first of all of the need to collect taxes and second of all to perform the expanding functions of modern states.

The major expanding function has been the provision for certain popular demands. This has not been an optional expense.

The growth of these provisions has been a principal means of ensuring relative political stability in response to growing discontents of the lower strata concerning the increasing polarization of real income, which has been a steady feature of the world-system. Social welfare efforts by governments have been the pay-off utilized to tame the "dangerous classes," that is, to keep the class struggle within limited bounds.

We call the response to these popular demands "democratization," and it has also been a very real secular trend. There are three principal varieties of such popular demands: educational institutions, health facilities, and guarantees of income across the lifetime of individuals (especially, unemployment insurance and social security for the aged). There are two things to be noted about such demands. They have been made in more and more zones of the world-system, and are today nearly universal. And the levels of the demands have risen steadily within each country, with no clear limit in sight.

This has meant, has had to mean, steadily rising tax rates in virtually every country, with at most occasional slight reductions. But, of course, at a certain point, such redistributive taxation reaches levels where it interferes seriously with the possibility of accumulating capital. Hence the reaction today to what is perceived as the "fiscal crises of the states" is for capitalists to demand a rollback, and to seek popular support on the grounds that taxation of individuals is also rising sharply. The irony is that while there is often popular support for limiting taxes, there is zero popular support for cutting back welfare provisions (of education, of health, or of income guarantees). Indeed, at the very time that there are complaints about high taxation, the levels of popular demand on government services are growing. So here, too, we have a structural pressure on the accumulation of capital.

So there we are—three major structural pressures on the ability of capitalists to accumulate capital, the result of secular trends, which continuously ratchet upward. This crisis, not in growth but in capital accumulation, is further complicated by a different phenomenon, the loss of legitimation of the state structures. States are a crucial element in the ability of capitalists to accumulate capital. States make possible quasi-monopolies, which are the only source of significant profit levels. States act to tame the "dangerous classes," both by repression and by appeasement. States are the principal source of ideologies that persuade the mass of the population to be relatively patient.

The major argument for patience has been the inevitability of reform. Things will get better—if not immediately, then for one's children and grandchildren. A more prosperous, more egalitarian world is on the horizon. This is of course official liberal ideology, and has dominated the geoculture since the nineteenth century. But it has also been the theme of all the antisystemic movements, not least those that have proclaimed themselves most revolutionary. These movements have particularly emphasized this theme when they held state power. They have said to their own working classes that they were "developing" their economies, and these working classes must be patient while the fruits of economic growth eventually improve their life situations. They have preached patience about standards of living but also about the absence of political equality.

As long as such antisystemic movements—whether they were Communist or social democratic, or national liberation movements—were in their mobilizing phase against inegalitarian, militaristic, dictatorial, fascist, colonial, or even simply conservative regimes, this theme was muted and did not interfere with the ability of antisystemic movements to secure extensive popular support. Once, however, such movements came to power, as they did extensively throughout the world during the period from 1945 to 1970 (the Kondratieff A-phase period of which we have been speaking), they were put to the test. And worldwide they have been found wanting. The record of post-"revolutionary" regimes has been that they have not been able to reduce worldwide or even internal polarization to any significant degree nor have they been able to institute serious internal political equality. They have no doubt accomplished many reforms, but they promised far more than reforms. And because the world-system has remained a capitalist world-economy, the regimes outside the core zone have been structurally unable to "catch up" with the wealthy countries.

This is not merely a matter of academic analysis. The result of these realities has been a monumental disillusionment with the antisystemic movements. To the extent that they retain support, it is at most as a reformist group better perhaps than a more right-wing alternative, but certainly not as a harbinger of the new society. The major result has been a massive disinvestment in state structures. The masses of the world, having turned toward the states as agents of transformation, have now returned to a more fundamental skepticism about the ability of the states to promote transformation, or even to maintain social order.

This worldwide upsurge of antistatism has two immediate consequences. One is that social fears have escalated, and people everywhere are taking back from the states the role of providing for their own security. But of course this institutes a negative spiral. The more they do so the more there is chaotic violence, and the more there is chaotic violence, the more the states find themselves unable to handle the situation, and therefore the more people disinvest the state, which further weakens the ability of the states to limit the spiral. We have entered into this kind of spiral at varying paces in the various countries of the world-system, but at a growing pace virtually everywhere.

The second consequence is one for the capitalists. States that are delegitimated find it far more difficult to perform their function of guaranteeing the quasi-monopolies capitalists need, not to speak of maintaining their ability to tame the "dangerous classes." Thus, at the very moment that capitalists are faced with three structural squeezes on the global rates of profit, and hence on their ability to accumulate capital, they find that the states are less able than before to help them resolve these dilemmas.

Thus it is that we can say that the capitalist world-economy has now entered its terminal crisis, a crisis that may last up to fifty years. The real question before us is what will happen during this crisis, this transition from the present world-system to some other kind of historical system or systems. Analytically, the key question is the relation between the Kondratieff cycles I first described and the systemic crisis of which I have been talking now. Politically, there is the question of what kind of social action is possible and desirable during a systemic transition.

Kondratieff cycles are part of the "normal" functioning of the capitalist world-economy. Such so-called normal functioning does not cease because the system has entered into a systemic crisis. The various mechanisms that account for the behavior of a capitalist system are still in place. When the present B-phase has exhausted itself, we shall undoubtedly have an A-phase of a new cycle. However, the systemic crisis interferes seriously with the trajectory. It is a bit as though one tried to drive a car downhill with a motor still intact but with a damaged body and wheels. The car would no doubt roll forward but surely not in the straight line one would have previously expected nor with the same guarantees that the brakes would work efficiently. How it would behave would become rather difficult to assess in advance. Supplying more gas to the motor might have unexpected consequences. The car could crash.

Schumpeter accustomed us a long time ago to the idea that capitalism would not collapse because of its failures but because of its successes. We have tried to indicate here how the successes (modes of counteracting downturns in the world-economy, modes of maximizing the accumulation of capital) have, over time, created structural limits to the very accumulation of capital they were intended to ensure. This is concrete empirical evidence of the Schumpeterian assumption. No doubt, to continue the analogy of the damaged automobile, a wise chauffeur might drive quite slowly under these difficult conditions. But there is no wise chauffeur in the capitalist world-economy. No individual or group has the power to make the necessary decisions alone. And the very fact that these decisions are being made by a large number of actors, operating separately and each in his or her own immediate interests, virtually ensures that the car will not slow down. Probably, it will start to go faster and faster.

Consequently, what we may expect is recklessness. As the world-economy enters a new period of expansion, it will thereby exacerbate the very conditions that have led it into a terminal crisis. In technical terms, the fluctuations will get wilder and wilder, or more "chaotic," and the direction in which the trajectory is moving ever more uncertain, as the route takes more and more zigzags with every greater rapidity. At the same time, we may expect the degree of collective and individual security to decrease, perhaps vertiginously, as the state structures lose more and more legitimacy. And this will no doubt increase the amount of day-by-day violence in the world-system. This will be frightening to most people, as well it should be.

Politically, this situation will be one of great confusion, since the standard political analyses we have developed to understand the modern world-system will seem not to apply or will seem to be outdated. This will not really be true. But these analyses will apply primarily to the ongoing processes of the existing world-system and not to the reality of a transition. This is why it is so important to be clear on the distinction between the two and on the ways in which this double reality will be playing itself out.

In terms of the ongoing reality, it will be almost impossible for political action to affect it very much. To return to the analogy of the damaged car going downhill, we may correctly feel somewhat helpless, and the most we may be able to do is to try to maneuver so as to minimize immediate harm to ourselves. But in terms of the transition as a whole, the opposite is true. Precisely because its outcome is unpredictable, precisely because its fluctuations are so wild, it will be true that even the slightest political action will have great consequences. I like to think of this as the moment in historical time when free will truly comes into play.

We can think of this long transition as one enormous political struggle between two large camps: the camp of all those who wish to retain the privileges of the existing inegalitarian system, albeit in different forms, perhaps vastly different forms; and the camp of all those who would like to see the creation of a new historical system that will be significantly more democratic and more egalitarian. However, we cannot expect that the members of the first camp will present themselves the way I describe them. They will assert that they are modernizers, new democrats advocates of freedom, and progressive. They may even claim to be revolutionary. The key is to be found not in the rhetoric but in the substantive reality of what is being proposed.

The outcome of the political struggle will be in part the result of who is able to mobilize whom, but it will also result in large part from the ability to analyze better what is going on and what are the real historical alternatives with which we are collectively faced. That is to say, it is a moment when we need to unify knowledge, imagination, and praxis. Or else we risk saying, a century from now, "Plus ça change, plus c'est la même chose." The outcome is, I insist, intrinsically uncertain, and therefore precisely open to human intervention and creativity.

CHAPTER FOUR

*Racism: Our Albatross**

"God save thee, ancient Mariner,
from the fiends, that plague thee thus!—
Why look'st thou so?"—"With my crossbow
I shot the albatross."

SAMUEL TAYLOR COLERIDGE
"THE RIME OF THE ANCIENT MARINER"

I n Coleridge's poem, a ship was driven astray by the winds
into hostile climate. The only solace of the seamen was an albatross, which came to share their food. But Coleridge's
mariner shot him, for some unknown reason—perhaps sheer arrogance. And, as a result, all on the ship suffered. The gods were
punishing the misdeed. The other sailors hung the albatross
around the mariner's neck. The albatross, symbol of friendship,
now became symbol of guilt and shame. The mariner was the
sole survivor of the voyage. And he spent his life obsessed with
what he had done. The live albatross is the other who opened
himself to us in strange and far off lands. The dead albatross that
hangs around our neck is our legacy of arrogance, our racism.
We are obsessed with it, and we find no peace.

* This paper was originally given on March 9, 2000 in Vienna at a dramatic
moment in Austrian history.

I was asked more than a year ago to travel to Vienna to speak on "Social Science in an Age of Transition." My talk was to be in the context of a series of lectures in 2001 entitled "Von der Notwendigkeit des Überflüssigen—Sozialwissenschaften und Gesellschaft" ("On the Necessity of Superfluity—Social Sciences and Society"). I happily accepted. I believed I was coming to the Vienna that had had a glorious role in the building of world social science, especially in the era of *Traum und Wirklichkeit* (Dream and Reality), *1870–1930*. Vienna was the home of Sigmund Freud, whom I believe to have been the single most important figure in social science in the twentieth century. Or at least Vienna was his home until he was forced by the Nazis to flee to London in 1939, his dying year. Vienna also was home, for an important part of their lives, to Joseph Aloïs Schumpeter and Karl Polanyi. Men of strikingly opposite political opinions, they were in my view the two most important political economists of the twentieth century, underrecognized and undercelebrated. And Vienna was the home of my own teacher, Paul Lazarsfeld, whose combination of policy-oriented research and pathbreaking methodological innovations began with *Arbeitlosen von Marienthal,* a study he did with Marie Jahoda and Hans Zeisel. It was to this Vienna I was coming.

Then came the last Austrian elections, of 1999, with their far from inevitable consequence, the inclusion of Jörg Haider's far-right party, the Freiheitliche Partei Österreichs (FPÖ), in the government. The other states in the European Union (EU) reacted strongly to this change of regime, and suspended bilateral relations with Austria. I had to consider whether I still would come, and I hesitated. If I am here today, it is for two reasons. First, I wished to affirm my solidarity with *des andere Österreich* ("the other Austria"), which has manifested itself so visibly since the new government was installed. But second, and even more important, I came to assume my own responsibilities as a social scientist. We have all shot the albatross. It hangs around all our necks. And we must struggle with our souls and our minds to atone, to reconstruct, to create a different kind of historical system, one that would be beyond the racism that afflicts the modern world so deeply and so viciously. I therefore retitled my talk. It is now "The Racist Albatross: The Social Science, Jörg Haider, and *Widerstand.*"*

The facts of what happened in Austria seemed quite simple on the surface. For a number of successive legislatures, Austria had been governed by a national coalition of the two major and mainline parties, the Sozialdemokratische Partei Österreichs (SPÖ) and the Österreichische Volkspartei (ÖVP). One was center-left and the other was center-right and Christian democratic. Their combined vote, at one time overwhelming, declined throughout the 1990s. And in the 1999 elections, the FPÖ for the first time came in second in the vote, surpassing the ÖVP, albeit by only several hundred votes. The subsequent discussions between the two mainstream parties on forming still one more national coalition failed, and the ÖVP turned to the FPÖ as a coalition partner to form a government. This decision of the ÖVP upset many people in Austria, including President Tomas Klestil. But the ÖVP persisted, and a government was formed.

The decision also upset—and, it must be added, surprised—the political leaders of the other EU states. They decided collectively to suspend bilateral relations with Austria, and despite some voices that have questioned the wisdom of this, the EU maintained its position. The EU action in turn upset many Austrians, and not only those who supported the formation of the

---

* *Widerstand,* which means "resistance," was the slogan of the Austrians demonstrating against the new government. It was the term used between 1933 and 1945 for those actively opposing the Nazis. Jörg Haider was the far-right, populist leader of the FPÖ.

present government but also many of its opponents. Many of the latter argued that the EU was overstating the dangers of including the FPÖ in the government. "Haider is no Hitler" was a common formulation of this position. Others argued that the equivalents of Haider could be found in all the EU states, and to some extent even in their governments. And hence, these people argued, it was hypocritical of the EU to take the action that it did. And finally, some Austrians argued (as did some other Europeans) that the appropriate action by the EU would have been to wait and see, and that if eventually the new Austrian government did something reprehensible, then and only then would it be time to take action. Meanwhile, within Austria itself, there was launched a *Widerstand*.

I would like to take as my object of analysis not the FPÖ as a party and what it stands for but the strong reaction of the EU to the inclusion of this party in the Austrian government and the Austrian counterreaction as well as the *Widerstand*. Both the reaction and the counterreaction can only be understood if we shift our analytic focus from Austria proper to the world-system as a whole, its realities, and to what social scientists have been telling us about these realities. I propose therefore to look at this larger context in four time frames: the modern world-system since 1989; the modern world-system since 1945; the modern world-system since 1492; and the modern world-system after 2000. These are of course symbolic dates, but symbols in this case are very important. They help us to discuss both realities and the perception of realities. In doing this, I hope that I am expressing solidarity with the Austrian *Widerstand,* and I hope that I am assuming my own responsibilities, both moral and intellectual, as a social scientist.

THE WORLD-SYSTEM SINCE 1989

In 1989, the so-called socialist bloc of nations collapsed. The countries of eastern and central Europe, which had been held in check by the Brezhnev Doctrine (and, even more importantly, by the Yalta agreement), effectively asserted their political autonomy from the Soviet Union, and each proceeded to dismantle its Leninist system. Within two years, the Communist Party of the Soviet Union itself was dissolved, and indeed the U.S.S.R. broke up into its fifteen constituent units. If the story of the Communist states was different in East Asia and Cuba, this changed little in the consequences that these eastern European happenings had for the geopolitics of the world-system.

Since 1989, a great deal of world attention has been concentrated on these European former Communist countries. There have been endless conferences of social scientists on their so-called transition, to the point where we talk of "transitology." And in the zones that formerly constituted the Federal Republic of Yugoslavia and in the Caucasian areas of the Soviet Union, there have been a large number of quite nasty civil wars, in which in several cases outside powers have been actively engaged. Many social scientists have analyzed this violence under headings such as "ethnic purification," a phenomenon asserted to be the result of long-enduring ethnic hostilities. Even in states that have escaped a high level of internal violence, such as the Czech Republic, Hungary, and the Baltic states, there have occurred unpleasant reminders of seemingly resurgent ethnic tensions. At the same time, similar kinds of full-scale and also low-level civil wars have been occurring in many parts of Africa as well as in Indonesia, to take only the most obvious cases.

In the pan-European world (by which term I mean western Europe plus North America and Australasia but not east-central Europe), the analysis of these civil wars has centered on the presumed weakness of the civil societies in these states and the low level of their historic concern for human rights. Anyone who has read the press in western Europe cannot miss the degree to which, in what is being called a post-Communist world, the attention to these formerly Communist areas has been focused on a "problem." And the "problem" has been defined de facto as the absence in these areas of the higher level of modernity presumably to be found in the pan-European world.

Meanwhile, it is equally striking how little attention—by the press, by politicians, and especially by social scientists—has been paid to what has changed since 1989 in the pan-European world itself. Political regimes that had built their national logics on the fact that they were involved in a "Cold War" suddenly discovered that the arrangements they had sustained for forty years now seemed pointless, to their voters and to the politicians themselves. Why have a system of *pentapartiti* (and its *tangentopoli*)* in Italy built around the permanent majority of Democrazia Cristiana, if there was no Cold War? What was there now to hold together a Gaullist party in France, or even the Christlich-Demokratische Union in Germany? Why should the Republican Party in the United States continue to be bound by the constraints of a "bilateral foreign policy"? The result of these self-doubts? The major conservative parties in the pan-European world are crumbling, torn apart by divisions between the new ultras of economic liberalism and a more social conservatism, whether it be of the variety that wishes the state to rectify the degraded morality of the citizenry or the variety that retains a paternalist concern for social safety nets. And these factions fight each other amidst supporters who are fearful that, in the

---

* The *pentapartiti* refers to the five parties that were in almost every Italian government over a forty-year period, all organized around the Christian-Democratic Party. *Tangentopoli* is an invented word referring to the widespread corruption in all these parties.

turmoil, their existing social positions and income may be seriously threatened.

Well, then, what about the center-left parties, most of which call themselves social democratic? These parties, too, are in trouble. The collapse of the Communisms was in fact only the culmination of a spreading disillusionment with the Old Left in *all* of its three main versions—Communist parties, social democratic parties, and national liberation movements—a disillusionment that was signaled dramatically by the 1968 world revolution. This disillusionment was the consequence, not so paradoxically, of the very political success of these same movements. For once they were in power, these movements showed themselves not really capable of carrying through with their historic promise that, if only they achieved state power, they could and would build a new society, that is, transform society substantially in the direction of a more egalitarian, more democratic world.

In western Europe, the Old Left meant primarily the social democrats. And what has happened, since 1968 but even more since 1989, is that people may vote for such parties as a lesser evil, but no one dances in the streets when they win an election. No one expects them to bring about a revolution, even a peaceful one. And the most disillusioned of all are these parties' own leaders, who are reduced to talking the centrist language of the "third way." Furthermore, with this disillusionment in the Old Left parties has come a disengagement from the state structures themselves. The states had been tolerated by their populations, even lauded as potential agents of social transformation. Now they were coming to be seen primarily as agents of corruption and of the use of unnecessary force, no longer the citizen's rampart but now the citizen's burden.

You can see from this description that Austria is merely one more instance of a general pan-European pattern. Why have a national coalition in a post-Communist era? And why even vote for parties that seem primarily interested in the *Proporz* (system in which the two major parties divided up the patronage)? It is in this context that the FPÖ received its 26.9 percent of the vote on October 3, 1999. This is, to be sure, the highest percentage achieved by any far-right party in any European country since 1945. In 1995, Le Pen's Front National got 15.1 percent in France, and this already was a shock. But at that time, the two main conservative parties insisted that they would refuse the support of the FN at any level. And when, in the regional elections of 1998, the results were such that the conservative parties could form majorities in a large number of regions only with the support of those elected on the ticket of the FN, five regional leaders ignored this directive and obtained FN support for their regional governments. However, these regional leaders were promptly expelled from the two main conservative national parties, the RPR and the UDR. On the other hand, in Italy Berlusconi did form a government with the support of Gianfranco Fini and his Alleanza Nazionale, which was a party similar to that of Haider, with nonetheless the nuance that Fini had specifically renounced its neo-Fascist past before the elections.

Still why then, as many Austrians insist, did the EU take such a strong position on what happened in Austria? The answer is really quite simple. The EU countries were all afraid, precisely because their countries were not that different from Austria, that they would be faced with similar choices in the near future, and that they might be tempted to follow the path of the ÖVP. It was their fears of themselves that led to the strong EU reaction. At the same time, Austrians' incomprehension that they had indeed crossed a line that all of western Europe had set for itself not in 1999 but in 1945 accounts for the Austrian counterreaction. Let me make my own position quite clear. I approve of the EU decision to suspend bilateral relations with Austria. I consider that, had the EU not done this, we could indeed be swamped by an ideological tide that might tear western Europe apart. But I also agree that there was considerable hypocrisy, or rather considerable self-deception, in the EU decision. To see why this is so, we must look at the world-system since 1945 and not since 1989. Before I do that, however, let me say a word more about world social science since 1989. It has been lamentable. All anyone talks about—and that almost irrespective of political tendency—is globalization, as though this concept were more than a passing rhetorical device in the continuing struggle within the capitalist world-economy over the degree to which transborder flows should be unimpeded. It is dust in our eyes. So also is the endless litany about ethnic violence, and here not only the social scientists but also the human rights activists are responsible. My point is not that ethnic violence is not a terrible and terrifying reality, but that it is distinctly not the domain of some less fortunate, less wise, less civilized others. It is the absolutely normal result of the deep and growing inequalities within our world-system, and cannot be addressed by moral exhortation, or by an *ingérence* * by the pure and advanced into the zones controlled by the impure and backward. World social science has offered us no useful tools to analyze what has been happening in the world-system since 1989, and therefore no useful tools to understand contemporary Austrian reality.

THE WORLD-SYSTEM SINCE 1945

In 1945, the Nazi experience and the Nazi horror came to an end. Hitler had not invented anti-Semitism, nor had Germans. Anti-Semitism had long been the major European internal expression of the deep racism of the European world, and in its

---

* *Le droit d'ingérence,* "the right to interfere," was a slogan adopted by French human rights organizations in the 1990s with regard to the Balkans.

modern version it had been endemic on the European scene for at least a century. Anyone who compares Paris to Berlin on this score as of 1900 would not think that Berlin comes off the worse. Nowhere was active anti-Semitism absent, even during the Second World War, even in the United States.

So why was everyone so upset with Nazism, at least after 1945? The answer stands out and cannot be missed. It was the *Endlösung*—the Final Solution. Although almost everyone in the pan-European world had been openly and happily racist and anti-Semitic before 1945, almost no one had intended this anti-Semitism to result in an *Endlösung*. Hitler's Final Solution missed the entire point of racism within the capitalist world-economy. The object of racism is not to exclude people, much less to exterminate them. The object of racism is to keep people within the system, but as inferiors (*Untermenschen*) who can be exploited economically and used as political scapegoats. What happened with Nazism was what the French would call a *dérapage*—a blunder, a skid, a loss of control. Or perhaps it was the genie getting out of the bottle.

One was supposed to be racist just up to the point of an *Endlösung,* but no further. It had always been a delicate game, and no doubt there had been *dérapages* before—but never on such a large scale, never in so central an arena of the world-system, and never, never so visibly. The Allied troops who entered the concentration camps in 1945 were truly shaken at a personal level. And collectively, the pan-European world had to come to terms with the genie that had escaped from the bottle. They did this by a process of banning public usage of racism, and primarily of the public usage of anti-Semitism. It became taboo language.

The social scientists joined the game. In the years after 1945, they began to write book after book denouncing the meaningfulness of the concept of race,[1] the illegitimacy of assuming that differences in any current social measurement of social groups could be traced to innate genetic characteristics. The memory of the Holocaust came to be subject matter for school curricula. The Germans, a bit reluctantly at first but eventually with some moral courage, have tried to analyze their own guilt and thereby reduce their shame. And, after 1989, they have been joined, somewhat reluctantly no doubt, by other countries of the pan-European world. Allied powers such as France and the Netherlands began to admit their own guilt as well, guilt for permitting this *dérapage* to occur, guilt because at least some of their citizens actively participated in the process. One of the reasons that the EU reacted so strongly to Haider is that Austria as a country has refused to assume its share of the guilt, has insisted that it was primarily a victim. Perhaps a majority of Austrians had not desired *Anschluss* in 1938, although it is hard to know this when one sees the newsreel clips of the cheering crowds in Vienna. But what is more to the point is that no non-Jewish, non-Roma, Austrian was considered other than a German in the Third Reich after *Anschluss,* and the majority gloried in that fact.

This realization that racism had been undone by going much too far had two major consequences in the post-1945 pan-European world. First, these countries sought to emphasize their internal virtues as integrative nations unspotted by racist oppression, countries of liberty facing the "evil empire" of the Soviet Union, whose racism in turn became a regular theme of Western propaganda. All sorts of sociopolitical actions flowed from this attempt: the 1954 Supreme Court decision in the United States outlawing racial segregation; the philo-Israel policies of all the pan-European world; even the new emphasis on ecumenicism within the Western Christian world, as well as the invention of the idea that there was such a thing as a joint Judeo-Christian heritage.

Second, and just as important, was a need to restore a sanitized racism to its original function, that of keeping people within the system, but as *Untermenschen*. If Jews could no longer be treated thus, nor Catholics in Protestant countries, one would have to look farther afield. The post-1945 period was, at least at first, an era of incredible economic expansion and simultaneous demographic transformation in the direction of a radically reduced rate of reproduction of the pan-European world. This world needed more workers and was producing less than ever before. And thus began the era of what the Germans gingerly called "guest workers" (*Gastarbeiter*).

Who were these *Gastarbeiter?* Mediterranean peoples in non-Mediterranean Europe, Latin Americans and Asians in North America, West Indians in North America and western Europe, Black Africans and South Asians in Europe. And, since 1989, persons from the former socialist bloc coming to western Europe. All these migrants have come in large numbers because they wanted to come and because they could find jobs, indeed were desperately needed to make the pan-European countries flourish. But they came, almost universally, as persons at the bottom of the heap—economically, socially, and politically.

When the world-economy entered its long Kondratieff B-phase in the 1970s, and unemployment grew for the first time since 1945, the immigrants became a convenient scapegoat. The far-right forces, which had been absolutely illegitimate and marginal since 1945, suddenly began to reemerge, sometimes within the mainline conservative parties, sometimes as separate structures. In the latter case, they ate into the support not only of the conservative parties but of the center-left workers' parties as well. By the 1990s, these parties began to seem more serious, for reasons I've already suggested.

The mainline parties were not at all sure how to handle this resurgence of more or less openly racist parties. They were panicked that the genie might get out of the bottle once again and undo the social placidity of their states. Some argued that these far-right forces could be undermined by coopting their anti-immigrant themes in a mildly edulcorated form. Others said these forces constituted a virus that had to be isolated as fast as possible.

Once again, the social scientists did not help us very much. They sought to analyze the Nazi phenomenon in terms of some peculiarity of the German historical situation, instead of seeing that the whole world-system had been playing with fire for a long time, and it had been just a matter of time until sparks would ignite somewhere, somehow. Social scientists sought to proclaim their own moral virtue (the merits of which we shall come to in a moment) and to absolve the pan-European world because of its current supposedly nonracist rhetoric, when the pan-European racism after 1945 was in fact just as virulent as its racism before 1933 or before 1945. They had simply substituted other objects of hatred and fear. Do we not debate these days the so-called clash of civilizations, a concept invented by a social scientist?

Indeed, the very denunciation by the EU of Austria, much as I approve of it, smacks of racism. For what is it that the European Union is saying? It is saying in effect—Haiders are possible, perhaps even normal, outside the pan-European world, even perhaps in such nearby countries as Hungary and Slovenia. But Haiders are impermissible, unthinkable, within civilized Europe. We Europeans must defend our moral superiority, and Austria threatens to make this impossible. It is true: Austria does threaten to make this impossible, and Austria must somehow retreat from its present untenable position. But the grounds of the EU complaint are themselves not above suspicion of moral taint. For western Europe's universalist values are themselves deeply encrusted with the chronic, constitutive racism of the pan-European world.

To appreciate this, and to appreciate the failure of social science to unmask this, we must look at the story of the modern world-system after 1492.

THE WORLD-SYSTEM SINCE 1492

When Europeans landed in the Americas and claimed to conquer it, they encountered indigenous peoples who were extremely strange to them. Some were organized as fairly simple hunting and gathering systems. And some were organized in sophisticated and elaborate world-empires. But in both cases neither the weapons of these peoples nor their acquired physiological immunities (or rather the lack of them) made it possible for them to resist the invaders successfully. Thereupon, the Europeans had to decide how to treat these peoples. There were those Europeans who, acquiring vast lands (often for the first time), wished to exploit them as rapidly as possible, and were ready to enslave and use up indigenous laborers. The justification they gave for this was that the indigenous peoples were barbarous, undeserving of anything but harsh servitude.

But there were also Christian evangelists who were both horrified by the inhuman treatment meted out to these indigenous peoples by the European *conquistadores* and fiercely insistent on both the possibility and the importance of winning the souls of the indigenous peoples for Christian redemption. One such person was Bartolomé de Las Casas, whose passions and militancy culminated in a famous and classic debate in 1550 about the nature of the "other." Already in 1547, he had written a short summary for the Emperor Charles V (and all others) recounting the horrors of what was going on in the Americas in some detail, and summarizing what had happened in this way:

> If Christians have killed and destroyed so very many souls of such great quality, it has been simply in order to have gold,

to become exceedingly rich in a very short time and to raise themselves to high positions disproportionate to their station. . . . [T]hcy have for [these people so humble, so patient, and so easy to subdue] neither respect nor consideration nor esteem. . . . They have not treated them as beasts (would to God they had treated them as well and been as considerate to them as beasts); they have treated them worse than beasts, as less than manure.[2]

Las Casas was, to be sure, the impassioned and crusading defender of the rights of the peoples. He was, in a connection worth noting, the first bishop of Chiapas, home today to the neo-Zapatistas, where it is still necessary to defend the same cause that Las Casas was almost 500 years ago, the rights of these indigenous peoples to their dignity and their land. These peoples find themselves little better off today than they were in the time of Las Casas. There are those who would therefore classify Las Casas and other neoscholastic Spanish theologians, philosophers, and jurists as precursors of Grotius and as the "true founders of the modern rights of man."[3]

The emperor at first had been seduced by the arguments of Las Casas and named him his Protector of the Indians. But later he had second thoughts and convened at Valladolid in 1550 a special junta of judges to hear a debate between Las Casas and one of the emperor's other advisers, Juan Ginés de Sepúlveda, on the underlying issues. Sepúlveda, a staunch opponent of Las Casas, gave four arguments to justify the treatment of the Indians to which Las Casas had been objecting: They were barbarous and therefore their natural condition was that of submission to more civilized peoples. They were idolatrous and practiced human sacrifice, which justified intervention to prevent crimes against natural law. Intervention was justified to save innocent lives. Intervention would facilitate Christian evangelization.

These arguments seem incredibly contemporary. All we have to do is substitute the term democracy for the term Christianity.

Against these arguments Las Casas asserted: No people may ever be forced to submit to another people on the grounds of a presumed cultural inferiority. One cannot punish a people for crimes of which they were unaware that they were crimes. One is morally justified in saving innocent people only if the process of saving them does not cause still greater harm to others. And Christianity cannot be propagated by the sword. Here too the arguments seem incredibly contemporary.

For some therefore Las Casas should be seen as the last of the *Comuneros,* that understudied first great movement of social protest which took place in Spain in the first third of the sixteenth century, a movement that was both democratic and communitarian. The implications of what Las Casas was arguing seemed to put in question the vary basis of the Spanish empire, which is in fact the probable reason that Charles V withdrew his early support for Las Casas.[4] Indeed, in his discussion of the concept of what a barbarian is, Las Casas insisted that "no one is unable to locate a barbarian to dominate," reminding Spaniards of their own treatment by the Romans.[5] But others have argued that Las Casas was really simply the theorist of "good" colonization, a reformer who "proposed tirelessly, to the end of his life, substitute solutions for the problems of the colonial system founded on the *encomienda.*"[6]

The fascinating thing about the great debate before the Junta at Valladolid is that no one is quite sure what the Junta decided. In a sense, this is emblematic of the modern world-system. Have we ever decided? Can we decide? Was Las Casas, the antiracist, the defender of the downtrodden, also the person who was seeking to institutionalize a "good" colonization? Should one ever, can one ever, evangelize by the sword? We have never been given answers to these questions that were logically consistent or politically so persuasive that they ended all discussion. Perhaps no such answers exist.

Since Las Casas we have constructed a capitalist world-economy, which then expanded to encompass the entire globe, and which has always and at every moment justified its hierarchies on the basis of racism. It has always, to be sure, also had its quota of persons who have sought to alleviate the worst features of this racism, and they have had, it must be admitted, some limited success. But there have also always been brutal massacres, *Endlösungen* before the *Endlösung,* though perhaps less bureaucratically, systematically, and effectively planned, and certainly less publicly visible.

Ah, you will say, but then came the French Revolution and the *Déclaration des droits de l'homme.* Well, yes, but well, no! The French Revolution did incarnate a protest against hierarchy, privilege, and oppression, and made this protest on the basis of an egalitarian universalism. The symbolic gesture that displayed this protest was the rejection of "Monsieur" as a form of address and its replacement by the appellation "Citoyen," citizen. Ay, there's the rub, as Shakespeare put it. For the concept of citizen was intended to be inclusive. *All* citizens were to have a say in their government, not just a limited group of aristocrats. The rub is that if one is to include everyone who is in a group, someone has first to decide who constitutes the membership of this group. And this necessarily implies that there are persons who are nonmembers.

The concept of the citizen inevitably excludes every bit as much as it includes. The exclusionary thrust of citizenship has in fact been as important as its inclusionary thrust in the two centuries since the French Revolution. When Mayor Karl Lueger of Vienna said in 1883, "Wir sind Menschen, christliche Österreicher" ("We are male, Christian Austrians"),[7] he was offering a definition of the limits of citizenship, one that Viennese voters seemed to appreciate, even if the emperor did not. Lueger was not ready to include the Judeo-Magyars,[8] who were for him as much foreigners as the foreign capitalists he also denounced. Was this proto-fascism, as many contend, or merely "calculated extremism," as John Boyer wishes to insist?[9] Today, some pose this same question about Jörg Haider. But what difference the answer? The political result is virtually identical.

At that very moment in modern history when the French Revolution was bequeathing to us all this minefield of the concept of citizen, the world of knowledge was going through a major upheaval. This upheaval followed on the successful secularization of knowledge achieved by the detachment of philosophy from theology, a process that had taken several centuries. But now it was to be more than a question of secularizing knowledge. More or less in the latter half of the eighteenth century, two terms that had hitherto been if not synonymous then heavily overlapping, science and philosophy, came to be defined as ontological opposites. The two cultures, that singular feature of the structures of knowledge of the modern world-system, had become accepted as a defining cleavage of knowledge. And with this cleavage came the intellectual and institutional separation of the search for truth on the one hand (the domain of science) and the search for the good and the beautiful on the other (the domain of philosophy or the humanities). It is this fundamental rupture which explains the subsequent form of development of the social sciences as well as, I believe, their inability to speak to the constitutive racism of the capitalist world-economy. I now turn to this story.

The two great cultural legacies of the French Revolution were the idea that political change was normal, and that sovereignty resided neither in the ruler nor in a group of notables but in the people.[10] The latter was simply the expression of the logic of the concept of citizen. Both ideas were extremely radical in their implications, and neither the downfall of the Jacobin regime nor even the end of its Napoleonic successor regime could keep these ideas from suffusing the world-system and becoming widely accepted. Those in power were forced to deal with this new geocultural reality. If political change was to be regarded as normal, then it was important to know how the system operated, the better to control the process. This provided the basic impulse for the institutional emergence of social science, that branch of knowledge which purports to explain social action, social change, and social structures.

This is not the place to analyze the institutional history of the social sciences, which was done succinctly in the report of the international commission I headed, *Open the Social Sciences.*[11] There are just two things I wish to discuss here: the place of the social sciences amidst the two cultures, and the role the social sciences have played in the understanding of racism.

The two cultures divided up the domains of knowledge along lines that today we think are self-evident, although no one would have thought so in the seventeenth century or earlier. Science appropriated the domain of the natural world as its exclusive realm. And the humanities appropriated the world of ideas, cultural production, and intellectual speculation as its exclusive realm. When, however, it came to the domain of social realities, the two cultures contested the domain. Each argued that this realm really belonged to it. What happened therefore when the social sciences began to be institutionalized in the renascent university system of the nineteenth century is that they were torn apart by this epistemological debate, this *Methodenstreit.* The social sciences emerged in two camps, with some of what were now called disciplines leaning heavily, at least at first, toward the idiographic, humanistic camp (history, anthropology, Oriental studies) and others leaning heavily toward the nomothetic, scientistic camp (economics, sociology, political science). The implication of this for the problem with which we are dealing here is that the social sciences were deeply divided over the issue of whether they were to be concerned only with the search for the true or were also to be concerned with the search for the good. The social sciences have never resolved this issue.

As for racism, the most striking thing about social knowledge throughout the nineteenth century and right up to 1945 was that the social sciences never confronted this issue directly. And indirectly, their record is deplorable. Let us start with history, the only modern social science that existed as a name and as a concept long before the nineteenth century. History underwent a so-called scientific revolution in the nineteenth century, whose central figure was Leopold von Ranke. You will all know that Ranke insisted that historians must write history *wie es eigentlich gewesen ist* ("as it really happened"). This meant reconstructing the past primarily out of materials contemporary to the past being studied. Hence, the importance of archives, depositories of written documents of the past, documents that had to be analyzed critically as *Quellen,* sources.

I will ignore now later criticisms of this approach as limiting us inevitably to the study almost exclusively of political and diplomatic history, using as sources the writings of persons linked to the states and their rulers. I will also ignore the fact that the insistence on archives as the crucial source of data forced history exclusively into the past, whose temporal boundaries were defined by the degree of willingness of states to let scholars peruse their archives. Allow me to insist merely on one element of history, at least as it was practiced before 1945. History was the history only of so-called historical nations. Indeed it had to be, given the methods used.

In the Austro-Hungarian Empire, as elsewhere, the concept of historical nations was not merely a scholarly concept; it was a political weapon. It is clear who or what are the historical nations. They are the nations located in powerful, modern states that can fund and constrain their historians to write about them. As late as the 1960s, H.R. Trevor Roper made the incredible assertion that Africa has no history. But one might ask, how many courses were offered in the nineteenth century in the University of Vienna on Slovenian history? How many, indeed, are offered today? The very term "historical nation" intrudes a racist category into the very heart of historical practice. It is no accident then, if one regards world historical production before 1945, that 95 percent of it (at the very least) was the story of five historical nations or arenas: Great Britain, France, the United States, the Germanies (I choose this formulation deliberately), and the Italies. And the other 5 percent is largely the history of a few less powerful European states, such as the Netherlands or Sweden or Spain. I should add that a small percentage was also written about the European Middle Ages as well as about the presumed founts of modern Europe, ancient Greece and Rome. But not ancient Persia, or even ancient Egypt. Were the historians who constructed the history of the Germanies of any use in illuminating the public debate that Karl Lueger and others launched in Vienna in the last third of the nineteenth century? I think not.

Did the other social sciences do better than history in addressing racism? The economists were busy constructing universal theories of *Homo economicus.* Adam Smith, in his famous formulation, told us that *all* humans seek to "truck, barter, and trade." The whole object of his book *The Wealth of Nations* was to persuade us (and the British government) that everyone should cease interfering with this natural tendency of all humans. When David Ricardo created a theory of international trade based on the concept of comparative advantage, he used, again famously, a hypothetical illustrative example in which he inserted the names of England and Portugal. He did not tell us that the example was drawn from real history, nor did he explain to us the degree to which this so-called comparative advantage had been imposed by British power upon the weaker Portuguese state.[12]

Yes, some economists insisted that the processes of recent English history did not constitute an illustration of universal laws. Gustav von Schmoller (1838–1917) led a whole movement, *Staatswissenschaften,* which sought to historicize economic analysis.[13] It was a Vienna economist, Karl Menger (1840–1921), who led the assault against this heresy, eventually to bring it down, despite its previously strong hold in the Prussian university system. On the other hand, an even more powerful critique of classical economics than the one made by Schmoller was the one Karl Polanyi made in *The Great Transformation,* a book written in England after he left Vienna in 1936. But economists do not read Polanyi. Economists tend not to deal with political economy at all if they can help it, and the major attempt to deal with racism by a mainstream economist involved discussing it as a market choice.[14]

The scorn of the mainstream economists for analysis of any situation outside the parameters of *ceteris paribus* ensures that economic behavior that does not follow the norms of the market, as economists define these norms, is not worth analyzing, much less taking seriously as possible alternative economic behavior. The feigned political innocence that follows from such presumptions makes it impossible to analyze the economic sources or consequences of racist movements. It erases this subject from the purview of scientific analysis. Worse, it suggests that a good deal of political behavior that can be analyzed as racist or as *Widerstand* to racism is economically irrational behavior.

The political scientists have not served us too much better. Their early concentration on constitutional issues, derived from their historic links to law faculties, turned the analysis of racism into an issue of formal legislation. Apartheid South Africa was racist because it ensconced formal discriminations in the legal system. France was not racist because it did not have such legal discrimination, at least in the metropole. In addition to the analysis of constitutions, political scientists before 1945 also developed what they called the study of "comparative government." But which governments did they compare? Our old friends, those of the five major pan-European countries: Great Britain, France, the United States, Germany, and Italy. No one else was worth studying, because no one else was truly civilized, not even, I fear, that strange beast, the Austro-Hungarian Empire.

Well, then, at least the sociologists, who have had the reputation of being the hearth of political radicalism in the university system, surely at least they did better. Far from it! They were the worst of all. Before 1945 there were two brands of sociologists. There were those, especially in the United States, who explicitly justified the concept of White superiority. And there were those who, coming from a background of social work or religious activity, sought to describe the underprivileged of the large urban centers and explain the "deviance" of their denizens. The descriptions were well intentioned if patronizing, but the assumption that this behavior was deviant and had to be rectified to meet middle-class norms was unquestioned. And since in most cases the lower classes, and not only in the United States, were also ethnically distinguishable from the middle classes, the racist underpinnings of this group are clear, even if they themselves did not recognize it.

And worst of all, all four basic disciplines—history, economics, political science, and sociology—only analyzed the pan-European world, considered to be the world of modernity and of civilization. Their universalisms presupposed the hierarchies of the modern world-system. The analysis of the extra-European world was consigned to separate disciplines: anthropology for the barbaric "peoples without history," and Oriental studies for the non-Western "high civilizations" that were, however, incapable of proceeding to modernity without European intrusion and reorganization of their social dynamics. Ethnography specifically rejected the historicity of its "tribes"; they were unchanging, at least before "culture contact." And Oriental studies saw the histories of these high civilizations as "frozen."

The extra-European world represented "tradition"; the pan-European world represented modernity, evolution, progress. It was the West versus the rest. Note well that, in analyzing the modern world, social science invented not one but three disciplines to describe the regularities of the present: economics, political science, and sociology. But in analyzing the extra-European world, there was not only no need for history but no need for the trinity of approaches required for the pan-European world. This was because the "differentiation" into separate arenas of social action—the market, the state, and the civil society—was thought to be an achievement of modernity, indeed its very essence. Because of the disjunction of science and philosophy, there was no one to remind the practitioners that this was merely an assumption of liberal ideology and not a plausible accounting of social reality. No wonder that the social sciences could not help us understand Nazism. And their post-1945 evolution, while rectifying the aim a bit, has not been very helpful in helping us understand Haider. And, most of all, there was no way of accounting for *Widerstand,* except as one more deviant activity, to which one could perhaps be sympathetic, in a slightly patronizing way.

Social scientists were so busy fighting the battles of the birth of the modern world-system that they could not fight the battles of the functioning world-system. Social scientists' search for scholarly neutrality was their struggle against the Church's, and by derivation the states', seeking to impose themselves on the scholars. When Max Weber spoke of the disenchantment of the world, the very language was theological, even though he was in actuality inveighing against Prussian nationalism. It is only in the wake of the terrible destruction of bourgeois values brought about by the First World War that Weber would begin to remember once again, in his famous speech to the students at the University of Munich, "Wissenschaft als Beruf" ("Science as a Vocation"), that social science cannot separate itself from the ways in which the world is always enchanted:

> Not summer's bloom lies ahead of us, but rather a polar night of icy darkness and hardness, no matter which group may triumph externally now. Where there is nothing, not only the Kaiser but also the proletarian has lost his rights. When this night shall have slowly receded, who of those for whom spring apparently has bloomed so luxuriously will be alive? [15]

THE WORLD-SYSTEM AFTER 2000

The strong vote for the FPÖ and the strong EU reaction are annunciatory, though not the first signs, of our present crisis. The shift from an underlying optimism about the future, from the certainty that things would in fact get better, to an underlying fear that this may not be so has reached the wealthy part of the world. In Austria, too, in western Europe, too, in the United States, too, faith in centrist rational reformism, slow-moving but always in the right direction, has been replaced by a skepticism about all the promises of the mainstream political forces, whether they call themselves center-left or center-right. The centrist consensus informed by nineteenth-century liberal ideology is no more. It was fundamentally challenged in 1968 and was buried in 1989.

We have entered into a long period of chaotic transformation of the world-system of which we are a part. Its outcome is intrinsically unpredictable. But on the other hand we can influence its outcome. This is the message of the sciences of complexity.[16] This is the message that social science should be conveying today. This is the context in which we must place Jörg Haider and *Widerstand*.

In a world-system that is collapsing because its structural possibilities of adjustment have exhausted themselves, those with power and privilege will not stand by idly and do nothing. They will organize to replace the present world-system with one equally hierarchical and inegalitarian, if based on different principles. For such people Jörg Haider is a demagogue and a danger. He understands contemporary reality so little that he is not even aware that, for Austrians to maintain their present standard of living, the country would have to double, triple, or quadruple the number of immigrants it took in annually in the next twenty-five to fifty years merely to maintain a workforce large enough to sustain the pensions of the aging Austrian population.[17] The danger is clear, that the demagoguery will lead the pan-European world even more quickly down the path of destructive civil wars. Bosnia and Rwanda loom on the horizon. The leaders of the European Union see that. So does President Klestil. But apparently not the ÖVP leadership.

Meanwhile, there is a *Widerstand*. Those who resist represent forces of transformation amidst this structural crisis of the capitalist world-economy different from those of the FPÖ but also different from that of the leadership of the EU. But have they a clear vision of what it is they want? Only perhaps in a blurred fashion. This is where social science can play a role, but only a social science that refuses to separate the search for the true and the search for the good, only a social science that can overcome the split of the two cultures, only a social science that can fully incorporate the permanence of uncertainty and bask in the possibilities such uncertainty affords for human creativity and a new substantive rationality (Max Weber's *Rationalität materiel*).

For we desperately need to explore alternative possibilities for a more substantively rational historical system, to replace the mad and dying one in which we live. We desperately need to uncover the deep roots of racist privilege that permeate our existing world-system and encompass all of its institutions, including the structures of knowledge and indeed including the forces of *Widerstand* itself. We are living amidst rapid change. Is that so bad? We shall have much disorder and many changes in the coming decades. And yes, Vienna will change. But there has always been more change than we remember and the change has been more rapid than we imagine. The social sciences have let us down, too, in its understanding of the past. They has offered us a false picture of a traditional world that moved oh so slowly. Such a world never really existed. It doesn't exist now, neither in Austria nor anywhere else. Amidst the immense uncertainty about where we are heading, we must strive to locate in our pasts, as we invent them now, what is good and beautiful, and build these visions into our futures. We need to create a more livable world. We must use our imaginations. And we may thereby begin to eradicate the deep racisms that lie within us.

In 1968, during the great student uprising in France, the leader of the students, Daniel Cohn-Bendit, called Dany le Rouge, made the tactical error of briefly visiting Germany. Since he was a German citizen and not a French citizen, de Gaulle's government could block his return to France, which it did. Thereupon the students marched in Paris, protesting under the slogan "We are all German Jews; we are all Palestinian Arabs." It was a good slogan, one we might all adopt. But we might also all add, with some humility, "We are all Jörg Haider." If we wish to combat the Jörg Haiders of the world, and we must, we have to look within first. Let me give you one small but telling example.

When the new Austrian government was formed, the Israeli government correctly withdrew its ambassador in protest. Yet only a month or so later, the Israeli Knesset placed Prime Minister Ehud Barak in great difficulty by passing a motion insisting that any referendum on a withdrawal from the Golan required a "special majority," code language for a provision that would effectively disfranchise Arab citizens of Israel on this issue. And one of the main proponents of this motion was Natan Sharanksy and his party made up of Russian émigrés, the same Natan Sharansky who was the famous dissident in the Soviet Union protesting against the de facto anti-Semitism of governmental policy there. The struggle against racism is indivisible. There cannot be different rules for Austria, for Israel, for the U.S.S.R., or for the United States.

Let me recount one more anecdote, a curious one. In the 2000 presidential race in the United States, there was a crucial Republican primary in South Carolina. During the primary race, George W. Bush sought to ensure strong support from among the so-called Christian right by speaking at Bob Jones University, a fundamentalist Protestant institution and a stronghold of these forces. The problem was that Bob Jones University is known for two things: its denunciations of the pope as the Antichrist (the university being a fundamentalist Protestant institution), and the fact that it forbade its students to date persons of a different race. This became a major political issue subsequently, embarrassing George W. Bush, who said he regretted not having spoken against these two positions—the ferociously anti-Catholic attitude and the refusal of interracial dating—when he was at the university.

The anecdote does not concern Bush's embarrassment, which does however speak to the taboos established after 1945. The interesting thing is the reaction of Bob Jones III, the president of the university, in the light of the public controversy. Bob Jones

III appeared on the CNN program of Larry King. The first question Larry King posed to Bob Jones III was: Why did the university forbid interracial dating? The answer was that those running the institution gave was that they were against the philosophy of "one world," that there are no differences. Larry King suggested that it seemed to him a far reach from opposition to one world and opposition to two young people dating. Bob Jones demurred, but then insisted that neither he nor the university was racist (the big taboo) and that the university had that very day repealed the rule, since it was secondary and not fundamental to their objective of promoting Christianity. I suppose this shows that public protest makes some racists backtrack in public, at least tactically. This should be a lesson for conservative forces faced with the nightmare of a far-right offensive against them. But quite apart from the tactical shift, the fact is nonetheless that the racism persists.

The albatross is around our necks. It is a fiend that plagues us. *Widerstand* is a moral obligation. It cannot be intelligently and usefully pursued without analysis, and it is the moral and intellectual function of the social sciences to help in providing that analysis. But just as it will require an enormous wrench on all our parts to extirpate the racism within each of us, so it will require an enormous wrench for social scientists to unthink the kind of social science that has crippled us and to create in its place a more useful social science. I return to my original title, "Social Science in an Age of Transition." In such an age, all of us can have an enormous impact on what happens. In moments of structural bifurcation, the fluctuations are wild, and small pushes can have great consequences, as opposed to the case in more normal, more stable periods, when big pushes can at best have small consequences. This offers us an opportunity but also creates a moral pressure. If at the end of the transition the world is not manifestly better than it is now, and it could well not be, then we shall have only ourselves to blame. The "we" are the members of the *Widerstand*. The "we" are the social scientists. The "we" are all ordinary, decent people.

NOTES

1. UNESCO sponsored an entire series of such books.
2. Bartolomé de Las Casas, *Très brèves relations de la déstruction des Indes* (1547; reprint, Paris: La Découverte, 1996), 52.
3. Angel Losada, "Ponencia sobre Fray Bartolomé de las Casas," in *Las Casas el la politique des droits de l'homme* (Aix-en-Provence: Institut d'Etudes Politique d'Aix and Instituto de Cultura Hispánica, October 1974; Gardanne: Esmenjaud, 1976), 22.
4. See Vidal Abril Castello, "Bartolomé de Las Casas, el último Comunero," in *Las Casas et la politique des droits de l'homme.*
5. Henry Mechoulan, "A propos de la notion de barbare chez Las Casas," in *Las Casas et la politique des droits de l'homme,* 179.
6. Alain Milhou, "Radicalisme chrétien et utopie politique," in *Las Casas et la politique des droits de l'homme,* 166.
7. Helmut Andics, *Ringstrassenwelt, Wien 1867–1887: Luegers Anstieg* (Wien: Jugend und Volk, 1983), 271.
8. Lueger also denounced *Judensozi, Judeoliberalismus,* and *Judenfreimaurer* (Jewish Freemasons).
9. John W. Boyer, *Political Radicalism in Late Imperial Vienna: Origins of the Christian Social Movement, 1848–1897* (Chicago: University of Chicago Press, 1981), xii.
10. See Immanuel Wallerstein, "The French Revolution as a World-Historical Event," in *Unthinking Social Science* (Cambridge, England: Polity Press, 1991), 7–22.
11. Immanuel Wallerstein et al., *Open the Social Sciences: Report of the Gulbenkian Commission on the Restructuring of the Social Sciences* (Stanford: Stanford University Press, 1996).
12. See S. Sideri, *Trade and Power: Informal Colonialism in Anglo-Portuguese Relations* (Rotterdam: Rotterdam University Press, 1970).
13. See Ulf Strohmayer, "The Displaced, Deferred or was it Abandoned Middle: Another Look at the Idiographic-Nomothetic Distinction in the German Social Sciences," *Review* 20, nos. 3 and 4 (Summer–Fall 1997): 279–344.

14. See Gary S. Becker, *The Economics of Discrimination,* 2nd ed. (Chicago: University of Chicago Press, 1971).

15. Max Weber, "Science as a Vocation," in H.H. Gerth and C. Wright Mills, eds., *From Max Weber: Essays in Sociology* (New York: Oxford University Press, 1946), 128.

16. See, first of all, Ilya Prigogine, *The End of Certainty* (New York: Free Press, 1997).

17. See the report published in March 2000 by the United Nations Population Division entitled "Replacement Migration: Is It a Solution to Declining and Aging Populations?" Austria is not discussed in the report. But for Germany, the report argues that merely in order to keep the size of its working-age population constant at 1995 levels, Germany would have to admit 500,000 migrants per year each year from now to 2050.

CHAPTER FIVE

Islam: Islam, the West, and the World

My title, "Islam, the West, and the World," has two geographic terms in it. So I think it best to start with taking a look at the geography. There are three so-called world religions—Judaism, Christianity, and Islam—that have their historical origins in the same rather small area of the world, the southwestern corner of the Asian continent. They all claim some special relationship to this region, which is seen as their spiritual home. None of the three religions, however, remained localized in this region.

As a result of their being conquered and the destruction of their states, Jews were relocated (or relocated themselves) to Egypt, then to Babylonia, then in Roman times to various parts of the Mediterranean, then later throughout much of Europe, and finally in modern times to the Western Hemisphere and to many other zones of the world. All of this created what is called a diaspora. And, as we know, in the twentieth century, many Jews returned to the original area and a new political structure was created, the state of Israel, which asserts itself to be the reconstructed homeland of the Jewish people.

Christianity started as a religious movement among the Jews

in this home area. Relatively soon, however, the Christians cut their ties with the Jewish community and proselytized among non-Jews, primarily within the then-extensive Roman Empire. A mere three centuries later, Christianity had become the state religion of the empire, and in the succeeding five hundred to seven hundred years Christians pursued a policy of conversion, primarily throughout the continent of Europe. Later, the construction of the modern world-system involved a so-called expansion of Europe, one that was simultaneously military, political, economic, and religious. Within this context, Christian missionaries spanned the globe, but were noticeably more successful in parts of the world that were not dominated by other so-called world religions. The number of converts in largely Islamic, Buddhist, Hindu, and Confucian-Taoist zones was relatively low, and there were particularly few in Islamic zones.

Finally, Islam appeared in the same home area some six centuries after Christianity. It too was a proselytizing religion, and spread very rapidly throughout what we now call the Middle East, northern Africa, and the Iberian peninsula. In the sixteenth century, it was pushed out of Iberia but simultaneously penetrated what we now call the Balkans. Meanwhile, it had been extending its geographic zone eastward toward southeastern Asia and southward into the African continent. In the twentieth century, the process of spread continued and eventually, by migration and conversion, reached into the Western Hemisphere and western Europe.

I have not done more than resume some schoolboy knowledge. I have reviewed this geography in order to point out that despite the fact that all three religions, and particularly Christianity and Islam, are worldwide in scope and claims, we tend to think and to speak of Christianity as the "West" and Islam as the "East." To be sure, there is no doubt some geographic basis for this shorthand, but less than we assume, and it is diminishing.

Hence, we have a question as to why we insist on using this geographical shorthand. It obviously has more political than geographic meaning.

We have had some answers recently that are well known to you. Samuel Huntington sees the West and Islam as two antithetical "civilizations" that are in long-term geopolitical conflict. Edward Said sees Orientalism as a false construct erected for ideological reasons by the Western world, one both pervasive and pernicious in its effects. I prefer to approach the question another way, and ask the question, why is it that the Christian world seems to have singled out the Islamic world as its particular demon, and not merely recently but ever since the emergence of Islam? Actually the reverse has probably also been true, that Islam has regarded Christianity as its particular demon, but I do not feel I have the competence to discuss the question of why that is so or the degree to which it is so.

Although my emphasis will be on the modern world, I do not believe we can explain what happened without some reference to the European Middle Ages, for it is out of this period that we have derived our mythologies about this relationship. As we all know, Christianity and Islam at that time held sway in large zones that more or less bordered each other. Although each zone was rent with internal strife of multiple kinds, each zone appeared to regard itself as a cultural unit, and one in conflict primarily with the other. In part, the reasons for this lay in the dominant theologies, the sense of each that it incarnated the entire and only possible truth, and probably also the very fact that they had both originated in the same small area. The Christians claimed that they had fulfilled the Jewish law and therefore supplanted it with a new and final revelation. The Moslems in turn claimed that they had built on the wisdom they had inherited from Jews and Christians with a new and truly final form of commitment to Allah. So, one part of the quarrel was an intrafamily quarrel about heritage and truth. This is the kind of quarrel that has often turned out to be the most divisive, the most bitter, because in some sense it is the one most filled with both affection and competitiveness.

There was another part to this quarrel, one less about ideas than about resources and power. In the rolling back and forth of conquests—the eighth-century Ommayad thrust into Iberia and France, the Christian Crusades into the Holy Land, the Saracen pushback of the Christian conquests, the Reconquista of Spain by Christians, the expansion of the Ottoman Empire into the Balkans, the eventual pushback of the Ottomans—it is true that the Christian world and the Islamic world were struggling over control of vast areas of land—their resources and their populations—and that for each the other represented the main military threat. To be sure, both were faced at specific points in time with other conquering groups from northern Asia. However, not only were these other conquerors eventually forced back, but many of these conquering groups were converted religiously and thus tamed as a cultural menace.

All this set the scene for the modern world-system, where a capitalist world-economy came into existence in western Europe and began to expand its economic frontiers to encompass more and more of the world. The core of this system was western European and Christian. But here we have to observe that the European geographic focus changed. The initial expansion of Europe in the sixteenth and seventeenth centuries tended to jump over the Islamic world, or at least its Middle Eastern core. European powers went west, they thought to India, but came instead to the Americas. And they circumnavigated Africa, again to reach out to Asia. In part, this was because they sought what they thought to be the wealth of Asia. But in part this was because it was easier. The Islamic world seemed a hard nut to crack, particularly at that moment, at the height of Ottoman power. In any case, it is as though there was a hiatus, a break in the centrality of the medieval Christian-Islamic struggle. The struggle was not forgotten, but it seemed to take second place for the time being in western European concerns in terms of their immediate geoeconomic and geopolitical projects.

If we look at the history of the modern world-system from its beginnings in the long sixteenth century to the beginning of the twentieth century, we shall observe that European dominance sometimes took the form of direct colonial rule and sometimes took a more indirect form, one that has sometimes been termed the establishment of semicolonies, by which has been meant an economic subordination mixed with politico-military intrusions that stopped short of establishing actual imperial rule. Once again, a quick overview of world geography would be useful. The colonized areas were the Americas, most of Africa, most of South and Southeast Asia, and Oceania. The main areas that were not fully colonized were eastern Europe, the Far East, and the Middle East. This is of course a very crude summary, and needs to be specified and nuanced in many ways.

In each case there are very obvious explanations why full colonization was neither sought nor possible in the particular regions, and why it was sought and was possible in the others. I shall not review what led to the difference in European attempts to control different regions, but rather ask what was the difference in the consequences for the peoples of any given region depending on whether their relationship with Europe in the modern world has been that of a colony as opposed to a semicolony. (Of course, as of the late nineteenth century, the term Europe should be considered a cultural term and should be understood to include the United States.)

For the moment, I restrict myself to observing that the fiercest political conflict with Europe in the twentieth century has come from precisely the three regions that were only "semicolonized":

the Soviet Union, the Chinese People's Republic (and North Korea), and "Islam." Of course, "Islam" is not a state but a region, and Iran, Iraq, and Libya only begin the list of states that have been in fierce conflict with the pan-European world. Since these are the three regions which have been in sharpest conflict with Europe, it is quite comprehensible that, in the imaginary of European discourse, the demons have been located there: Communism, the Yellow Peril, Islamic terrorism. In the West, today the demon of Communism seems like historical memory, and China, a difficult but cultivated friend—even ally. There remains primarily Islamic terrorism—a demon much discussed and much feared in the West, but essentially an imprecise construct representing a blurred vision of reality.

How did so-called Islamic terrorism become such a central image in the world today, and especially since the collapse of the Communisms in 1989–91? As we know, for several decades now there have been important social and religious movements in Islamic countries, which are often labeled "Islamic fundamentalist" and, somewhat more rarely, "Islamic integrist." These labels are not, to my knowledge, self-designations, but are those used in the Western world and in the Western media. In Islamic countries, these movements are more likely to be called "Islamist."

Where do these Western designations come from, and to what do they refer? Note that the two terms originate not in the Islamic sphere but in the Christian world. "Fundamentalism" is a term derived from the early-twentieth-century history of Protestantism in the United States, where certain groups, particularly within Baptist churches, called for a return to "fundamentals." By this they meant that they believed that various modernist, even secularist, ideas had invaded Christian theology and practice, leading it astray. They called for a return to beliefs and practices of an earlier era. "Integrism" as a term derives from Catholic history in western Europe, particularly France, and referred to a similar call for the "integral" faith, without dilution from modernist or nationalist views and practices.

By analogy, "Islamic fundamentalism," or "integrism," became the label given to those groups in the Islamic world who feel that modernist views and practices have led the faithful astray and call for a return to older, purer, more correct views and practices. The main target of so-called fundamentalists is always those who bear the same religious label but who either are totally secular in practice or observe what the "fundamentalists" consider to be a diluted and distorted version of the religion. Historians of religious ideas constantly point out that "fundamentalist" groups never represent with full accuracy what were the supposed older, purer, more correct versions of belief and practice. These historians have no trouble demonstrating that these so-called fundamentalist groups always reinvent the tradition with numerous differences, sometimes considerable ones, from the actual beliefs and practices of yesteryear.

But of course these movements are not groups of Rankean historians, searching for religious truth *wie es eigentlich gewesen ist.* They are movements of the present putting forth a claim that everyone should believe certain things and engage in certain practices. And pedantic exercises examining the verisimilitude of their historical claims are of no interest to them whatsoever. Nor are they of very much use to those others in the present, not members of these groups, who wish to understand what the "fundamentalists" are doing and proclaiming, and why.

The fact that the terminology in use derives from Christian religious history gives us a first clue to what is going on. Whatever it is, it is not peculiar to Islam. In the twentieth century, we have had not only Christian and Islamic "fundamentalists" but Jewish, Hindu, Buddhist versions as well, and they all seem to share certain common features: the rejection of "modernist," secularist tendencies within the group; the insistence on a puritanical version of religious practice; a celebration of the integrity of the religious tradition, and its eternal, unchangeable validity. But they share a second feature, even in their Christian versions: an opposition to the dominant power structures of the modern world-system. It is this combination—a reformist demand of a return to "fundamentals" within the religious group, and an antisystemic rhetoric that goes beyond merely religious issues—that is both their defining feature and the key to an analysis of their significance in the evolving history of the modern world-system.

Let us step away from religious issues for a moment and look at the political economy of the world-system. What do we see? The capitalist world-economy is a historical system that has combined an axial division of labor integrated through a less than perfectly autonomous world-market combined with an interstate system composed of allegedly sovereign states, a geoculture that has legitimated a scientific ethos as the underpinnings of economic transformations and profit making, and liberal reformism as a mode of containing popular discontent with the steadily increasing socioeconomic polarization that capitalist development has entailed. This system originated in western Europe and over the centuries expanded to incorporate the entire globe.

In the nineteenth century there emerged within this system antisystemic movements which were based on the interests of oppressed groups within the system. These movements set themselves the object of transforming the system into something else, something more democratic and more egalitarian. The two main forms they took were those of social and national movements. By the post-1945 period, such movements were well organized throughout the world, and a de facto tripartite geographic division seemed to exist. By the First World War the so-called social movements had split into two main camps: social democrat and Communist—which organized themselves internationally as the Second and Third Internationals. Both varieties of social movement claimed to represent the interests of the working classes. Both kinds of movements were distinct from the nationalist movements within "empires," which spoke in the name of "peoples" whose national identity was not recognized and who sought to create national states.

All three kinds of movements had emerged in the period between 1850 and 1945, and were originally politically quite weak. All three kinds of movements had, however, believed that history was on their side and that their cause would eventually be fully realized. All three kinds of movements, after much internal debate, had decided upon a two-stage historical strategy: first gain control of the a state structure; then transform the world. In the twenty-five years after 1945, one could say that all three kinds of movements achieved stage one of their strategy, an achievement that might have amazed observers at the beginning of the twentieth century but one that seemed to validate their own certainty that history was on their side.

Geographically, the three main varieties of movements divided the world. The Communist movements came to power in a zone that went from central Europe to the northern Pacific, and encompassed about a third of the world's area. The social democratic movements came to power (at least to alternating power) in the Western world—western Europe, North America (if one counts New Deal Democrats as social democrats), and Australasia. And nationalist movements, now frequently called national liberation movements, came to power in Asia and Africa, and somewhat similar populist movements came to power in Latin America.

There are two things to note about this remarkable political surge forward of the antisystemic movements. It occurred at the very moment of time when United States power in the world-

system was at its height, and therefore at a moment when prosys-
temic forces were at their most coordinated, most integrated,
presumably at their strongest. Secondly, virtually all of these
movements had fulfilled stage one of the strategy— they had
achieved state power—and thus, having achieved power, could
be judged on the degree to which they were able to accomplish
the changes promised as stage two of their announced strategy,
the transformation of the world.

The world revolution of 1968 constituted the world reaction
to this double reality: the worldwide hegemony of the United
States and the establishment of its world order on the one hand;
and the worldwide realization by the antisystemic movements of
stage one, the coming to power of the various movements often
grouped together under the label of the Old Left, on the other
hand. The revolutionaries condemned the first actor, the United
States, for its oppressiveness, and they condemned the second
actor, the Old Left movements, for their inadequacy as opposition movements to, if not their actual collusion with, the hegemonic project. Although the first denunciation was obvious for a
radical world movement, the second loud denunciation, that
against the traditional antisystemic movements, was to be the
more consequential.

The second denunciation was the cry of deception. To understand the deception we have to assess expectations, and perhaps
illusions. From the standpoint of 1968, the world was looking
back on a history of antisystemic struggle that went back in popular imagination at least to the French Revolution, although the
struggles may have begun locally at a later date, some as late as
the early twentieth century. In any case, there existed a long historical memory.

What were the major elements in this historical memory?
First of all, there had been a difficult struggle in which the actual
movements originated as a weak force and slowly gained

strength through mobilization of popular support, both locally and fraternally from elsewhere. Furthermore, there was the memory not only of struggle but of repression, often severe repression by the powerful forces in the local region, a repression that was actively abetted and supported by worldwide powerful forces—most immediately the United States government.

The second memory was of the opposite tactic of the forces of oppression, co-option, which had historically split the movements between those who received the fruits of co-option and those who necessarily could not. The latter, when not depressed, were angry and sought ever more radical spokespersons. But since the process of co-option, of concessions that ameliorated the lot of some but not of all, was an ongoing, repetitive process, it was also a confusing process, since the lessons needed to be relearned in each successive generation, and this weakened the ability of various segments of the oppressed to make common cause with each other and to achieve fundamental change.

And there was the third memory, which neutralized the other two memories, those of repression and co-option. It was the memory of achievement—achievement measured in the growing strength of the movements themselves in terms of the numbers of persons they could mobilize and in terms of their public recognition as actors in the political realm; and achievement measured in the accumulating concessions that were part of the co-option processes.

This third memory was the source of political and historical hope—the firm expectation that "history was on their side," that a better life was in store for the children and grandchildren of those living now. This third memory was based on what might be called a quantitative reading of recent history—more members in the associations, and improvements in the style of life (that is, more money in the lifetime bank, more gadgets in the style of life). This sense of deep hope in the future, this sense of certainty that there would be more equality and more democracy, especially when it was based on the fact that the oppressed were struggling hard to achieve this and that their struggle was responsible for achieving it, was paradoxically the most depoliticizing worldview possible. It allowed one to discount the paltry results of the present in the light of the significant results anticipated in the future.

This vision was in fact the essential message of liberal reformism, as promoted, ironically but efficaciously, by the antisystemic movements themselves. And the more radical such movements claimed to be, the better they could persuade those they mobilized to be patient about the results of their impatient and vigorous demonstrations. In this way the various antisystemic movements of the Old Left served paradoxically as the most important guarantor of political stability of the world-system in the long run, despite their frequent calls for political turbulence.

There was only one negative in this call to latent passivity beneath the facade of manifest activity, a call justified by a quantification of achievements, measured both locally and worldwide. It was that, eventually, one could do the arithmetic and assess how significant were the changes that had been realized and what was the real pace of this change. It was precisely at the moment of maximum visible achievement of the antisystemic movements that this eventual moment of overall calculation seemed to come. The world revolution of 1968 was the outcome of this assessment of the effectiveness of the century-long strategy. And the verdict was negative. Disillusion followed the illusion of success. The success was deemed less than real, the beneficiaries of the changes a small group (what in the Soviet system was called the Nomenklatura), the real gap between the privileged and those underneath more polarized than ever, despite all the presumed reforms and successes of the Old Left.

It is time to return from this general worldwide assessment to the Islamic world. Of course, the processes described here were as true of it as of most other regions of the world outside the core zones—no more, no less. But of course, each region had its historical specificity and the reactions took a local guise. What was the historical specificity of the Islamic world, and in particular its historic Arab core?

If one looks at all the successive movements in the various Arab countries from, say, 1900 on, the calls for *nahda,* for an Arab revolt, for a nationalist awakening, all tended to be modernist in their rhetoric. These movements analyzed the oppression they felt as the result in part of outside control (imperialism) and in part of internal "traditionalism." They called therefore for a simultaneous rejection of outside control and an internal cultural change. The two went together and reinforced each other, indeed might be said to make each other possible. To be sure, the movements to which these sentiments gave rise were diffuse in their social base and multiple in their visions of the social future. Some had more conservative and some more radical views of the good society.

Generally speaking, however, for all these movements, Islam as a religion played only a small role, and for many of them, a somewhat negative one. To be sure, they might insist on the fact that they were Moslems, but this was thought of as a sort of cultural affiliation, and perhaps as a necessary claim to appease less-enlightened potential followers. The future they envisaged was a modern one, by which they meant a secular one. The various Arab movements shared many of the premises of Kemalism in Turkey. The Moslem League in colonial India was not very different.

These movements, especially the more radical ones, were by and large successful in the post-1945 period. They came to power in various forms: Nasserism in Egypt, the Baath in Syria and

Iraq, the Neo-Destour in Tunisia, the Front de Libération National (FLN) in Algeria. These regimes all tended to join with parallel movements in other parts of what was now called the Third World in movements of the so-called nonaligned powers, movements inspired by the Bandung Conference. Indeed, as we know, Gamal Abdel Nasser personally played an important role in the creation of this world network, and the Algerian FLN provided an inspirational model across this network, similar to that of the Vietnamese movement.

On the other hand, the post-1945 period saw some major difficulties for the Arab world, and by extension for the Islamic world as a whole. The biggest was the creation of the state of Israel. I would not like to discuss here the whole history and merits of this story. I merely wish to underline a few facts. The Zionist movement came into existence more or less at the same time, the turn of the twentieth century, as Arab nationalist movements. It shared much of the same rhetoric—the need to create an independent state, the sense of oppression by the powerful of the world-system, the sense that there should be an internal transformation of the psychology of the Jewish people, the ambiguous (and reticent) relationship with Judaism as a religion. In the Zionist imaginary, the Arabs did not play a real role before 1948. The enemy was the Christian world, and of course, after 1918, Great Britain in particular.

But this imaginary changed radically with the creation of the state of Israel. The military resistance of the Arab states to the creation of Israel meant that for Zionists the primary opponent became the Arab world, and this was largely an Islamic world. This attitude was all the more reinforced by the Israeli victory in the 1967 wars, which brought a large Arab population under Israeli rule. It was at this moment that a modern Palestinian nationalist movement, the Palestinian Liberation Organization (PLO), became important. The PLO was a movement of the same type and rhetoric as the other modernist, nationalist movements I have mentioned. And it had the same reticent, ambiguous relationship with Islam as a religion, all the more so since in Palestine there is a significant Christian Arab population, which in fact supports the PLO.

Without reviewing the history of Israeli-Arab and Israeli-Palestinian relationships from 1948 to today, one can say that, by and large, the Israelis have had the upper hand militarily and politically. But we can also say that the Palestinian mobilization has been sufficiently successful to force the Israelis, on the whole reluctantly, to enter into what became very protracted, inconclusive, and frustrating so-called peace negotiations, negotiations that eventually collapsed completely.

The existence of Israel has posed a problem for Arab nationalism in that it added a locally based enemy to the more remote Western world, one that was less ready to make concessions than the collective West. The only real parallel in the non-European world in the twentieth century was the existence of an apartheid state in South Africa, and this situation has now been resolved with the change in the constitution and the coming to power of the African National Congress.

The Arab world has had, in addition, a second special problem, almost as great as that of Israel, and imbricated with it. This is the fact that it is the locus of a large part of the world's oil supply. This was not known in the nineteenth century. It only became a consideration after the First World War, but it has been a central geopolitical reality ever since, and especially since 1945. The United States has not been at all indifferent to the politics of the region for this reason. Nor has Russia or Western Europe. Maintaining a continuous flow of oil supply, and a reasonable limit on oil rent, has been a major concern of the great powers. This has given them an additional reason both to support Israel and to invest in an effort to encourage and stabilize relatively more conservative regimes in Arab countries.

If one looks at Islamist movements in the Arab world, they actually have a history as long as that of nationalist movements, and in some countries could be confused with them. The Wahhabite movement in the Arabian desert, and the Senussi movement in Cyrenaica (Libya) shared some features with the secular nationalist movements. They too worried about outside oppression, and they too called for an internal renewal that laid stress on purer, more puritanical, behavior. They too moved toward the creation of a modern state structure. But of course they used a religious rhetoric, unlike the secularist movements. They too came to power. The Senussi regime was replaced by a more secular regime in 1969. The Saudi regime has successfully resisted such a fate up to now.

When we look at so-called Islamist movements, what do we see? We see groups who say two things. They say, first of all, that all these movements that have come to power in the various countries have not succeeded in removing or undoing the role of outside powers in their internal affairs, even if they are technically independent states. They take note of the continuing role of the United States in the region, and of the powerful presence of Israel, which is regarded as primarily an outpost of the West, a settler state akin to the Crusader states of the Middle Ages. And they say, second, that this situation is abetted and indeed made possible by the very regimes that assert they are opposing this— not only the secularist regimes but also, be it noted, presumably religiously based regimes such as that of Saudi Arabia.

Hence, what Islamists say is that if one wishes to overthrow outside oppression and foster internal renewal, one has to get rid of these modernist Arab regimes, and they include in this category the Wahhabites. Of course, this is the same thing that Ayatollah Khomeini said about the Shah's regime in Iran, and the Taliban have said about the pseudo-Communist regime in Afghanistan, as well as about its various successors. Thus far, in the Arab world no Islamist regime has come to power, except in the Sudan.

Furthermore, if one looks at the ways these Islamist groups have mobilized politically, one can see that they have not merely put forth an alternative rhetoric, and hence an alternative analysis of the mode of functioning of the modern world-system to that of modernist movements they have been opposing, but that they are also saying that these modernist regimes have failed in the primary task of modern states: providing for the minimal ongoing welfare and security of the citizens. It is well known that the Islamist organizations provide extensive social service to those in need and frequently fill serious voids in state functions. Another noted feature of Islamist movements is that they recruit extensively and successfully among students in technical and scientific branches of the universities, and then make use of these students' skills in advancing their cause.

Now both these features—the social-service function and the attractiveness of Islamism to young engineers and scientists—demonstrates that the Islamists are not romantics nostalgic for a bygone agricultural society. They are, rather, purveyors of an alternative form of modernity, one that is open to technological advance but rejects secularism and its attendant values. Where they are ambivalent is in their attitude to the state structures. Out of power, they are a powerful antistatist force, not merely in politics but in ideology. They reject the centerpiece of secular modernism, the centrality of the embracing, presumably neutral state as a moral and political fulcrum. They insist on the priority of a set of spiritual values, as expounded by an authorized group of interpreters. This priority creates problems when the Islamists actually achieve political power, as today in Iran, for example, and has the potential of creating an ongoing tension between state and religious authorities, the exact problem the modern secular state was intended to resolve. Thus far, Islamism as a political force has continued to give priority to its extrastatist rhetoric.

So how may we interpret what has been happening in Islamic countries in the last twenty years or so? I think the prime element has been the disillusionment, among both the educated elite and the populations at large, with the performance of the historic antisystemic movements, the movements of national renewal and liberation, that were the major expressions of popular struggle in the twentieth century. These movements, in all their variants, have been found wanting. They are condemned for having pursued a futile strategy. They are condemned for permitting a small group to profit venally from the struggle. They are condemned for having failed in their primary objective, to enable the peoples of their region to attain either real political autonomy or real economic advancement compared to the dominant zones of the world. Whether or not this condemnation represents a balanced judgment on the activity of these movements is irrelevant; the fact is that this disillusionment is massive.

The disillusionment has had the consequence that the underlying long-term reformist strategy of the antisystemic movements seems pointless, especially two of their central tactics: the transformation of mores via secularization and the creation of strong state structures. The way was open for an alternative vision, one that used neither of these allegedly pointless tactics. In the Islamic world, this alternative vision has been Islamism. In other parts of the world, the same disillusionment has bred different visions, all of which, however, share the feature that they reject the allegedly pointless tactics.

From the point of view of the holders of power in the world-system, such alternative visions are both better and worse than the now antiquated tactics of the movements of national liberation. They are better in the sense that the Old Left is always pointing out. The alternative visions push people away from a penetrating analysis of the actual structures of the modern world-system, and thereby make it easier for the privileged in the world-system to maintain these structures on a day-by-day basis. The charge is that when the holders of alternative visions such as Islamism come to state power, they find either that they have no real foreign policy or that they have an ineffective one or that they can in fact be easily co-opted into operating within the framework of the system. Up to a point, this charge is true.

On the other hand, the rise of forces with an alternative vision is desperately bad for the holders of power in the world-system, for one simple reason. One of the key stabilizing features of the modern world-system is the confidence populations put in their state structures as their efficacious political defenders vis-à-vis the whole range of outside forces that impinge on their daily lives. In this sense, these state structures, especially after secularist antisystemic movements come to state power, are veritable political demobilizers. They preach confidence in the leadership, and hence they preach patience. When the alternative movements break down confidence in the state structures, they remove the constraint that caused political demobilization.

This calculation of the pluses and minuses, from the point of view of the powerful in the world-system, of the rise of these alternative movements explains much in the current demonization of Islam in the West. Although the option of cooperative co-option of Islamist forces is constantly played with by the West, in general, Western holders of power have emphasized the dangers in the breakdown of popular confidence in their own state structures. This has been reinforced in the case of the Islamic world by two factors that are special to Islamic countries there: the existence of Israel, and role as a locus of oil supply.

These latter two factors alone explain little, but as reinforcement for the choice of tactical response to Islamism, they are crucial.

If the existence of oil resources is both a blessing and a curse for the Arab world, it is nonetheless a reality outside their control, even if it is a reality that may not go on forever. The existence of Israel, on the other hand, is a historically contingent reality, one that is therefore more changeable, and therefore one that has been the focus of acute struggle. Thus, we must look briefly at the source of the very strong support the Western world has given to the state of Israel. It was never inevitable. And I remind you that it was very uncertain as of 1945, even as of 1948. I don't believe in fact that it was locked in as a policy priority, in either the United States or western Europe, until 1967.

There are three elements in this policy. One is that the historic anti-Semitism of the Christian world, which was pervasive virtually from the beginning of Christianity, reached a morally repulsive acme in Nazism and the Holocaust, and this caused a very deep reaction of guilt. It would be a mistake to underestimate the role this sense of Christian guilt plays in the current situation. It has led to dramatic changes in the rhetoric of a range of major social groups in the West—secular intellectuals, the Catholic church, and fundamentalist Protestant sects, some of whom are now talking a language of the necessity of the existence of the state of Israel as a prerequisite for the second coming of Christ.

The guilt complex might not have withstood other geopolitical considerations had it not been for the Israeli victory in the wars of 1967. This victory did two things. On the one hand, it created an overwhelming support for Israel on the part of world Jewry, a level of support that had not been there before. This victory over Arabs had the psychological effect of being at one and the same time a compensation for the Holocaust and a belief that the Arab world threatened to initiate a second version of it. Once again, I do not discuss the degree to which such a vision was justified, but I insist on its occurrence.

The second consequence was doubtless that for the first time the Western world was persuaded that Israel might serve a function as a military control on restless Arab countries, and Israel became integrated to Western geopolitical strategy. The price of this second decision went up severely once the Intifada began, in December 1989, which accounts for Western concern with the so-called peace process and the increasing disgruntlement of Western powers with the Israeli government. But the basic support of Israel has not yet disappeared.

In any case, the combination of Christian guilt about anti-Semitism, worldwide Jewish support of Israel, and the Western view of the utility of Israel as an element in the political stabilization of the world's major oil zone has resulted in the mediatization of so-called Islamic terrorism as the grand demon of the 1990s. This is all the more the case since the demons of Soviet Communism and of the Yellow Peril seem to have evaporated. And it is all the easier to demonize Islamism to the degree that Islam is culturally a cousin of Christianity, unlike Buddhism or Hinduism. The family-feud tonality adds to the irrationality and the persistence of the demonization. Another element that adds to choosing Islam as the demon is the fact that most of the core of the Islamic world was never truly colonized. In an important sense, the West feels somewhat confident in dealing with ex-colonies. After all, they had conquered these areas once militarily and governed them, and think they know their weaknesses. The noncolonized or only semicolonized zones retain an aura of mystery and therefore of danger.

Let me resume my arguments. On the one hand, what has been happening in the Islamic world, in particular the rise of Islamism as a social and political force, is simply one variant of what has been going on everywhere in the peripheral zones of the world-system. The basic interpretation of these events has to revolve around the historic rise of antisystemic movements, their seeming success and their real political failure, the consequent disillusionment, and the search for alternative strategies. All of this is part and parcel of the development of the modern world-system as a historic social system.

On the other hand, there are some special elements in the relationship of the West and Islam that result in the quite extraordinary demonization of Islam in the West. I have tried to indicate the complex of these elements: the millennial relationship of Christianity and Islam and the millennial relationship of Christianity and Judaism as well as the fact that all three religions are linked by what could be termed extended family ties. I added an unbudgeable but theoretically accidental geoeconomic reality, the location of oil. And finally, I added the disappearance of alternative possible demons from noncolonized areas of the world.

This brings me to my very last theme. Can the West do without a demon? I doubt it at the moment. The West is facing a massive crisis—not merely economic, but fundamentally political and social. The capitalist world-economy is in crisis as a historical social system. I cannot review here the crisis in detail, something I have done elsewhere on several occasions,[1] but I raise these issues to insist that the consequence is a great deal of confusion and self-doubt in the West, a situation that always evokes the need for demons. This same confusion and self-doubt pervades the Islamic world, as is evident from the zigzagging tactics of all the main actors. The secularist forces are in disarray. The Islamist forces are not very clear, and are not at all agreed among themselves, what their real political program is or ought to be.

Once again, we should put this in the context of the world-system as a whole, and not limit our attention to the Islamic world. Systems that are in crisis enter into a chaotic period, out of which eventually a new order emerges. Their trajectories bifurcate, and it is intrinsically impossible to predict the branch that will prevail. In practice this means two things. Even small pressures in one direction or another may be decisive, since the system is far from equilibrium. Second, the social struggle is therefore extremely acute. The question that arises, therefore, is how the sides in the struggle for shaping the successor social system will align themselves.

When the struggles were less acute, the lines seemed to be sharp. That is why we can speak of antisystemic movements within the modern world-system. These movements thought they knew what they were about and who their primary enemy was. So did the forces that defended the existing system. What the last twenty-five years has taught us all—I think of it as the lesson of the world revolution of 1968—is that our vision of the struggle was deeply flawed, that opponents were not real opponents and allies, not real allies, whichever side one was on. In this sense the Islamists are profoundly correct in saying that we have to recalibrate our understanding of what the issues that divide the existing historical system and what the alternative historical possibilities of a possible reconstructed world-system are.

Their critique is on the mark, but what of their solution? As I have said, I do not believe they are sure of what solution they really intend. Those of us who do not share some or most of their premises and are heirs of a more secularist tradition find it difficult to accept most of what they offer as first steps to a better future. What I do feel is that there is a need for a genuine dialogue, or multilogue, about the essential limitations of our existing world-system and the parameters of our historical alternatives. Personally, I think the basic conflict is that between those who seek to establish or reestablish a hierarchical world-order in which some are privileged and most others not and those who wish to construct a maximally democratic and egalitarian order. I think that goal requires different kinds of value systems to undergird it and that the historic world religions may have much to teach us about what is crucial in such value systems.

The real problem is that in the secularist and the fundamentalist camps in all parts of the world there are persons on both sides of what I anticipate will be the great politico-social struggle of the coming fifty years. I think myself that posing the issue as one of secularism versus fundamentalism is distracting us in a very major way from clarity of vision. And clarity, not demons, is what we need most at the present time.

NOTES

1. See in particular *Utopistics, or Historical Choices for the Twenty-first Century* (New York: New Press, 1998).

CHAPTER SIX

The Others: Who Are We?

Who Are the Others?

> Recognizing the power of raciology, which is
> used here as a shorthand term for a variety of
> essentializing and reductionist ways of thinking
> that are both biological and cultural in character, is
> an essential part of confronting the continuing
> power of "race" to orchestrate our social, economic,
> cultural, and historical experiences.
>
> PAUL GILROY, *Against Race*[1]

Not so long ago, there was a Cold War. Everyone talked of it as an ideological battle. For some this was the battle between the free world and the evil empire of Communism; for others it was the battle between the exploiting capitalist class and the workers of the world. But everyone purported to believe that this was a life-and-death struggle over fundamental political values.

One day the Cold War ended. The end was in fact rather sudden, and most unexpected. The European regimes that purported to be Marxist-Leninist almost all ceased to exist. The

Asian countries with Communist parties in power and Cuba continued to wear the same ideological clothing, it is true, but in general, the world seemed to accept that there was no more "Cold War," and by and large this was regarded with some relief.

This new situation was greeted spectacularly by some as "the end of history," although most people seemed to think that history was continuing its ceaseless path. A new word, "globalization," did become common currency to describe the marvelous new world about to begin or that had presumably already begun, and to which (in Mrs. Thatcher's unforgettable prose) TINA—there is no alternative. The very same moment of history saw the maturing of a strong new academic emphasis, one that had begun in the 1970s but seemed to reach an acme in the 1990s. It came to be known generically as cultural studies.

"Culture" was once a benign word. High culture was something of which to boast. No one cared to be described as uncultured. Culture meant restraint, cultivation, taste. But the new field of cultural studies harbored a more feisty mood. It was an academic upstart and announced in no uncertain terms that it was remedying a deep neglect in the structures of knowledge. Cultural studies was often associated with, allied with, the pursuit of something called multiculturalism. And multiculturalism was a political demand, a demand of groups that felt they were downtrodden, or ignored, or repressed. Meanwhile, in a different camp and from within the world Establishment, there were voices using the concept of culture in quite a different way. They were telling us that the twenty-first century was going to be the century of a "clash of civilizations," and that we had to gird ourselves politically (and implicitly militarily) to meet the challenge. What the proponents of multiculturalism took as a liberating prospect, namely, the successful reassertion of themselves by non-Western cultures, the proponents of the clash of civilizations considered to be the prime menace.

What is going on here? And first of all, in what capacity do I speak of it? * Am I speaking as an American in China—a citizen of the currently strongest state in the world-system speaking to an audience of the most ancient civilization in the world? Or am I a pan-European addressing an audience of the non-Western world—a White among non-Whites? Or am I am a modern-worlder addressing an audience at a university whose very name bespeaks modernity—a university of science and technology? Or am I simply an academic scholar among his peers—peers who happen to be working or studying in Hong Kong? Or am I a social scientist trying to cope with a concept whose primary locus is in the humanities—the concept of culture?

To be honest, I'm not sure which of these roles describes me, or describes me best, if any of them do. Nor am I sure which of these roles I wish to affect. We are far less in control of our biographies than we like to think, and we can find it extraordinarily difficult to be "objective" in our analyses, if it means that we are required to shed our biographies in our scholarly work. Nor are any of us so easy to classify. Biographies are complex mixtures, and the weights of different locations in which we find ourselves are not necessarily easy to discern, by others or by ourselves. Nor do these weights remain constant over time. What I am today is not necessarily identical to what I was yesterday.

I think I am coming to you now as a social scientist who is attempting to understand the world in which we live, one who is deeply concerned about the trajectory of this world and who believes he has a moral duty to act within it and upon it. I think I am coming as a modern-worlder who has nonetheless deep reservations about what the modern world has been and who is no longer at all sure that it has represented progress over earlier

* This paper was originally delivered as the Y.K. Pao Distinguished Chair Lecture at the Center for Cultural Studies, Hong Kong University of Science and Technology, on September 20, 2002.

world-systems. I probably cannot escape being an American and a pan-European, and I see no good reason to try to do so. And, at my age, I certainly bear the sins as well as the virtues of a life as a scholar.

I am going to talk about time, about universalism, and about particularism, and I am then going to use this discussion to talk to you about who the "we" are and who the "others" are in our thoughts and in our politics. But I should immediately amend that, because I shall be talking of time, universalism, and particularism only in the plural number, since I do not believe those words have any meaning otherwise. There are multiple temporalities, multiple universalisms, and multiple particularisms. And a good deal of our confusion in discussing culture comes from suppressing this multiplicity in the analysis.

Let us start with temporalities. I opened my remarks by referring to the Cold War. The Cold War is usually dated as going from 1945 to 1989. Actually, André Fontaine insisted a long time ago that it began in 1917.[2] And starting it in 1917 changes the analysis considerably. But no matter. It is supposed to be over. Yet, when one listens to some voices in the United States, and some in China or Russia, it does not seem to be over for everyone. Such voices seem to take the ideological rhetoric of the Cold War as a continuing marker of how they define the current world reality. Perhaps we should not take them too seriously. Proponents of *Realpolitik* have always argued that ideology was merely rhetoric that was meant to mask the *raison d'état* of the states, and that the ruling strata never paid too much attention to the ideology they officially espoused. Charles de Gaulle seemed to have little doubt that the Soviet Union was first and foremost the Russian empire and the United States, the American empire, and he made his analyses and calculations on this basis. Was he wrong? When Richard Nixon went to China to meet Mao Zedong, was each subordinating ideology to *raison d'état,* or was each simply pursuing more long-range ideological objectives? Historians will no doubt continue to argue over this for centuries to come.

Today, the United States and China seem to share a common commitment to encouraging production for the world market. Yet each defines the roots of this commitment differently. American politicians and pundits persist in describing the United States as a country committed to free-enterprise capitalism, whereas Chinese politicians and pundits persist in describing China as a country committed to socialism, now sometimes called market socialism. Are we as social scientists to take such self-descriptions at face value? And if not, how should we really describe the structures of each country?

Of course, one factor in these self-descriptions is the chronosophy[3] common to each country, or at least to its leaders and to most of its citizens. Each country is committed to a long-range optimism based on the assumption of linear progress. Each seems to be sure it is on the path to the more perfect society. These self-descriptions are, however, in some sense as much statements of the teleological objective toward which these countries are heading as analyses of the present. But there are other chronosophies that would give us different temporalities. And even within any chronosophy, there are other periodizations, which again give us different temporalities.

What is most important to remember is that we live in many of these social temporalities simultaneously. We can, for example, analyze the world in terms of the modern world-system as a historical system, which would lead us to take as temporal boundaries the long sixteenth century to the present. And one of the many ways in which we could describe this system is the periodic shift of centricity, seeing the system as having a succession of hegemonic powers, whose hegemony is always temporary. If we did this, we could talk of the rise of American hegemony beginning in the 1870s, reaching a peak in the period between 1945 and 1970, and now in the early stages of its decline. And we could of course ask the question, one indeed frequently asked, as to who might the successor hegemonic power be. Some argue the case for Japan, and a few for China, and there are others who think that U.S. hegemony is still too much with us for us to think clearly about such an issue.

Or, still within the time boundaries of the modern world-system, we could see the history of the past two centuries as a pan-European project of world domination (the "expansion of Europe") and debate when this expansion peaked—in 1900, in 1945, in 1989? And when did the pushback begin—with the Japanese defeat of Russia in 1905, with the entry of the Chinese Communists into Shanghai in 1949, with the Bandung Conference in 1955, with the U.S. defeat in Vietnam in 1973? And then we could discuss the question of whether this pushback is the signal of a structural crisis in the modern world-system, or (as some would have it) nothing but the end of a phase in a far longer historical process in which Asian global centrality had been temporarily displaced by a brief Western or European moment.

The multiple temporalities in which we live may cause us some analytic confusion, but they are far easier to think about and to handle than multiple universalisms. "Multiple universalisms" is of course an oxymoron. "Universalism" is supposed to mean the view that there exist laws or truths that apply to all persons, all groups, all historical social systems *at all points in time and space.* Hence it is unitary, unique, and unified. How can there be multiple versions of that which is one? Well, I could refer to some versions of Christian theology, which have long argued that there is a trinity in which God is both one and three, or to the Hindu idea that the gods have many avatars. These are theological, not scientific, ideas, but they do indicate a wisdom, the kind of wisdom science has often, to its peril, ignored, and often found validated at a later point in its own evolution.

But I do not wish to appeal to theological insights. It is quite clear that there are multiple universalisms both at the level of popular, community-based claims and also at the level of scholarly assertions. Speaking from within the framework of one of these claims, we can of course reject the others as patently false or at least badly worded, and this is regularly done. All nomothetic social science is based on precisely this procedure. There are many who would insist that the term "science" is reserved for those who, in any domain of knowledge, are working to build a unique universalism. I want to argue not only that no unique universalism exists, nor could it ever exist, but also that science is the search for how multiple universalisms can best be navigated in a universe that is intrinsically uncertain, and therefore hopefully creative.[4]

The modern world has been for most of its history a prisoner of Aristotle's doctrine of the excluded middle. Something is either A or not-A. There is no third possibility. But of course quantum mechanics has gotten us used to the idea that things can be two different things at the same time, or at least can be measured in two quite different ways or can satisfy two different equations. Light is a swarm of particles and a continuous wave as well. We do not have to choose, or, rather, we cannot.

We face the same problem in social science. In the arena of public policy, groups regularly contend on the basis of different so-called basic values, or different priorities in values. We are in fact constantly faced with such issues in our personal lives. I read in the newspapers of the tragic situation of two European infants who are Siamese twins. The doctors say that, since the twins have only one heart and one lung, they can only be separated in such a way that one twin lives and the other dies. The doctors also say that if they do not separate the twins, both will die within months. The parents say that they cannot allow one child to be killed in order that the other might live. And the British courts were asked to resolve juridically this moral dilemma, this differ-ence in moral priorities.

Not all such choices are tragic. Not all of them require that we choose between competing rights to life. But the underlying is-sues are omnipresent, and we are all collectively being constantly asked to make historical choices. All the debates about outside intervention in the "internal affairs" of any country invoke on the one side claims about universal human rights and on the other side the right of countries not to be subordinate to the im-perial and imperious imposition of the values of others on them. And it is this last debate that has been central to the modern world-system since its outset and that has come to the fore again in the last decade.

The reality of the modern world-system, the capitalist world-economy, is that it is a hierarchical, unequal, polarizing system, whose political structure is that of an interstate system in which some states are manifestly stronger than others. In furtherance of the process of the endless accumulation of capital, stronger states are constantly imposing their will on weaker states, to the degree that they can. This is called imperialism, and is inherent in the structure of the world-system. Imperialism has however, always had, its moral defense. It has been justified on the basis of the "civilizing mission," the presumed moral necessity to force oth-ers to conform to the norms prescribed by universal values. It seems a curious coincidence that the values that are said to be universal are always those primarily observed by the imperial power. Resistance by the victims to such specious morality seems a self-evident virtue.

Yet, on the other hand, local despotisms have always thrived on their ability to maintain closed frontiers and to reject any and all "outside interference" with their nefarious doings. And we have become increasingly sensitive to the evils of noninterven-tion, given the enormity of the crimes that are sometimes committed under the cover of sovereignty. In this current era when so many governments and churches are apologizing for past misdeeds, we are constantly adjured to remember those, especially those who are seemingly powerful, who failed to protest (and perhaps thereby to prevent) the misdeeds of still others. From the Holocaust to Rwanda, the albatross of guilt is laid around our necks. But of course the guilt of nonintervention didn't start with the Holocaust. Before the Holocaust there was the Middle Passage of the Atlantic slave trade, and the countless slaughters of indigenous peoples, not to speak of the child labor that to this day pervades the globe.

So we cannot fail to confront these evaluations of the past and the present by pretending that to do so is an exercise of the political and not of the scientific world. It is after all a discussion of multiple universalisms, which we have all been sedulously avoiding. Since, however, there are many, many universalisms, should we give them all equal weight and place? This is another way of asking whether we should be totally relativistic. And the answer is surely not. Because if there are formulas of accommodation between many universalisms, it is also true that there are some universalisms which are truly incompatible with others. And we are thereby forced into a meta-debate: Is there a singular hierarchy of universalisms, some of which are reasonable and acceptable and others of which are deeply repugnant? And if the answer is yes, and I suspect it is, is this not simply another way of returning to the unique universalism we are trying to escape? In any case, to say there is a hierarchy of universalisms solves nothing, since we still must decide on what basis we can judge which claims we should firmly exclude.

There is no easy or immediate answer to such a question. The attempt to draw fuzzy lines instead is the only real alternative. It is our continuing quest for unifying the true and the good. The journey, rather than reaching some utopian arrival point, is the positive action. It is a moral action, but it is an intellectual one as well, one, furthermore, that can only be conducted plausibly by a truly worldwide collectivity of participants in the quest. Each will bring to the quest a different biography, a different experience with priorities, a different insight into the possible consequences of alternative paths. Each may restrain the worst impulses or the weakest judgment of the other.

In practice, there are three major varieties of universalisms that have a hold on the modern mind. There are those that derive from the world religions (and of course there are many religions). There are those that derive from the secular Enlightenment ideals that have been central to modernity. And there are those that express the sense of the powerful that the basis of their power has been their righteous actions and that therefore imperial stretch is a virtue, not a vice.

We have learned once again in the last two decades not to underestimate the hold of religions on the minds of people and therefore on the politics of the world-system. Religions are universalist almost by definition. Even when they originate in very local situations, they almost always lay claim to being universal truth, applicable to all persons. Often, however, religious universalisms are thought to be more than merely applicable to all; they are seen as mandated for all. And even when the rhetoric is less compulsory in tone, almost all religions teach the uniqueness of their path to truth or to salvation. Some religions are more exclusionary than others, but all insist on the virtue of their particular path of doctrines and practices. The three most widespread religions in the world—Christianity, Islam, and Buddhism—are all proselytizing, the first two aggressively so. This is no doubt why they are the most widespread, or at least that might be the view of an uncommitted observer.

So what do the religions of the world tell us? To love each other, to love everyone, and to love particularly those who share

the faith or the practice. One cannot say that this is an unambiguous message. And the results of course have been highly ambiguous. For although it is clear that religious authorities have
regularly been a force for peace and tolerance, it is equally clear
that they have regularly been a force for violence and intoler-
ance. No doubt God moves in mysterious ways, but we simple
humans may feel impelled to try to make sense of these ways
and, dare I suggest it, to draw more coherent conclusions from
our faiths and our sciences than mere fatalism.

It was of course in revolt against the dominance of religions
that Enlightenment humanism-scientism staked its claim to a
truly universal universalism, one to which all persons had equal
access via their rational insight and understanding of eternal verities, via their verification of these truths in ways that all could
replicate. The problem here, as we know, is that when all persons
exercised their insight and understanding they came up with different lists of truths. Of course one could (and did) argue that this
situation was temporary, to be resolved by rational debate. But in
practice, this solution did not seem to eliminate the problem.
And Enlightenment humanism-scientism was thereby forced
to create a hierarchy of human beings, according to their degree
of rationality. Some were clearly more rational than others,
whether because of their education, their experience, or their
natural intellectual gifts. These persons were specialists in
knowledge. And it did seem to follow that a more rational world
required the imposition by more rational persons of the practical
implications of the eternal verities they had perceived. So Enlightenment humanism-scientism entered the same ambiguous
path as the world's religions. On the one hand, we were adjured
to regard all humans as rational, and on the other hand we were
adjured to respect the preeminence and political priority of those
who were more rational. We were adjured to respect each other,
to respect everyone, and to respect particularly those who shared

our meritocratic skills and merited positions of advantage. Once again, a not unambiguous message.

Those who based their universalisms on the imperative of might makes right were at least more straightforward. Essentially, they told us that whatever is had to be and that polarizing hierarchies are and must be the result of unequal skills, wisdom, and moral virtue. This was theorized in the nineteenth century as somehow biological in origin. Biologically based explanations have come into disfavor, ever since the Nazis took these theories to their logical conclusion. But never fear! It has been easy to replace these biological explanations with cultural ones. Those who have power and privilege are said to have it because they are heirs to a culture that provided them with skills, wisdom, and virtue. Do note the coming to the fore, in this context too, of the concept of culture.

What none of the three varieties of universalisms—the religious, the humanist-scientific, or the imperialist—have offered us, however, is a theory of multiple universalisms, or even a theory of a hierarchy of universalisms. For each it has seemed to be a competitive race to the top. This may explain why the twentieth century, the most universalizing century in the history of humanity, was also the most brutal and the most destructive of human beings.

When universalisms are used to destroy or oppress, people take refuge in particularisms. It is an obvious defense, and most of the time a very necessary one. And it works, up to a point. Particularisms by definition deny universalisms. They say, in effect, "We are different and difference is a virtue. Your rules do not apply to us, or have negative effects on us, or are designed specifically to do us harm. We therefore amend them, or reject them outright, and our rejection has a status of at least moral equality with your assertion of the universalistic rules." It turns out, however, that there are multiple stances from which one can assert particularisms, and the cultural claims made in the name of the multiple particularisms can have quite different political meanings.

There are first of all the particularisms asserted by the current losers in the universalism races. The current losers are generically those to whom we refer as "minorities." A minority is not primarily a quantitative concept but one of social rank; it is those who are defined as different (in some specified way) from the group that is dominant—dominant in the world-system, dominant in any institutional structure within the world-system such as the state-system, or the class structure, or the meritocracy scales, or the constructed race-ethnic hierarchies we find everywhere. Minorities do not necessarily begin by proclaiming particularisms. They often try first to appeal to the universalistic criteria of the winners, demanding equal rights. But they quite frequently find that these criteria are then applied in such a way that they lose anyway. And so they turn to particularisms with which to confront the so-called majority.

The mechanism of these confrontational particularisms is quite familiar. It is to assert that the losers had in fact been ahead of the winners on the universalistic criteria over the long term, but that they had been pushed temporarily behind by some act of illegitimate force, and that the rank order is destined to be reversed once again. Or it is to assert that the universalistic criteria are in reality particularistic criteria, no better (indeed worse) than the particularistic criteria of the minority, and therefore the rank order is destined to be reversed. Or it is to deny that any truly universalistic criteria can possibly exist, that the rank order is always a matter of force, and that since the minorities are a quantitative majority, the rank order is destined to be reversed. Or it is to proclaim all these theses simultaneously. The emphasis in this variety of particularism is always on "catching up" to, and quite often on "exceeding," the presently dominant group. It is seldom the search for a new universalism, except one that may be achieved by the total elimination of the currently dominant group.

There are then the particularisms of the declining middles. Social science has written much about this. These groups may define themselves in any way—class, race, ethnicity, language, religion. Given the ceaselessly polarizing pressures of the capitalist world-economy, there are always clusters of people whose status in the prestige hierarchy and whose standard of living is declining with reference to a recent past. And such people are naturally anxious, resentful, and combative. Sometimes they may focus their angers on those responsible for this decline, who will defend themselves on the basis of the inevitability of the changes in terms of maximizing overall economic efficiency of production. But quite often it is not easy to perceive what actions of the powerful have led to the decline. And thus it is that those who are suffering such declines come to scapegoat groups that seem even weaker than they (but who are perceived, often incorrectly, to be improving their status and income levels).

This is such a familiar story around the world over the past centuries that it is scarcely worth spending time elaborating it. But it should be noted that in such situations we see fierce particularisms, often of a particularly nasty nature. And it follows that the groups who are the target of these angers, these hatreds, respond by forging their own strong particularisms. Thus we enter into a cycle of senseless violence, which can last a very long time, until the groups are exhausted, and the rest of the world, too, and some kind of truce is imposed on the contending groups. In the process, scapegoating becomes the game of the third parties as well. They define the conflict as the result of eternal enmities. Frequently such claims are patently false assertions, but they do have the consequence of blaming both sets of victims—the original group that is declining because of the imperatives of capital accumulation and the still weaker group it is blaming for this—and minimize our ability to analyze the relevant causes of the fierce internecine combats. Invoking cultural particularisms in such situations is in no way a positive action, even if we can understand how those particularisms arose. In the end, we can only emerge from this vicious cycle by an appeal to relevant universalisms.

There is a third variety of particularism, that of the persistently bottom groups, again however defined. That these groups are thought of, and think of themselves, as particular is of course basic to social definitions of identity. They are the pariahs of our system—Blacks, Roma, Harijan, Burakumin, Indios, Aborigines, Pygmies. The assertion of their particular identities has been in the twentieth century, particularly the late twentieth century, an essential element in their political mobilization to achieve minimal political, economic, and social rights. That they have overstated their arguments in some cases, that they have from time to time indulged in a counterracism, seems less relevant than the fact that, despite all their efforts, they have at best been only very moderately successful in emerging from the pariah category. The fact is that the social dice are still loaded against all these groups. And one of the major weapons used to keep them down is to assert the primacy of universalistic norms every time they demand compensatory intervention or assistance in overcoming the cumulative negative effect of centuries (if not more) of discriminatory treatment, what in the United States is called affirmative action. Over all, however much the particularisms of the declining middles may have devastating social consequences, the particularisms of the persistently bottom groups tend to have positive consequences for all social strata, and not only for them. The greatest beneficiaries of affirmative action over the long run will be the so-called majorities.

There is a fourth variety of particularism with which we are all familiar. It is the particularism of the effete snobs, those who pride themselves on their high culture (that word again) and denounce the vulgarity of the masses. Not that the masses are not vulgar. The word "vulgar" comes after all from the Latin term for the "common people." In days of yore, the members of the aristocracy defined their own behavior as high culture, and forbade the common people to engage in practices of high culture. For example, there were dress codes. But the modern world-system has created a superficial democratization of culture. We are all permitted to engage in these practices. And more and more people everywhere do.

The effete snobs are really that segment of the upper strata, sometimes especially found among those declining in wealth, who are determined to hold on to their cultural separation from the masses. This creates a curious game. As each cultural practice and artifact that is defined as "high" is copied or indulged in by the common people, it becomes redefined as vulgar. And the effete snobs rush to find new artifacts and practices. One of the places they find such new practices is precisely in the protesting, antisystemic practices of the persistently bottom groups. This creates a constant strain, as everyone constantly reevaluates such artifacts and practices, amidst much confusion, frequent relabeling, and much struggle to appropriate the rights to them.

A fifth kind of particularism is that of dominant elites. This is not quite the same as that of the effete snobs. For it does not garb itself as high culture but as a basic set of cultural presuppositions, what I have called the geoculture, "the underside of geopolitics."[5] This form of particularism hides itself behind the screen of universalism—in today's world, as the universalism of rationality. This form of particularism uses the denunciation of particularism as the most effective means of asserting its own primacy. In the United States we have come to call the debates that result the "culture wars"—again that word!

These multiple varieties of particularisms of course are no more governed by the law of the excluded middle than are the multiple varieties of universalisms. We all move back and forth through all these varieties constantly, and espouse several of them at any given time and space. Nor are the political implications of each etched in stone. Their role is a function of the total social situation in which they occur and in which they are perceived. But we can of course evaluate these roles and we can support, ignore, or oppose them in terms of our own priorities in values.

If we look at the long historical evolution of the modern world-system we see that the choices among temporalities, universalisms, and particularisms have constituted a central locus of our political struggles. One of the weapons the powerful have had has been to misdefine these debates, and thus to obscure them, using an imagery that implies that time and space are simply contexts within which we live rather than constructs that shape our lives. And universalism and particularism are defined as a critical antinomy that we can use to analyze all social action and between whose priority we all have to choose, and once and for all. This has been helpful to the winners and not at all to the losers, which is the most urgent reason why we must unthink this antinomy and make far more complex our appreciation of the options that are available to all of us.

Culture, too, is not just there. Its very definition is a battlefield, as I have previously argued.[6] Furthermore, the uses of the concept of culture are manifold, as I have tried to show in this discussion. One of the most urgent tasks of cultural studies today is to take more emotional distance from culture, to regard the concept of culture itself, as well as the students of the concept, as an object of study. Equally, we need to deepen our understanding of the politics and the economics of culture. The sacred trinity of liberal ideology—the political, the economic, and the sociocultural—is one of the most oppressive weapons of the particularism of the dominant strata. This trinity is probably the concept that is most difficult and most necessary to unthink. I would, if I could, abolish all three adjectives from our vocabulary. But I do not think I can, yet—for one thing, because I am not sure with what to replace them.

So, are cultures in conflict? Undoubtedly, but saying that does not tell us very much. We need to be aware that the historical system within which we live thrives by the effort to commodify everything. High culture has been commodified for at least two centuries, and the last half-century has seen a spectacular rise in the degree to which high culture is a profitable enterprise for all concerned—the manufacturers of cultural products and the artists whose products are packaged.

In the last twenty years we have seen how the culture of protest can be commodified as well. One doesn't assert one's identity, one pays to assert it, and one pays to observe others asserting theirs, and some people even sell us our identity.[7] One copyrights culture. These days, there is a struggle going on between the producers of music in the form of CDs who seek to sell these CDs and those who operate web sites on the Internet that enable consumers to download these CDs at no cost. But of course, the web site expects to make its money from the advertisements that will be placed on its web site. Virtually no one in this dispute speaks in favor of the true decommodification of cultural products.

Is the culture that we pay to display the expression of our heritage or our souls or even our political demands or is it the internalization of values imposed on us for the profit of those who gain rent from the transmission of these displays? Or can we even distinguish the two? Not even folklore, traditionally defined as a noncommodity, escapes this deep involvement in the endless accumulation of capital.

Who then are we? Who are the others? The answer depends on which battle we are fighting. Is it local, national, or global? It also depends on our assessment of what is happening within our historical system. I have been arguing for some time now that our historical system, the capitalist world-economy, is in structural crisis. I have said that we are in the middle of a chaotic period, that a bifurcation is occurring, and that over the next fifty years, not only will our current system cease to exist but a new one will come into existence. Finally, I have argued that the nature of this new system is intrinsically unknowable in advance, but that nonetheless its nature will be fundamentally shaped by our actions in this era of transition in which "free will" seems to be at its optimal point. Finally, I have argued that the uncertain outcome may result in a historical system that is better, worse, or about the same morally as the present one, but that it is our moral and political duty to seek to make it better.

I will not rehearse here the case I have made for the existence of such a structural crisis, nor for the chronosophy I am employing. Rather I want to outline the possible "we's" and the corresponding other's in this crucial period of a struggle that is simultaneously political, economic, and cultural.

Let me start by rejecting some possible "we's." I do not believe we are really living through, or should be living through, a clash of civilizations in which the Western world, the Islamic world, and an East Asian world find themselves arrayed against each other. Some people would like us to believe this, in order to weaken our hands in the real battles. But I see little real evidence of such a clash, outside the rhetoric of politicians and commentators. The multiple universalisms and particularisms that I have outlined exist within each of these presumed civilizational arenas, and in not significantly different proportions.

To be sure, the clash of civilizations is one formula for defining North-South conflicts. While I believe that North-South conflicts are a fundamental political reality of the contemporary world—how could they not be in a constantly polarizing world-system?—I do not draw the conclusion that virtue derives from geography, or that the spokespersons for each side at any moment necessarily reflect the interests of the larger group they purport to represent. There are too many cross-cutting interests at play, too many tactical follies, for anyone to commit himself or herself unreservedly to one side or the other in the endless skirmishes. However, on the basic issue that there must be an end to the polarization and a drastic move toward equalizing the uses of the world's resources I feel there cannot be any equivocation. It is for me a moral and political priority.

Is then the "we" those delineated in the class struggle? Well, of course, but what exactly does that mean? We can draw a line between those who are living off the surplus value produced by others and those who are not retaining all of the surplus value they are producing, and we can call this line that between the bourgeoisie and the proletariat, or use some similar language. But in fact, of course, within each of these categories there exists a complex, overlapping internal hierarchy. The existing system has not created two homogenized classes (much less one homogenized humanity), but a subtle skein of privilege and exploitation. That is why we have so many varieties of particularisms. Reducing this picture to two camps is no simple task, as none other than Karl Marx demonstrated in his classic political analysis, *The Eighteenth Brumaire of Louis Napoleon*. If even Mao Zedong insisted that the class struggle continued within a socialist society, we are made aware of how prudently we have to be in assigning "we-ness" on the basis of class.

Then there is the "we-ness" of nationhood. Nationalism has proved to be an extremely powerful appeal to solidarity in the last two centuries, and there is little sign that this appeal has disappeared from the horizon. We are all aware of the conflicts nationalism has bred between states. But I wish to remind us of the conflicts that nationalism has bred within states. For nationalism is not a cost-free good.

Look at Japan. In the post-Meiji period, nationalism became a strong weapon for constructing a modern state, a state that was powerful, that achieved its objectives in terms of advancing the relative status of Japan in the world-system. It led ultimately to the seizure of Korea, the invasion of China, the conquest of Southeast Asia, and the attack on Pearl Harbor. Japan lost the Second World War, and suffered the atrocious price of Hiroshima. After the war, nationalism became itself an element of internal conflict within Japan. There are those who fear that any resuscitation of nationalist symbols might trigger a restoration of a militarist, aggressive, internally repressive regime. And there are those who feel that Japan alone is being denied its national(ist) identity, to the detriment of so-called traditional values.

Japan is not alone in this conflict about the utility of national(ist) identity. Both China and the United States are afflicted by the same latent (and not so latent) conflict. But so are a long list of states around the world. I draw from this the conclusion that invoking national identity is akin to risky surgical intervention. It may be essential for survival (or merely for improved health) in some situations, but beware the surgeon (political leader) whose hand slips, or the side effects that no surgeon (political leader) could have prevented.

If I thus reject civilization, class, and nation as easy, straightforward criteria of "we-ness" (not to speak of race, a totally malicious and invented criterion), with what are we left to navigate the difficult waters of a chaotic transition over the next fifty years from the historical system in which we live to some alternative system in which our descendants shall live? Nothing easy to define.

Let us begin by asserting moral and political objectives. When a historical system is in crisis, one can move, it seems to me, in one of two basic directions. One can try to preserve the hierarchical structure of the existing world-system, albeit in new forms and perhaps on new bases. Or one can try to reduce, if not altogether eliminate, the inequalities to the extent possible. And it will follow that most of us (but not all of us) will opt for one of the two alternatives in consequence of the degree of privilege we enjoy in the present system. It will follow that there could emerge two broad camps of persons, and that such camps could not be identified either by civilization, by nation, or even by current definitions of class status.

The politics of the two camps is not hard to predict. The camp favoring hierarchies will enjoy the benefits of its current wealth, its power therefore to command intelligence and sophistication, not to speak of weaponry. Nonetheless, its strength, though manifest, is subject to one constraint, that of visibility. Since by definition this camp represents the numerical minority of the world's populations, it must attract others to support it by appealing to themes other than hierarchy. It must make its priorities less visible. This is not always easy, and to the extent it is achieved it can cause confusion and reduce solidarity among its core members. So it is not guaranteed victory.

Arrayed against it would be the camp of the numerical majority. But this is a highly divided camp, divided by the multiple particularisms and even by the multiple universalisms. The formula that can overcome this disunity has already been proclaimed. It is the formula of the rainbow coalition. But this is far easier said than done. Each participant's advantages in such a formula is middle-run, and short-term considerations force themselves upon all of us with great regularity. We seldom have the discipline, or even the resources, with which to ignore short-run advantage. We live after all in the short run as individuals. It is only collectively that we live in the middle run, and can place such an alternate temporality into our schema of priorities. And when one thinks of creating not a national rainbow coalition but a global one, we realize what a formidable political task this is, and how little time there is to forge such a coalition.

How then does one go about trying to do this? In part, this is a political task that has to be pursued simultaneously at the local, the national, the regional, and the global levels. One has to concentrate, if one is to succeed in pulling together a meaningful coalition, on the middle-run question of the kind of replacement system we wish to construct while not ignoring the short-run problem of alleviating the miseries under the existing system. I feel it is not my function to go further in outlining a political strategy. Rather, I wish to concentrate on the intellectual contributions that social science can make in this era of transition.

I think the first thing we can do is to unthink the social science categories that have been bequeathed to us by the existing world-system and that have so hobbled us in our analyses not only of current reality but of the possible alternatives to it we might construct. Recognizing the existence of multiple temporalities, multiple universalisms, multiple particularisms is a first step. But we need to do far more than simply acknowledge their existence. We have to begin to figure out how they fit together, and what is the optimal mix, and in what situations. This is an agenda for major reconstruction of our knowledge systems.

I have not spoken up to now of the "two cultures"—that presumed fundamental epistemological split between the humanities and the sciences. This split, reproduced within the social sciences as the *Methodenstreit* between idiographic and nomothetic methodologies, is in fact a recent invention. It is no more than 200 to 250 years old, and is itself a prime creation of the modern world-system. It is also deeply irrational, since science is a cultural phenomenon, a prisoner of its cultural context, and the humanities have no language that is not scientific, otherwise they could not communicate coherently their message to anyone.[8]

One thing we all need to do is read far more widely. Reading is a part of the process of theoretical discovery, of uncovering the clues and the links that lie buried in the mass of deposited knowledge products. We need to point our students toward reflection on fundamental epistemological issues. We must cease fearing either philosophy or science, since in the end they are the same thing, and we can only do either by doing both, or by recognizing that they are a single enterprise. In the process, we shall become fully aware of the multiple universalisms that govern our universe, and begin for the first time to be substantively rational, that is, to reach a consensus, however interim, on the priorities of values and of truths in a universe where we must constantly make choices, and therefore be creative.

If social scientists—no, if all scholars of whatever field—can succeed in thus reconstructing their enterprise, and that is a very big if, we shall have contributed massively to the historical choices that all of us are necessarily making in this era of transition. This will not be the end of history, either. But it will allow us to proceed on a better footing.

There is said to be a Qing dynasty saying: "People fear the rulers; the rulers fear the foreign devils; the foreign devils fear the people." Of course, the Qing already had experience with the modern world-system. But we, the people, we are also the foreign devils. In the end there are no others, or at least no others that we cannot control if collectively we set our minds to it, discuss it, weigh alternatives, and choose, creatively. In a socially constructed world, it is we who construct the world.

NOTES

1. Epigraph from Paul Gilroy, *Against Race: Imagining Political Culture Beyond the Color Line* (Cambridge, Mass.: Harvard University Press, 2000), 72.

2. André Fontaine, *Histoire de la guerre froide,* 2 vols. (Paris: Fayard, 1983).

3. On the concept of chronosophy, see Krzysztof Pomian, "The Secular Evolution of the Concept of Cycles," *Review* 2, no. 4 (Spring 1979):563–646. Pomian uses the term in contrast to "chronometry" and "chronology," saying, "It speaks of time; it makes time the object of a discourse or rather of discourse in general" (568–69).

4. See Ilya Prigogine, *The End of Certainty* (New York: Free Press, 1997). It should be noted that the original title in French, *La Fin des certitudes,* uses the plural, "certainties."

5. This is the title of part 2 of Immanuel Wallerstein, *Geopolitics and Geoculture: Essays on the Changing World-System* (Cambridge; England: Cambridge University Press, 1991).

6. "Culture as the Ideological Battleground of the Modern World-System," *Hitotsubashi Journal of Social Studies* 21, no. 1 (August 1989):5–22, reprinted in Wallerstein, *Geopolitics and Geoculture,* 158–83.

7. See an excellent discussion of this phenomenon in Gilroy, *Against Race,* Chapter 7 and passim.

8. My arguments to elaborate this thesis are to be found in part 2, "The World of Knowledge," in Immanuel Wallerstein, *The End of the World As We Know It: Social Science for the Twenty-first Century* (Minneapolis: University of Minnesota Press, 1999).

CHAPTER SEVEN

Democracy:
Rhetoric or Reality?

DEMOCRACY AND THE WORLD-SYSTEM
UP TO NOW

Democracy has become everyone's slogan today. Who does not claim that democracy is a good thing, and which politician does not assert that the government of which he is a part practices it and the party that he represents wishes to maintain and extend it? It is hard to remember that not so very long ago, in the period from the French Revolution up to 1848 at least, "democracy" was a word used only by dangerous radicals.[1] "Democrat" was the label of multiple extreme-left organizations in the 1830s and 1840s.[2] For the powers that were in the period of the Holy Alliance, to accuse someone of being a democrat was a bit like accusing someone in the post-1945 Western world of being a Communist.

When, after 1848, Mazzini (who called himself a democrat) fell into a major quarrel with the socialists, the latter added the term "social" to their slogan; they talked of being "for a universal democratic and social republic."[3] This is probably the origin of the later term "social democrats," the distinction "social" now being deemed necessary because "democrat" alone no longer denoted radical, having been appropriated by others as well whose politics were more centrist. It would take another half-century at least before conservatives also appropriated the word.

It all depends on the content we put into a word, any word. One possible usage of "democracy," one widespread definition today, is freedom from arbitrary political power. According to this definition, democracy is more or less the realization of an individualist liberal political agenda. Its outward measures of how democratic a country is become whether or not there are free elections in which multiple parties contend, whether or not there exist communications media not under the direct political control of the government, whether or not one can pursue one's religious faith without state interference—in short, the degree to which all those things that are usually summarized as "civil liberties" are in fact practiced within the bounds of a particular state.

Using this definition, the historical development of democracy tends to be described as having followed a linear curve. The usual theoretical model starts implicitly with the moment of an "absolute monarch" or its equivalent. Wresting decision-making away from the chief executive, or at least forcing him to share his powers with an elected legislature, is part of the story. Limiting the degree to which the state is permitted to intrude in the so-called private arena is another part of the story. Ensuring that critics are neither silenced nor punished is still another part. Employing these criteria, we find that the picture seems to be brightest today in the pan-European world (western Europe, North America, Australasia) and less good, to quite varying degrees, elsewhere in the world. One part of the furor raised by the inclusion of Jörg Haider's party in the Austrian government last year was the fear that Austria would begin to look less good on this kind of scorecard.[4] When today Western politicians talk about how democratic a particular country is, this is usually how they are measuring it. Indeed, for a number of years now, the U.S. government has annually issued formal scorecards of other governments using precisely such criteria.

To be sure, civil liberties are indeed very important. And we know exactly how important they are whenever they are seriously constricted. Under regimes that constrict civil liberties, which we usually label "dictatorships," there is to be sure always a certain amount of resistance, particularly by persons who wish to speak out publicly (intellectuals, journalists, politicians, students), an opposition that may be deeply underground if the repression is sufficiently severe. When for whatever reason the regime becomes weaker and is somehow overthrown, one of the things that people tend to celebrate is the end of such kinds of repression. So we know that such civil liberties are valued, appreciated, and utilized when and where they exist.

But we also know that, for the average person, while civil liberties are seen as desirable, they are seldom at the top of his or her political agenda. And in those states in which a regime largely respects civil liberties, civil liberties seldom seem to be enough to fulfill the average person's sense of what should define a democratic society. If they were, we would not have so much political indifference and so much political abstention. When we look at the so-called liberal states, those with relatively high levels of civil liberties, we discover a whole series of other issues that are of concern to most people, give rise to their complaints, and inflect their political priorities.

The complaints, it seems to me, can be grouped in three major categories: complaints about corruption; complaints about material inequalities; complaints about the inadequate inclusiveness of citizenship. Let us start with corruption. There is an incredible amount of cynicism on this subject, as well there might be. It would be hard to name a single government in the world in the last one hundred years that has not known one, several, many corruption scandals. Of course, here again, it is a bit a matter of definition. If we mean by corruption the private purchase of the services or decisions of a public figure, a politician or civil servant, this of course occurs all the time, often in the form of kickbacks from government contracts. This is possibly more frequent in poorer countries, or more frequently reported. In the case of the poorer countries, the corrupters are quite often noncitizens, persons from wealthier states, both capitalists and representatives of other governments. However, overt bribery is the least of the story.

A much more fundamental issue is the degree to which money buys access. This kind of corruption is pervasive in the operations of the regimes of the wealthier states—precisely those with the better records on civil liberties. Politics in a multiparty system is an expensive game to conduct, and it is getting more expensive all the time. Most politicians and most political parties have financial needs that go far beyond what can be supplied by the relatively small contributions of the mass of their supporters. We all know what happens as a result. Wealthier contributors (individuals and corporate groups) offer large sums of money, sometimes to multiple competing parties at the same time. And in return, they expect a certain amount of tacit sympathy for their needs and explicit access for their lobbying.

In theory, capitalists operate via the market and wish governments to stay out of market operations. In practice, as every capitalist knows, the governments are crucial to their market success in multiple ways—by making possible or impossible relative monopolies, in being large-scale near-monopsonistic purchasers of expensive items, and as manipulators of macroeconomic decisions, including of course taxation. No serious capitalist can afford to ignore governments, his own and those of any other country in which he operates. But given that politicians must give priority to getting into power or remaining in power, and have great financial needs, no serious capitalist can afford to ignore this obvious source of pressure on governments, or he will lose out to competitors or to hostile interests. Therefore no serious capitalist does ignore governments, and all serious capitalists have in the forefront of their consciousness the fact that politicians have great financial needs. Consequently, corruption is absolutely normal and unexpungeable from the ongoing political life of the capitalist world-economy.

Still, corruption is not merely illegal; it is against the norms, regularly proclaimed, of honest government and a neutral bureaucracy. When a major norm is violated daily, the only possible result is widespread cynicism. And that is what we have. Cynicism can lead to quite different responses. One response is to get our guys in there. Another is to wage battle to limit the damage of corruption. A third is to withdraw from active participation in politics. Each response has its limitations. The problem with "getting our guys in there" is that it seldom changes the gap between norm and reality. The problem with seeking to limit the damage is that it is so difficult to do—almost impossible—that it often seems not worth the trouble to try. And this leads more and more people to opt for the third response, withdrawal, which leaves the corrupt to reign undisturbed.

Another possibility, however, is to redefine what one means by democracy, enlarging on the previous definition, and insisting on substantive results in addition to mere electoral process. The electoral process of course has known an important evolution in the last two centuries. We have arrived, in virtually every state, at a norm of universal adult suffrage. Considering where the world was two hundred years ago, this is a major structural change. And as we have already noted, universal adult suffrage is regularly celebrated as the advent of democracy. If we look at the history of the expansion of suffrage,[5] we see immediately that it was always the result of a political struggle. And we see also that the widening of suffrage tended to be a concession by those in power to movements conducted by those who lacked the suffrage.

The principal debate among those who controlled the political machinery whenever such a widening of suffrage was discussed was always one between the fearful (who paraded as the tough-minded) and the sophisticated. The fearful were those who argued that allowing wider access to suffrage would result in significantly negative changes in the control of the state machinery, putting political power in the hands of persons who would undo the existing social system. This was the theme of the "unwashed masses" threatening to displace persons of social substance. The sophisticated were those who argued that, on the contrary, once they were accorded suffrage, the "dangerous classes" would become, by the very fact of their nominal inclusion in the political process, less dangerous, and the dreaded political changes would not occur or would turn out to be minor.

The incremental concessions advocated by the sophisticated were eventually widely adopted, and the sophisticates turned out to be correct indeed in their anticipations that widened suffrage would not lead to overturning the system. On the contrary, the concessions did precisely seem to undo the revolutionary inclinations of the unwashed masses. But of course, this is in part because the concessions went beyond those of suffrage alone. The second set of concessions are those we call generically the "welfare state." If we define this loosely as all state action that supported and made possible increases in wage levels plus the use of the state for a certain amount of redistribution of the global surplus, then of course we have had the welfare state to some degree for over a century and virtually across the world (though of course to very different degrees).

Actually, we can divide the welfare state redistributive benefits into three principal categories, the response to three kinds of
fundamental demands that average persons have put upon the
states. The categories are health, education, and lifetime income.
Virtually all people wish to prolong life and good health to the
extent possible, for themselves and their families. Virtually all
people wish to arrange education for themselves and their children, primarily in order to improve their life chances. And almost all people worry about the irregularities of real income over
their lifetime and wish not merely to increase their current income but to minimize sharp fluctuations. These are of course all
perfectly reasonable aspirations. And they have been regularly
reflected in ongoing political programs.

Actually, quite a bit has been accomplished along these lines
over the past two hundred years. In the field of health, we have
had governments active in improving sanitation, in providing
preventive medicine (such as mass vaccinations), subsidizing
hospitals and clinics, expanding medical education, and providing various kinds of health insurance as well as certain kinds of
free services. In the field of education, whereas two hundred
years ago virtually no one received a formal education, today
primary education is available almost everywhere, secondary
education is widespread (albeit unevenly), and even tertiary education is available for a significant number of people, at least in
the wealthier states. As for guaranteed lifetime income, we have
programs of unemployment insurance, old-age pensions, and
various other methods of evening out fluctuations over the life
span. To be sure, compared to health and education, programs to
guarantee lifetime income are far more unevenly distributed
across the world-system.

We should be careful how we evaluate these welfare-state
benefits. On the one hand, they constitute a remarkable struc-

tural difference with the situation two hundred years ago, when almost all such programs and mechanisms were unknown and politically inconceivable. On the other hand, these programs have benefited primarily that part of the world's population we might call the cadres of the system, or the middle strata. Such middle strata are not, it is important to note, evenly distributed across the world-system. In a Third World country, at most 5 percent of the population might fall within such a category, whereas in the wealthiest states, perhaps 40 to 60 percent of the population would fall within such a category.

Thus, looked at through the lens of national statistics, it is the case that in a minority of states the majority of the population is better off today than their ancestors were two hundred years ago. At the same time, the social polarization of the world-system has continued apace, not only between countries but within countries. Furthermore, this polarization is not merely relative, but for some portion of the world's population (difficult to measure but not too difficult to observe), the polarization is absolute.

And yet, although the redistributive effects of the welfare state have been far less good than we are wont to believe or than the propagandists of the world-system constantly tell us, it is simultaneously true that the cost of such redistribution as there has been is considerable and is reflected in the relatively high tax rates of the wealthier countries. Those who are taxed perpetually complain that it is too much. But it is true that the tax bill is far higher today than 50, 100, 200 years ago—for both the upper and middle strata of the world's population and for capitalist enterprises.

To be sure, there are advantages to capitalists in this redistribution, since it increases effective demand. But it is not at all sure that the increased effective demand is greater than the tax bite, as measured over the long run. And this is true for one simple reason. Politically, the popular demand for democratization has translated into an unceasingly upward curve in the level of demand of redistribution, spreading not only upward within countries, but also outward to more and more countries and therefore upward within the world-system as a whole.

Now this kind of democratization is less popular with capitalists in general than are civil liberties, and the struggle to limit the redistribution, to reverse the pattern and reduce the rate to the degree possible, is the bread and butter of conservative political programs. I have no doubt that conservative forces repeatedly win victories that enable them to stem the increase in or even reduce the levels of redistribution. But if one regards the picture over some two hundred years, it seems clear to me that taxation has followed an upward ratchet. Each reversal has been small compared to the next advance. The neoliberal offensive of the 1980s (Thatcherism-Reaganism) and the globalization rhetoric of the 1990s have been just such an effort to stem the increase. This effort has achieved something, but far less than its proponents had hoped, and the political reaction has already set in across the globe.

Let me now introduce the third set of complaints, that about the inadequate inclusiveness of citizenship. The term "citizen" we know is one thrust upon the world's political vocabulary by the French Revolution. The concept was intended to symbolize the refusal of a system of orders, in which nobility and commoners had different social rank and different political rights. The intent was inclusion. Commoners as well as nobility were to be included in the political process. All persons, that is, all citizens, were to be equal. All citizens had rights.

The problem is posed immediately of what is to be included in the "rights" of citizens. Various attempts to have these rights defined very extensively at one fell swoop were beaten back by "counterrevolutions." But there has been a slow extension over the past two hundred years, and this extension has accelerated particularly in the last fifty years. One element was the extension of suffrage, expanding from the propertied to the nonpropertied, from older to younger persons, from men to women, from the core ethnic group to so-called minorities. A second front was the struggle against slavery and then against other forms of servitude. A third front has been the effort to end formal discriminations, by eliminating them from state practices and forbidding them in private practices. Today, we have a long list of sources of discrimination that have become socially illegitimate: class, race, ethnicity, "indigenicity," gender, age, sexuality, disabilities. And this list is constantly being augmented.

One should point to one last level of complaint about democracy. It is the complaint that we are theoretically limited to complaining about, and doing something about, the amount of democracy in the countries of which we are citizens. There have always been persons who have been solidary with movements in other countries for social justice or for citizenship rights or for national liberation. There have been cosmopolitan individuals who have gone off to other countries to be active in their struggles, including their revolutions. But states have been constrained and have constrained themselves from becoming involved in other states' struggles on the principle of reciprocal recognition of sovereignty.

In the nineteenth century, the reciprocal recognition of sovereignty was accorded only to states considered part of the interstate system, which were defined as "civilized" states. Zones of the globe that were not considered "civilized" were subject to the self-proclaimed right of the "civilized" states to engage in a "civilizing mission," which involved conquest, administration, and forcible transformation of certain customs. In the heyday of imperialism, in the late nineteenth century, the term "imperialism" was a word of honor, at least in the countries in which it formed the basis of their policies.

The attitude toward the legitimacy of imperialism changed after the Second World War. Suddenly, it became a negative word. And we entered the era of the national liberation movements, which proceeded to achieve success more or less everywhere in the post-1945 period in their primary aim, local sovereignty for their states. As soon as this occurred, however, a new movement arose, largely in the Western world, in favor of "human rights," which were defined as the various kinds of democratic rights of which we have been speaking, from civil liberties to the citizenship rights.

Organizations founded outside the accused countries that tried to create political pressure directly upon the governments of the states defined as having inadequate human rights and indirectly via the governments of the states in which these human rights organizations were located. Pressure could take many forms—publicity, boycotts, and ultimately "the right to intervene." The recent activities of the NATO states in the Balkans have all been conducted under the rubric of "human rights" and the "right to intervene."

So where are we in this discourse about democracy? Is it a reality, a mirage, something in-between? Is it realizable, but not yet realized? The apologists for incremental advance assert that much has been accomplished. The spokespersons for the multiple groups that have come into existence to struggle for greater democracy in multiple ways argue for the most part that the goal of equal rights is nowhere near to being realized. I think that, if we are to speak to these dissonant evaluations, and in the light of the historical realities I have summarized, we must go over the ground a second time, a bit more analytically, dividing our assessment of democracy's progress into three categories: democracy as rhetoric; democracy as practice; democracy as possibility.

DEMOCRACY AS RHETORIC

Why did the term "democracy" evolve from being the expression of revolutionary aspiration to a universal platitude? Originally, in Western political philosophy, from the Greeks through the eighteenth century, democracy had always been taken to mean what its Greek roots indicate, the rule of the people—that is, the rule of the people as opposed not only to the rule of one person but even more to the rule of the *best* people, the aristocracy. So democracy was first of all a quantitative concept. It implied the call for equality in a basically inegalitarian situation, since if there were "best" people, then there must have been "less good" people—ignorant, unwashed, crude, poor.

Who the best people are does not really matter. They have been defined in terms of blood/descent/formal attributions. They have been defined in terms of wealth/property/economic managerial role. They have been defined in terms of education/intelligence/complex skills. And all of these modes of classifying the best have always been accompanied by assumptions that manners/style of life/being "civilized" is a characteristic of the best people. The crucial element has always been to distinguish between two groups, those defined as having the capacity to participate in the process of collective decisions and those said to be without this capacity. Democracy as an idea, as a movement, was originally intended to refuse such a distinction as the basis of organizing political life.

There was never really any important debate on this issue; there could not have been one until the time that the concept of "citizenship" became current in ordinary political discourse. And this cultural shift is the great rhetorical legacy of the French Revolution. We are all citizens now.

Or are we? The basic discussion about the implications of the concept of citizenship took place at two successive moments in time. In the beginning of the nineteenth century, it took the form of an internal national debate in Great Britain, France, the United States, and a few other countries, centering on the issue of the suffrage.[6] The basic alternative was that between suffrage of the propertied, what the French called *suffrage censitaire,* and universal suffrage. We know that eventually, in these countries and then elsewhere, universal suffrage won out; furthermore, what was included in the term "universal" was steadily expanded.

But once the principle of universal suffrage became accepted (even if not fully implemented), the debate shifted location. As suffrage became wider in Western countries (and other elements of civil liberties became more widespread as well in these same countries), the term "citizen" became more legitimate in these countries and was utilized to fulfill its inclusive intention. However, the concept of citizen always excludes every bit as much as it includes. For citizen necessarily implies noncitizen. If the dangerous classes are no longer dangerous, if the uncivilized working classes are now accepted as citizens, then the rhetorical line between civilized and uncivilized shifts to being one between civilized countries and uncivilized countries. This would then become the chief rhetorical justification of imperial rule, and the rhetorical basis for demanding and obtaining working-class participation in the glories of the civilizing mission.

At this point, "democracy" was no longer being used as a term to express the demands of the understrata in a national class struggle but rather as a term that justified the policies of the dominant forces in a world struggle between the so-called civilized and the noncivilized, between the West and the rest. Thus, because the resonance of the concept of democracy had changed, the very groups that had dreaded the word in the first half of the nineteenth century came to adopt it by the end of the century and were using it as their theme song by the second half of the twentieth century. At this point, the concept of democracy became primarily a symbol of, a consequence of, a proof of civilization. The West is democratic; the rest are not. The hegemonic forces in the world-economy proclaim themselves thereby the moral leaders. Their hegemony is the basis of progress throughout the world. They offer democracy as a Holy Grail. They therefore incarnate virtue.

DEMOCRACY AS REALIZATION

The new rhetoric would not have worked if there had not been some empirical bases to these claims. What were they? To appreciate this, we have to reflect on the fundamental difference between a capitalist and a precapitalist system in terms of social stratification. In a precapitalist structure, the upper stratum held power because it controlled the means of violence. It thereby laid claim to a disproportionate share of the wealth. Those who acquired wealth otherwise than by military appropriation—say, via the market—were not defined as part of the upper stratum and therefore lived in the eternal fear of confiscation. They sought to avoid this fate by buying their way into the aristocracy, which took time, sometimes as much as four generations, to complete.

The capitalist world-economy is just as deeply stratified as the precapitalist systems, but the relations of the strata are different. The upper stratum holds its rank not because of its past military prowess but because of its past economic prowess. Those who are not at the top but have skills, those we are calling the cadres or middle strata of the system, are not living in fear of confiscation. On the contrary, they are in effect being constantly solicited and appeased by the upper strata, who need their assistance to maintain the political equilibrium of the overall world-system, that is, to hold the dangerous classes in check.

The extension of suffrage, the benefits of the welfare state, the recognition of particularist identities, all are part of the program of appeasing these cadres, of securing their loyalty to the overall system, and most of all of obtaining their assistance in keeping the majority of the world's population in their place. Let us think of the capitalist world-system as socially a tripartite system divided (symbolically) into 1 percent at the top, 19 percent who are cadres, and 80 percent at the bottom. Then let us add the spatial element to which we have already referred. Within the bounds of the singular system that is the capitalist world-economy, the 19 percent are not spread out evenly among all the political units but rather are concentrated in a few of them.

If we make these two assumptions—a tripartite stratification system, with geographical lumpiness—then it seems obvious that the slogan of "democracy" has had enormous meaning for the 19 percent, since it implies a real improvement in their political, economic, and social situation. But we can also see that it has had very little meaning for the 80 percent, since they have received very few of the presumed benefits, whether political, or economic, or social. And the fact that a small group of countries has more wealth, and a more liberal state, and multiparty systems that function more or less—in short, the fact that a few countries are civilized—is not the cause but precisely the consequence of the deep inequalities in the world-system as a whole. And this is why the rhetoric rings true in some parts of the world-system and seems so hollow in other parts, the larger parts.

So, democracy unrealized? Of course. One doesn't even need to demonstrate, which can be done, that democracy, however defined, is constrained and limping even in the so-called liberal states. It is enough to note that it is not functioning to any significant degree at all in most of the world. When Western leaders preach the virtues of democracy to a Third World state, and they do this quite regularly, they are either being willfully blind to the realities of the world-system or they are cynical or they are asserting their countries' moral superiority. I am in no way defending or justifying the dictatorships of the world. Repression is not a virtue anywhere, not to speak of mass slaughters. It is simply to note that these phenomena are neither accidental nor the result of the fact that certain countries have uncivilized cultures, nor certainly the result of the insufficient openness of such countries to the flows of capital. Two-thirds of the world's people do not have liberal states because of the structure of the capitalist world-economy, which makes it impossible for them to have such political regimes.

DEMOCRACY AS POSSIBILITY

If democracy is in my view thus quite unrealized in our contemporary world, is it realizable? There are two possible answers: "Yes, by further increments"; and "No." There are many who say, "Yes, by further increments." The idea is that the benefits accorded to 19 percent could next be accorded to 21 percent and then to 25 percent and then and then . . . What is needed, say these people, is further organized pressure—by the social movements, by the NGOs, by enlightened intellectuals, or by the cultural reformation of the uncivilized peoples.

The major argument that such prognosticators have on their side is that this is how it has worked in the last two hundred years, where the concessions we may call democratization have indeed been won by struggle, have indeed been won in increments. What this prognosis leaves out of account is the cumulative impact of the incremental change on the functioning of the system. The basic reason for concessions by persons of privilege to demands for democratization is to defuse the anger, to incorporate the rebellious, but always in order to save the basic framework of the system. This strategy incarnates the di Lampedusa principle, that "everything must change in order that nothing change."

The di Lampedusa principle is a very efficacious one, up to a tipping point. Demands for further democratization, for further redistribution of the political, economic, and social pie, far from having exhausted themselves, are endless, even if only in increments. And the democratization of the past two hundred years, even if it has benefited only my hypothetical 19 percent of the world population, has been costly to the 1 percent and has consumed a noticeable portion of the pie. If the 19 percent were to become 29 percent not to speak of their becoming 89 percent, there would be nothing left for the privileged. To be quite concrete, one could no longer have the ceaseless accumulation of capital, which is after all the raison d'être of the capitalist world-economy. So either a halt must be called to the democratization process, and this is politically difficult, or one has to move to some other kind of system in order to maintain the hierarchical, inegalitarian realities.

It is toward this kind of transformation that I believe we are heading today. I shall not repeat here my detailed analysis of all the factors that have led to what I think of as the structural crisis of the capitalist world-system. Democratization as a process is only one of the factors that have brought the system to its current chaotic state, and imminent bifurcation. What I see, as a result, is an intense political struggle over the next twenty-five to fifty years about the successor structure to a capitalist world-economy. In my view this is a struggle between those who want it to be a basically democratic system and those who do not want that. I therefore am somewhat unhappy about the suggestion of some that democracy may be "an essentially unfinishable project." Such a formulation evokes the image of the tragic condition of humanity, its imperfections, its eternal improvability. And of course, who can argue with such an imagery? But the formulation leaves out of account the possibility that there are moments of historic choice that can make an enormous difference. Eras of transition from one historical social system to another are just such moments of historic choice.

Even if we can never have a perfectly democratic system, I do believe it is possible to have a largely democratic system. I do not believe we now have it. But we could have it. So, it then becomes important to go back to the drawing board and say what the struggle is about. It is not about civil liberties, although of course a democratic society would have civil liberties to warm the cockles of John Stuart Mill's heart. And it should have them. It is not about multiparty systems, a technique of democratic large-scale choice that is only one of many possible ones, and one not widely used in any arena today other than in national and subnational periodic votings.

Democracy, it must be said, is about equality, which is the opposite of racism, the pervasive sentiment of political life in the capitalist world-economy. Without equality in all arenas of social life, there is no possible equality in any arena of social life, only the mirage of it. Liberty does not exist where equality is absent, since the powerful will always tend to prevail in an inegalitarian system. This is why complaints about corruption are endemic to our system. This is why they are complaints about the uneven realization of citizenship. This is why there is cynicism. An egalitarian system might be relatively depoliticized but it would not be cynical. Cynicism is the psychological defense of weakness to power.

The call for a system that combines relative equality with a relatively democratic politics raises the question, is it possible? The main argument against the possibility is that it is historically unknown. This seems to me a very weak argument. Human societies have existed for a very brief time, when all is said and done. We cannot begin to rule out future possibilities on the basis of our short historic past. In any case, the only conclusion one can draw from pessimism is to give up the ghost. The second major argument against equality is the sorry showing of the Leninist regimes. But of course these regimes were never egalitarian at any point, although at early points they pursued an egalitarian rhetoric and may to some extent have believed in it. But their practice was deeply inegalitarian, a mere variant on other regimes in peripheral and semiperipheral zones of the capitalist world-economy. Their experience tells us absolutely nothing about the possibilities of an egalitarian social system.

The fundamental issue is that today, at this point in the evolving history of the capitalist world-economy, further incrementalism is not a real choice. We have, it seems to me, reached its limits within the framework of our present historical social system. The system is in crisis and will inevitably change. But it will not necessarily change for the better. This is the political and moral choice of this era of transition. I do not believe there is any reason to assume the inevitability of progress, of political or moral progress. I believe, however, in the theory of possible progress.

What do we then need to do? First of all, we need to be clear about where we are and about the fact that we have choices, because the system is bifurcating and therefore ending. Second, we need debate among ourselves (the "we" being those who would wish that the successor system be egalitarian) about what political tactics might offer us the possibility of creating such a system, and how one might construct the alliances that are necessary to achieve this. And third, we need to avoid the siren songs of those who would create a new but still hierarchical and inegalitarian system under the [aegis] of something progressive. None of this is easy. And there is no assurance we can succeed. What we can be sure of is that those with privilege intend to retain it in one form or another, and will fight both fiercely and intelligently to do so.

So, democracy? I feel about it like Mahatma Gandhi, when asked what he thought of Western civilization. He replied, "I think it would be a good idea."

NOTES

1. See the discussion of democracy as a talismanic word to rally the revolutionary Left in James Billington, *Fire in the Minds of Man* (New York: Basic Books, 1980), 244–46. Billington describes the evolution of such revolutionary language from "democracy" to "communism" in the period from 1789 to 1848.

2. Most of these groups were ephemeral and small, but see the names they chose: Democratic Friends of All Nations, Fraternal Democrats, Association Démocratique, Comité Central Démocratique Européen. See also the names of journals: *Democratisches Taschenbuch für das Deutsche Volk; Le Débat social, organe de la démocratie.* When, in England, a group seceded from the Working Men's Association in 1837 because it was too peaceable, they called themselves the Democratic Association. See A. Müller Lehning, *The International Association, 1855–1859: A Contribution to the Preliminary History of the First International* (Leiden: E.J. Brill, 1938), 4, 11–18. As late as 1872, Fustel de Coulanges, whose politics were conservative but republican, was accounting for the origins of the Second Empire in this way: "If the republicans who had just chased Louis-Philippe [from his throne] hadn't naively also been democrats and not instituted universal suffrage, it is extremely likely that the Republic would have continued to exist in France these past 24 years" (Coulanges, "Considérations sur la France," in François Hartog, *Le XIXe siècle et l'histoire: Le Cas Fustel de Coulanges,* Paris: Presses Universitaires de France, 1988, 238).

3. See Lehning, International Association, 24–25 and Appendix 10, 90–96.

4. This is only part of the story concerning Jörg Haider. See chapter 4.

5. See, for example, the work of Stein Rokkan, including the article on suffrage extension, "Electoral Systems," in *Citizens, Elections, Parties: Approaches to the Comparative Study of the Processes of Development* (Oslo: Universitetsforlaget, 1979), 147–68.

6. See Stuart Woolf on the distinction between nation and people in Enlight-

enment thought as it informed the thinking of the Napoleonic era: "The 'nation' was understood in a restrictive manner, as the 'educated' or, slightly more broadly, the ruling elites. . . . Enlightenment writers always made a sharp distinction between the educated, to whom their message was directed, and 'the most numerous and useful part of the nation.' The 'people,' by definition not depraved but easily influenced, required a moral, technical (and physical) education appropriate for their status, that best equipped them for the life of a laborer" (Woolf, "French Civilization and Ethnicity in the Napoleonic Empire," *Past and Present,* no. 124 [August 1989]:106).

CHAPTER EIGHT

Intellectuals:
Value-Neutrality in Question

I have argued in my recent book *The End of the World As We Know It: Social Science for the Twenty-first Century*[1] that the modern world-system is approaching its end and is entering an era of transition to some new historical system whose contours we do not now know, and cannot know in advance, but whose structure we can actively help to shape. The world that we have "known" (in the sense of *cognoscere*) has been a capitalist world-economy, and it is beset by structural strains that it is no longer in a position to handle.

I can give here only the briefest outline of the source of these strains and how they are operating. They are three. The first is the consequence of the deruralization of the world, which is far advanced and will probably be largely complete within the next twenty-five years. It is a process that is inexorably increasing the cost of labor as a percentage of total value created. The second is the long-term consequence of the externalization of costs, which has led to ecological exhaustion. This is driving up the cost of inputs as a percentage of total value created. And the third is the consequence of the democratization of the world, which has led to constantly greater demands for public expenditure on education, health care, and guarantees of lifetime income. This is pushing up the costs of taxation as a percentage of total value created.

The combination of the three is creating a massive long-term structural squeeze on profits from production, and is in the process of making the capitalist system unprofitable for capitalists. I will not argue the case in this text, since I have done so elsewhere.[2] I will assume this combination as a given for the purposes of the issues I wish to discuss.

As a part of the structural crisis of the capitalist world-economy, we are also seeing the end of the way we have "known" the world (in the sense of *scire*), that is, the end of the usefulness of the present frameworks of our knowledge-system. In particular, the concept that scientific knowledge and philosophic/humanistic knowledge are radically different, intellectually opposite ways of knowing the world—a concept we sometimes call "the two cultures"—is turning out not only to be inadequate to the task of providing an explanation of the massive social transition through which we are living, but also to be itself a major obstacle to our capacity to deal intelligently with the crisis. We should remember that the "two-cultures" concept is really only two centuries old, and had never existed in any other historical system.

The concept was invented as part of the ideological framing of the modern world-system and may be going out with the prospective demise of this system. For a transition from one historical system to another, the result of a bifurcation in our trajectory, is necessarily uncertain in its outcome taking the form of a chaotic whirl of destructuring the familiar, exaggerating the thrusts in all directions, and of course confusing us all in the process.[3] It is therefore appropriate to ask what the role of intellectuals is or could be or should be amidst the rapid, unsure, but very important transformations of our world through which we are all living.

We have always known that the pursuit of social knowledge involves not only intellectual questions but moral questions and political questions as well. In the modern world, there has been, however, extensive discussion about how these different questions relate to each other. In particular the debate has, for at least two centuries now, centered around the issue of whether one can and should keep radically separate the intellectual, the moral, and the political questions the ones from the others. Passions run high in this debate.

In the multiple cultures that predated the construction of the modern world-system there was far less debate. It had always been accepted that the three kinds of questions—intellectual, moral, political—were inseparable and that in any case, where they appear to be in conflict, moral considerations should take precedence and determine outcomes. The concept that one should keep these questions separate, like the concept of the two cultures, is an invention of the modern world-system. Indeed, the two concepts are logically linked. In the modern world, those who have called themselves scientists have asserted that science is the only domain of the pursuit of the true and have relegated philosophy, letters, and the humanities to the role of being the domain of the pursuit of the good and the beautiful. On the whole, this division of epistemic objectives has been accepted on both sides. Indeed, this set of credences has been cited regularly as one of modernity's great achievements, one of its very hallmarks.

How different this concept is from previous worldviews can be seen by looking at ancient Greece. Modern Western thinkers often assert that Greek culture is their intellectual fount and in any case is quite similar in its metaphysics by virtue of the centrality of "rationalism" in Greek thought. Of all premodern civilizations, that of ancient Greece is claimed as nearest to that of the modern Western world. Yet what is the great symbolic moment in the history of Greek culture that relates to this issue of separating the pursuit of the true from the pursuit of the good? It is Socrates being made to drink hemlock because he is charged with corrupting Athenian youth. Not only is he required to drink hemlock, but he does so without resistance, in a sense acknowledging the legitimacy of the demand. In the Western cultural itinerary, the Inquisition can be considered the continuation of the worldview that led to the Athenian judgment of Socrates. Intellectuals were a favorite target of the Inquisition.

In point of fact, in the modern world, despite "modernity," intellectuals are quite often still required to drink hemlock; they are still being burned at the stake. But today, such repression is no longer accepted by the victims as legitimate, nor is it, probably, by most people. The theme of intellectual tolerance is very strong in the imaginary of the modern world. Intellectuals have tried to use this theoretical validation of tolerance to provide themselves with some space. But there is much hypocrisy in this imaginary, since the actual practice is so far from the theory. Intellectuals have been in fact under constant pressure from those in power.

In the last 500 years, and particularly in the last 150 years, there have been two different modes by which intellectuals have struggled against the repression of their self-expression—two quite different ways, which reflect two quite different political stances.

The principal mode of argument within the social sciences has been the one that has built its case on the hypothetical distinction between science, the realm of truth, and politics, the realm of values. Most social scientists today argue that they speak as scholars only in the scientific realm and leave to the public arena all discussion of values and the conclusions one should therefore draw from the picture of reality that social scientists draw. They say that they advocate "value-neutrality," which, it is asserted, represents the only appropriate stance for the intellectual in general, and the empirical social scientist in particular. Such neutrality is said to justify the social and political tolerance of social science that the intellectuals demand in return.

The exact definition of value-neutrality is subject to much debate, but the fundamental idea is that the task of gathering data and interpreting their meaning should be pursued regardless of whether or not the results validate or counterpoise themselves to values espoused by the researcher, by the larger community, or by the state. Whether a description is correct or true is said not to have any connection with whether or not what it describes is desirable; that is, *what is* and *what ought to be* are asserted to be quite distinct. A further subargument is that it thereupon becomes the *moral* duty of the scholar to present fairly to the public the results of his research, whatever the implications this may have for public affairs. And conversely, it is the mark of a liberal society that it makes no impediment to the disclosure by the intellectual, scholar, or scientist of results that others will find disturbing because of their moral or political implications.

One of the most influential statements of this basic perspective within the social sciences, and one that is regularly cited, is that of Max Weber in his discussions of "value-freedom" and of "objectivity":

> [I]t may be asserted without the possibility of a doubt that as soon as one seeks to derive concrete directions from practical political (particularly economic and socio-political) evaluations, (1) the indispensable means, and (2) the inevitable repercussions, and (3) the thus conditioned competition of numerous possible evaluations in their *practical* consequences, are all that an *empirical* discipline can demonstrate with the means at its disposal. Philosophical disciplines can go further and lay bare the "meaning" of evaluations, i.e., their ultimate meaningful structure and

their meaningful consequences. . . . The social sciences, which are strictly empirical sciences, are the least fitted to presume to save the difficulty of making a choice, and they should therefore not create the impression that they can do so.[4]

Note the language Weber uses: social science cannot save one the difficulty of making a choice. He himself seems to be aware of how wrenching such ascetic self-denial is for the scientist. In his famous talk to Munich students right after the end of the First World War, in which he discussed science "as a vocation," he reminds us that Tolstoy said, "Science is meaningless because it gives us no answer to our question, the only question important for us: 'What shall we do and how shall we live?' " Weber acknowledges this: "That science does not give us an answer to this is indisputable."

But what does he thereupon conclude?

The fate of our times is characterized by rationalization and intellectualization and, above all, by the "disenchantment of the world." . . .

To the person who cannot bear the fate of the times like a man, one must say: may he return silently, without the usual publicity build-up of renegades, but simply and plainly. The arms of the old churches are opened widely and compassionately for him. . . .

[Intellectual] integrity, however, compels us to state that for the many who today tarry for new prophets and saviors, the situation is the same as resounds in the beautiful Edomite watchman's song of the period of exile that has been included among Isaiah's oracles:

"He calleth to me out of Seir, Watchman, what of the night? The watchman said, The morning cometh, and

> also the night: if ye will enquire, enquire ye: return, come."

The people to whom this was said has enquired and tarried for more than two millennia, and we are shaken when we realize its fate. From this we want to draw the lesson that nothing is gained by yearning and tarrying alone, and we shall act differently.[5]

This is a sober, even pessimistic, text, but Weber insists on holding on to his vision of a "disenchanted" world in the face all adversity, and hold high the ideal of objective science.

Of course, a close look at what Weber said shows the complexity of the position, not merely his personal position, but the position in general. As Runciman points out: "Weber did, despite his later advocacy of value-free social science, continue to use his influence where he could in matters of social policy. . . . But this is not inconsistent . . . as he had . . . written in the editorial of 1904, scientific objectivity and lack of personal convictions are quite separate matters."[6]

Nonetheless, whatever the complexities of Weber's own argumentation, his basic position in the end comes through clearly: "[T]o *judge* the *validity* of . . . values is a matter of *faith*. It may perhaps be a task for the speculative interpreter of life and the universe in quest of their meaning. But it certainly does not fall within the province of an empirical science. . . . The empirically demonstrable fact that these ultimate ends undergo historical changes and are debatable does not affect this distinction between empirical science and value judgments."[7]

I said that the position argued here represented a stance against intellectual repression. This stance is clearest in its early expressions in the modern world-system. The case for value-neutrality did not originate with social scientists, but with natural scientists and other philosophers, who were rebelling against the heavy hand of Christian theology on their lives and works.

The classic cult hero of this rebellion is Galileo, who was forced by the Inquisition to repent of his scientific argument about the orbit of the earth around the sun, but is said, romantically and no doubt apocryphally, to have ended his repentance by muttering "Eppur si muove!" The natural sciences to this day continue to feel they have to fight off what they think of as political intrusion into their work.

As for Weber, Runciman in 1972 noted that Weber's views may be the orthodoxy among the "great majority" in the post-1945 world but that this was not quite the case as late as Weber's lifetime: "Indeed, many readers of the essay on 'The Meaning of "Value-freedom,"' may have felt, as Halbwachs did, that Weber is making unncessarily heavy weather of the obvious. To this, however, there is the immediate answer that, obvious though it may be, Weber was on the losing, not the winning, side at the closed meeting of the Verein [für Sozialpolitik] for which the essay had first been written."[8]

Who Weber's immediate targets were has been subject to many interpretations. The most obvious target was Heinrich von Treitschke and those rightist professors in the German universities who felt that their primary allegiance was not to scientific truth in the abstract but to the German Reich.[9] And of course Marxists were a secondary target, often explicitly so.

What we can see, however, is that a position in favor of value-neutrality fits in most comfortably with the political arguments and presuppositions of the liberal center, and reinforces both its emphasis on the public-policy role of specialists and the political desirability of arriving at consensus via debates within certain constraints. Such centrist liberalism includes a wide gamut of positions and can tolerate almost anything that scholars/scientists say and do, provided that they do not in their work express political commitment to whatever is defined as the "extremes" of the political panorama at any moment. Expressing commitment to consensus values is, on the other hand, considered normal, even mandatory.

Thus, the proponents of value-neutrality present themselves as creators of space for the pursuit of knowledge in all its forms, defending its practitioners both against the established orders of church, state, and community and against the counter-orders of the antisystemic movements. The justification for value-neutrality is self-referential. Its practice is said to represent not merely the preferred but the only road to the acquisition of truth. Its defense is thought therefore to create per se a good for the entire society/state/world-system. Furthermore, this good, it is argued, is best served if all control over possible abuses of the privileges this system accords to specialists lies within the corporation itself.

The second possible stance concerning intellectual repression is quite different, since it rejects the concept of value-neutrality. This view has come historically from both the political left and the right and constitutes a claim that value-neutrality is a figleaf for the domination of centrist liberalism within the sphere of ideas. The most influential version of this argument was that of Antonio Gramsci. Gramsci argued that intellectuals were all necessarily rooted in their class affiliation commitment. Even more important, classes felt the need to create within themselves a group that Gramsci called "organic intellectuals":

> Every social class, coming into existence on the original basis of an essential function in the world of economic production, creates within itself, organically, one or more groups of intellectuals who give it homogeneity and consciousness of its function not only in the economic field but in the social and political field as well. . . .
>
> It can be seen that "organic" intellectuals which each new

class creates within itself and elaborates in its own progressive development are for the most part "specialisations" of partial aspects of the primitive activity of the new social type which the new class has brought to light.[10]

Note what Gramsci has done. He has questioned the neutrality of value-neutral intellectuals, insisting that they are linked to their class affiliation, organically. This of course raises the question of what if anything represents truth-value, and above all, who represents truth-value. As we know, this way of defining the role of the intellectual was used by the world's Communist parties to insist that intellectuals had to subordinate their personal analyses to those of the collectivity, which in turn was considered to be the Party, since the Party laid claim to representing the interests of the working class. Postmodernist scholars have essentially retained the core elements of Gramsci's claim of organicity, but have extended it to groups beyond "classes" while simultaneously refusing to recognize the existence of political groups that have the right to control their expression.

In a sense, Gramsci's concept led historically to jumping from the frying pan into the fire. To escape the dominance of right-wing nationalist intellectuals in the German academy, Weber insisted on the legitimacy of value-neutrality. To escape the dominance in the Italian intellectual arena of centrist liberalism represented by value-neutrality, Gramsci insisted on the organicity of the intellectuals which was interpreted to mean their subordination to political leadership. If the persecution of Galileo provided the moral tale underpinning for intellectuals' claiming freedom from those who said they incarnated Establishment (Christian) morality, the persecution of Soviet biologists by Lysenko/Stalin provided the moral tale underpinning their claiming freedom from the Party, which said it incarnated antisystemic morality.

And there the debate has stood throughout the nineteenth and especially the twentieth century, a true dialogue of the deaf, amidst ever more harsh infighting, as the recent "culture wars" have shown to us.[11] This kind of intellectual squabble is a natural reflection of the systemic tensions of an ongoing historical system but the quarrel is of little help to us when we are faced with a systemic transition, full of uncertainty about its outcome but full of certainty that we are living in the middle of a chaotic bifurcation that will mean the disintegration or disappearance of our existing world-system. We need a better grip on what is possible and not possible, what is desirable and not desirable, if we are to achieve optimal outcomes of the transition.

The modern world-system has one particularly curious feature. It puts forward a series of theoretical analyses of itself that are supposed to be realistically descriptive and simultaneously prescriptive but that, however, are inexact. We say that capitalism is based on competition in a free market, and ought to be. We say that the states, our mandatory political frameworks, are sovereign, and ought to be. We say that citizenship is based on equality of political rights, and ought to be. And we say that scholars/scientists practice value-neutrality, and ought to do so. Each of these statements is a description, and each a prescription. Not one of them, however, comes close to being an *accurate* description, and the majority of the world's populations and even of the elite defenders of the system seldom practice what is preached. Let us review each of these description-prescriptions.

The free (or competitive) market is the great shibboleth of the capitalist world-economy, yet is its supposedly defining characteristic. Yet every working capitalist knows that if a market is truly free as Adam Smith defined such freedom—a multitude of sellers, a multitude of buyers, and total transparence of operations, including full knowledge by all buyers and sellers of the true state of the market—it would be absolutely impossible for anyone to make any profit whatsoever. For the buyers would always force the sellers down to a price barely above the cost of production, if not below it (at least for a certain time). What is necessary in order to make profit is some kind of at least partial restriction of the market, some degree of monopolization. The greater the restriction or monopolization, the greater the potential profit available to the sellers. To be sure, monopolies have their downsides, which are regularly pointed out to us. But what ends monopolies is not a social awareness of their downsides but the fact that monopolies invite their own destruction through the rational and inevitable efforts of new producers/sellers to enter highly profitable markets. These efforts sooner or later succeed, but in the process they reduce the profitability of the particular market these new producers/sellers have entered.

So the market does indeed play an important role in the functioning of capitalism, but only as a mechanism whereby some producers/sellers constantly seek to undo the monopolies of others. The net result of this, however, is that those who have previously gained in a monopolized market, faced with the prospective end of their advantage, take their gains and move on, or try to move on, to find another—often newly—monopolized market. In this back and forth, the role of the states is central to everyone's maneuvers—states as guarantors or begetters of monopolies as well as "neutral" legitimators of monopolistic practices, but also states as disrupters of monopolies. Having the state on one's side is the royal road to large-scale profit. And if the state is not on your side but on someone else's side, then one's primary need as an entrepreneur is to change the politics of the state. Capitalists require states in order to make serious profits, but states that are on their side and not someone else's side.

Sovereignty in turn is the shibboleth of the interstate system. Every state in the modern world affirms its own sovereignty.

And every state claims to respect the sovereignty of others. But as we know, and as any proponent of *Realpolitik* will tell you, this isn't how things really work. There are stronger states and there are weaker states, the strength and weakness being a measure of the reciprocal relationship of states. And stronger states regularly interfere in the internal affairs of weaker states, while weaker states regularly try to become stronger so as to resist such interference. But even weaker states can insert themselves inside the politics of stronger states, albeit with greater difficulty. And all states, even the strongest, are constrained by the operations of the collectivity that is the interstate system. The phrase "the balance of power" refers precisely to such constraints.

If all states were truly sovereign, no state would have or would need an intelligence service, nor, for that matter, armed forces. But of course all states do have them, and they do need them if they hope to maintain a minimum of control over what goes on within their borders. It is not that the slogan of sovereignty is meaningless. It sets a normative limit on the degree and kinds of interference and can therefore be utilized by weaker states—up to a point—to limit the damage done to them by the stronger states. The United Nations is today one of the main vehicles through which such constraints are exercised. But how seriously is the United Nations taken in the foreign ministries of the world?

Ever since the French Revolution, every state has had "citizens" as opposed to "subjects." Citizens have rights. Citizens are equal participants in the political decision making of their state. Except that, ever since the concept was launched, virtually every state has tried hard to limit the applicability of the concept in reality. One of the ways this has been done is that the world-system has reified a whole series of binary distinctions and given them political importance to a degree unknown before: bourgeois-middle class/proletarian-working class; man/woman; White/

Black (or person of color); breadwinner/housewife; productive worker/unproductive person; sexually mainstream/sexually
aberrant; the educated/the masses; honest citizen/criminal; nor-
mal/mentally abnormal; of legal age/a minor; civilized/uncivi-
lized. And of course there are more.

What one has to note about these binary distinctions, all elab-
orated theoretically in great detail in the nineteenth century, is
that they build on ancient distinctions but give to them a salience,
an interconnectedness, and a rigidity that they seldom had before. What we have also to note is that the consequence of each
binary distinction that is made salient is the restriction of effective citizenship. Citizenship as a concept theoretically includes
everyone. The binary distinctions reduce this "everyone" to a relatively small minority of the population. This can be easily measured by looking at suffrage rights, and even more at the degree
of acceptability of real political participation.

Finally, we come to value-neutrality. This is a concept created
to constrain that rambunctious, difficult, and pseudo-intelligent
group, the intellectuals. In theory, all scholars and scientists are
devoted to the abstract truth and tell the story as it is really is, as
their research lets them understand the world. They claim they
choose their research topics in consideration only of their intrinsic scholarly or scientific interest, and select their research methods in terms of their validity and reliability. They draw no
conclusions valid for the public arena. They fear no social pressures. They take no cognizance of pressures, financial or political, to amend their results or their report of results.

It is a nice fairy tale, but any one who has frequented a university or a research institution for any length of time and still
believes this is consciously or subconsciously naive. The material
pressures are enormous, the career pressures almost as great, and
the political pressures always available if the others do not work.
It is not that there are not Galileos around. There are many, and

some do more than mutter "Eppur si muove." But dissent is courageous even in the most liberal of states.

One could easily explain why these four myths—the free market, the sovereign states, the equal rights of all citizens, and the value-neutral scholar/scientist—are necessary to the functioning of the modern world-system, why they are so loudly propagated and so widely believed (at least superficially). But that is not my concern here. My concern is to discuss what happens when the historical system in which one lives comes into a structural crisis and starts its bifurcation, the situation in which I believe we are today. And in particular, what happens to the value-neutral scholar/scientist, and what should happen to him or her?

I think the first thing we, the intellectuals, need to do is discard the myth and assert with some clarity the real situation, which is that all debates are simultaneously intellectual, moral, and political. This is, then, to recognize the real limitations of the complicated position of Weber, but without accepting the too-simple position of Gramsci. I have deliberately used three words—*intellectual, moral,* and *political*—to characterize the kinds of issues with which intellectuals deal because I believe that, although debates simultaneously involve all three modes of analysis, the three modes are not identical, and each mode has its claims. Furthermore, I believe that what is most useful is to address these three claims in a certain order: first, the intellectual assessment of where we are heading (our existing trajectory); second, the moral assessment of where we want to be heading; third, the political assessment of how we are most likely to get where we believe we should be heading. Each is difficult to do. To do the three in close concert and successively is even more difficult. But if we are not interested in assuming this task, then we should be in some other business.

Where are we heading? In order to answer this question, one

has to have a chronosophy, a unit of analysis, and an analytic perspective.[12] Mine are clear. My analytic perspective is something I call "world-systems analysis." My unit of analysis is a historical social system. And my chronosophy is based on the assumption of the existence of an arrow of time, in cascading bifurcations, which makes possible, but by no means inevitable, progress (which is a moral concept). I call this a theory of possible progress. Allow me to translate that specifically into more concrete language.

Our existing historical social system is the modern world-system, which is a capitalist world-economy. It has been in existence since the long sixteenth century. This system has expanded geographically to cover the entire globe, having squeezed out and incorporated all other historical social systems on the earth by the last third of the nineteenth century. Like all historical systems, once having come into existence it has operated by certain rules, which are possible to make explicit and which are reflected in its cyclical rhythms and its secular trends. Like all systems, the linear projections of its trends reach certain limits, whereupon the system finds itself far from equilibrium and begins to bifurcate. At this point, we can say the system is in crisis and passes through a chaotic period in which it seeks to stabilize a new and different order, that is, make the transition from one system to another. What this new order is and when it will stabilize is impossible to predict, but the choice are strongly affected by the actions of all actors during the transition. And that is where we are today.

The role of the scholar/scientist is to bring his or her skills to bear upon the nature of this transition, and, most importantly, lay out the historic choices that it offers to all of us, individually and collectively. Since the period is chaotic and it is also intrinsically impossible to predict the outcome, the intellectual task of analyzing the transition and the choices it offers is not an easy one or a self-evident one. Persons of good faith can and will differ, perhaps profoundly, on the intellectual analysis. This process involves an intellectual debate, using the rules that govern intellectual debates. I have sought to enter this debate, and so of course have many others.[13]

Is "Where are we heading?" the only intellectual question we can ask? No, but during a systemic transition, it is probably the most crucial one for our collective future. So it is both desirable and eventually inevitable that it become the center of our collective intellectual concerns. Of course, saying this presumes that the chronosophy, the unit of analysis, and the analytic perspective that I have chosen provide a basically correct starting point. Some, perhaps many, will deny this. And a certain amount of our energy has to go into confronting the debate on what might be called this set of preanalytic questions. But frankly, not too much. For those of us who are reasonably convinced that we are using the right set of premises, we cannot afford to spend so much time justifying the underlying premises that we cannot get to the knotty problems of diagnosing contemporary reality on the basis of these premises.

Once we have arrived at the debate concerning the nature of the transition, we have to engage in the tricky task of spelling out the vectors that are involved in the trajectory, the parameters within which they operate, and the likely alternative paths they could take, always bearing in mind that in a chaotic situation there will be many surprises and sudden reversals. The hardest thing is to distinguish between what is simply the continuation of cyclical patterns that are part of the old system and what is truly new. It is made harder by the fact that one of the characteristics of our existing world-system is its ideology of newness, one of whose expressions is the inclination of scholars and scientists and indeed of publicists to celebrate every twist in the real world as "new" and therefore either "wonderful" or "terrible." We need a certain coolness in our appreciation.

In a chaotic situation, the one thing of which we can be certain is that new paths will be offered us, and in a real sense we are being asked to choose among them. Here is where the moral issues enter and cannot be averted or neglected. The choice is never technical and never one of formal rationality. It involves what Weber called "substantive rationality," which means choosing among ends, not means. And when I speak of ends, I mean not ends that are narrowly and technically defined, but the overall shape and fundamental values of the new historical social system that we prefer to build.

This is of course an issue for everyone, and not merely or even primarily for scholars/scientists. But it is not one that scholars scientists can avoid by claiming that making such choices is the task of the "citizen" or some other social figure outside the domain of the intellectual. For our choices here impel the way we shall pursue the intellectual tasks. They are inescapably intertwined. Our choices determine what is formally rational, the inner domain of the scholar/scientist. What it means is that we have to open outward the number of factors we have to take into account in our analyses, as well as in our prescriptions. Whether, for example, a particular ecological or industrial policy makes sense, may be said to be rational, depends in part on the range of consequences and whether we are collectively willing to pay whatever the price is for these policies. And immediately the question becomes, who is the "we" that is paying the price? We have to open out the scope of people included in that "we," open it out in terms of all the social groupings within the system, open it out geographically, and open it out in terms of generations, including those yet unborn. No easy task!

Then, we must confront the reality that some today have

greater privilege than others, and that it is normal to expect that those who have greater privilege will desire to maintain it amidst the flux that an era of transition necessarily implies. In short, an era of transition is not a friendly sporting match. It is a fierce struggle for the future, and will lead to sharp divisions among us. When one asks, What is the biggest moral issue with which we are confronted in an era of transition? it is unquestionably a rather simple one: Will the successor historical system (or systems) be one(s) that maintain(s) the pattern of the existing and past systems, that of a hierarchical, inegalitarian system, or will it (or they) be relatively democratic, relatively egalitarian?

Right away we see that this is a moral issue: What is the good society? But it is also an intellectual issue: What kind of society is it possible to construct? Possible? Given what? Given a putative human psychology? Given a certain level of technology? Every major social science issue of the past two centuries has behind it this moral issue: What is the good society? And we are no nearer to a consensus on it today than we were in 1989, 1968, 1914–18, 1870, 1848, or 1789—to mention only a few of the great moments of social division in the modern world-system.

We can expect therefore a serious struggle between two moral camps, each of which will dress its claims in intellectual language as well as moral language. Furthermore, the intellectual language will not necessarily be honest—honest in the sense that the proponents truly believe that this is how things really work, as opposed to how they should work. Proponents do not always in fact know themselves when they are not being completely honest in this sense. Ergo, intellectual clarity is part of the moral struggle, involving the effort to delineate the distortions of analysis caused by the needs of propaganda, in the largest sense of that word.

And if, perchance, we successfully navigate the interface between intellectual and moral issues, giving each its due, we are still faced with the biggest hurdle of all, the political issues. For it is not enough to see clearly what is at stake intellectually, to measure clearly moral implications and assert moral preferences; we must also understand what is going on in the political sphere and how we can in fact be substantively rational, that is, how we can actually implement our vision of the true and the good. What fascism was, is, as an ideology is the rejection of both intellectual and moral claims in the name of the rights of force. "Whenever I hear the word 'culture' I reach for a revolver," said the Nazi leaders. There are still those who have revolvers and act this way. Historical choices are not garden parties, and they can get ugly, no matter how rational the analyses of scholars/scientists.

At this point we come to the question of how we might organize ourselves in an era of transition. Once again, this is not a question only, or even primarily, for the intellectuals, but once again it is one they cannot refuse to confront. Those who say they decline to confront it directly are either deceiving us or deceiving themselves. The great problem, however, for those who have opted to struggle for a more democratic, more egalitarian world is the legacy of disillusionment bred by the achievements and failures of the modern world's antisystemic movements in the past 150 years, and particularly in the last 50 years. We have all become wary of movements—of the triumphalism, the centralism, and the fierce intolerances they have displayed.

So what can one say about the politics of the transition? First of all, that lucidity takes precedence over mobilization. If we mobilize, we must know why, and not merely how. And why is both an intellectual and a moral question, and not merely a political one. I cannot underline this too strongly. It is here that intellectuals have their particular contribution to make. Presumably, intellectuals are defined as those who have spent more effort acquiring the skills of analysis that underlie lucidity than others. It is in the pursuit of lucidity that intellectual issues make their claims amidst the vortex of activities.

One of the intellectual realities of the modern world is that the groups with which we identify are multiple and overlapping and move in and out of salience, for us and for the world-system. This is in part the result of that plethora of binary distinctions the world-system institutionalized in the nineteenth century, from which we shall not be readily or easily liberated. We must live with these distinctions for the moment, even if we deplore their exaggerations. Centralism, however democratic, will not, cannot work. The lesson was made clear by the rebellions of 1968 and it has been partially learned and internalized by the movements since then. But only partially!

Those who wish to maintain hierarchy and privilege in the future historical social system we shall be creating have two great advantages over the rest of us. One, they have at their disposal enormous wealth, existing power, and the ability to buy the expertise they need. They are also intelligent and sophisticated. And they can organize more or less centrally. Those who prefer that the future historical social system we shall be creating be one that is relatively democratic and relatively egalitarian are at a disadvantage on both scores. They have less current wealth and power. And they cannot operate centralized structures.

It follows that their only chance is to turn a limitation into an advantage. They must build on their diversity. Whether we call this a "rainbow coalition" or "*la gauche plurielle*" or the "*frente amplio*" matters less than the basic idea that we cannot escape the necessity of creating a worldwide family of antisystemic movements that can have no, or anyway little, hierarchical structure. And this is organizationally difficult for two reasons. Such a loose structure may not be able to create a viable, coherent strategy. And such a loose structure is very open to infiltration and disruption from within.

In addition, such a loose structure, if it is to survive, requires mutual comprehension and respect. Here again there is a role for the intellectual. To the degree that the intellectuals can pull themselves back from the passions of the moment, they may be able to serve as the interpreters between the multiple movements, the ones who translate the priorities of each into the language of the other and into the mutual language that will enable all of them to understand the intellectual, the moral, and then the political issues they confront.

In the twenty-first century, I believe one could persuade Gramsci of the wisdom of such a revised view. I believe that one might even be able to persuade Weber, though that would be more difficult. But we have to try very hard. It is not sure that if one failed to persuade the Max Webers of the world, we could arrive at the kind of social transformation that we would want.

The outcome of the struggle is very uncertain. But in eras of transition, no one has the luxury of sitting on the sidelines.

NOTES

1. Minneapolis: University of Minnesota Press, 1999.
2. For a more detailed exposition of these arguments, see chapter 3.
3. See Ilya Prigogine, *The End of Certainty* (New York: Free Press, 1997).
4. Max Weber, "The Meaning of 'Ethical Neutrality' in Sociology and Economics," in Weber, *The Methodology of the Social Sciences* (New York: Free Press, 1949), 18–19.
5. Max Weber, "Science as a Vocation," in *From Max Weber: Essays in Sociology* (London: Routledge & Kegan Paul, 1948), 155–56.
6. W.C. Runciman, *A Critique of Max Weber's Philosophy of Social Science* (Cambridge: At the University Press, 1972), 6–7, n. 7.
7. Max Weber, " 'Objectivity' in Social Science and Social Policy," in Weber, *Methodology of the Social Science,* 55.

8. Runciman, *Critique of Max Weber's Philosophy,* 49.

9. See Arnold Brecht: "The original German relativists were scholars of democratic, liberal, or socialist inclinations who lived in a country run by a semi-authoritarian monarchic government. They were surrounded by a great majority of other scholars who accepted that type of government as ideal and often carried emotional patriotism and conservatism into their lectures and scholarly writings. Disinclined in their own work to bow to authoritarian forms and values, they were driven in self-defense to study the proper relation of science to political evaluations more carefully than their colleagues in democratically governed countries had reason to do" (Brecht, *Political Theory* [Princeton: Princeton University Press, 1959], 239).

10. Antonio Gramsci, "The Formation of Intellectuals," in *The Modern Prince, and Other Writings* (New York: International Publishers, 1957), 118. In a footnote after this sentence that is not translated in the English edition, Gramsci specifies what he means by this last statement, using the example of Gaetano Mosca: "The *Elements of Political Science* of Mosca . . . should be examined under this rubric. The so-called 'political class' of Mosca is nothing but the intellectual category of the dominant social group; the concept of 'political class' is similar to that of 'elite' of Pareto. . . . Mosca's book is an enormous mixture of sociological and positivist elements, with furthermore the tendentiousness of contemporary political reference, which makes it less difficult to digest and stylistically very lively" (Gramsci, *Gli Intellettuali e l'organizzazione della cultura* [Torino: Einaudi, 1949], 4).

11. See Lingua Franca, ed., *The Sokal Hoax: The Sham That Shook the Academy* (Lincoln, Neb.: University of Nebraska Press, 2000).

12. On chronosophy see chapter 6, n. 3.

13. See chapter 3.

CHAPTER NINE

America and the World:
The Twin Towers as Metaphor

I. AMERICA THE BEAUTIFUL

O beautiful for patriot dream
That sees beyond the years
Thine alabaster cities gleam
Undimmed by human tears!
America! America!
God shed his grace on thee
And crown thy good with brotherhood
From sea to shining sea!

—KATHERINE LEE BALES, "AMERICA THE BEAUTIFUL"

On October 24, 1990, I was invited to give the opening lecture of the Distinguished Speakers Series in celebration of the bicentennial of the University of Vermont. I entitled that lecture "America and the World: Today, Yesterday, and Tomorrow."[1] In that talk I discussed God's blessings to America: in the present, prosperity; in the past, liberty; in the future, equality. Somehow God had not distributed these blessings to everyone everywhere. I noted that Americans were very conscious of this unequal distri-

[193]

bution of God's grace. I said that the United States had always defined itself, had always measured its blessings, by the yardstick of the world. We are better; we were better; we shall be better. Perhaps blessings that are universal are not considered true blessings. Perhaps we impose upon God the requirement that She save only a minority.

Today, we live in the shadow of an event that has shaken most of us, the destruction of the Twin Towers on September 11, 2001, by a group of individuals so dedicated to their ideology and their moral fury at the United States that they conspired for years to find ways to deal a deadly geopolitical blow to America and those they deemed its supporters around the world, and did this in a way that required sacrificing their own lives. Most Americans have reacted to the events with deep anger, with patriotic resolve, and yet with considerable and persistent puzzlement. Puzzlement about two things: Why did this happen? And how could it happen? And the puzzlement has been laced with a good deal of uncertainty: What must be done, what can be done in order that such an event will not, could not, happen again?

As I look back on what I said eleven years ago, I do not wish to change anything I said then. But I do feel a bit of unease about the stance from which I spoke. I wrote as though I were an ethnographer from elsewhere, from Mars, perhaps, trying to understand this curious species, *Humanus americanus*. Today, I think that is not good enough. I am to be sure a human being, and am concerned with the fate of humanity. But I am also an American citizen. I was born here. I have lived here most of my life. And I share full responsibility, along with everyone else in my position, for what has happened here and what will happen here. I have a moral obligation to view America from inside.

So I wish to look at America and the world a second time. But this time I do not want to look at how Americans see themselves through the prism of the world, but rather at how Americans have seen the world, and how Americans might wish to see the world from here on in. And I am very aware that here I tread on contentious ground.

It is a rare president of the United States, in the twentieth century at least, who has not at some point made the statement that the United States is the greatest country in the world. I'm not sure our omnipresent public opinion polling agencies have ever put the question directly to the American public, but I suspect that the percentage of the U.S. population that would agree with such a statement is very large indeed. I ask you to reflect on how such a statement sounds, not merely to persons from poor countries with cultures that are very different from ours but to our close friends and allies—to Canadians, to the English, and of course to the French. Does Tony Blair think the United States is the greatest country in the world, greater than Great Britain? Would he dare think that? Does Pope John Paul II think it? Who, besides Americans and those who wish to migrate to the United States, believe this?

Nationalism is of course not a phenomenon limited to people in the United States. The citizens of almost every country are patriotic and often chauvinistic. Americans are aware of that, no doubt. But they nonetheless tend to note the fact that many people across the world wish to emigrate to the United States, and that no other locus of immigration seems to be quite as popular, and they take this as confirmation of their belief in America's superior virtue as a nation.

But in what do we consider that our superior virtue consists? I think that Americans tend to believe that others have *less* of many things than we have, and the fact that we have more is a sign of grace. I shall thus try to elaborate the many arenas in which this concept of "less-ness" may be thought to exist. I shall start with the one arena about which most Americans seem to be quite sure. Other countries are less modern, the meaning of modernity being the level of technological development. The United States has the most advanced technology in the world. This technology is located in the gadgets found in our homes across the country, in the networks of communications and transport, in the infrastructure of the country, in the instruments of space exploration, and of course in the military hardware that is available to our armed forces. As a result of this accumulation of technology, Americans consider that life in the United States is more comfortable, that our production competes more successfully in the world market, and that therefore we are certain to win the wars into which others may drag us.

Americans also consider their society to be more efficient. Things run more smoothly—at the workplace, in the public arena, in social relations, in our dealings with bureaucracies. However great our complaints about any of these practices, we seem to find, when we wander elsewhere, that others manage things less well. Others do not seem to have American get-up-and-go. They are less inventive about finding solutions to problems major and minor. They are too mired in traditional or formal ways. And this holds the others back, while America forges ahead. We are very ready therefore to offer friendly advice to all and sundry—to Nigerians, to Japanese, to Italians—about how they could do things better. The emulation of American ways by others is considered a big plus when Americans assess what is going on in other countries. Daniel Boone plus the Peace Corps comprise the bases of an evaluation of comparative political economy.

But of course most Americans would deny that the less-ness of others is merely material. It is spiritual as well. Or if the term "spiritual" seems to exclude the secular humanists, it is cultural as well. Our presidents tell us, and our patriotic songs remind us, that we are the land of liberty. Others are less free than we are.

The Statue of Liberty stretches out its hand to all those "huddled masses yearning to breathe free."

Our density of freedom is visualized in so many ways. Which other country has the Bill of Rights? Where else is freedom of the press, of religion, of speech so honored? Where else are immigrants so integrated into the political system? Can one name another country in which someone arriving here as a teenager, and still speaking English to this day with a thick German accent, could become the secretary of state, the chief representative of Americans to the rest of the world? Is there any other country where social mobility, for those with merit, is so rapid? And which country can match us in the degree to which we are democratic? Democratic not merely in the continuing openness of our political structures, the centrality of a two-party system, but also in our quotidian mores? Is the United States not the country that excels in maintaining the principle of "first come, first served" in the practices of daily life, as opposed to a system in which those who have privilege get preference? And these democratic mores, in the public arena and in social life, date back at least two hundred, if not almost four hundred, years.

From melting pot to multiculturality, we have prided ourselves on the incredible ethnic mix of real American life—in our restaurants, in our universities, in our political leadership. Yes, we have had our faults, but we have done more than any other country to try to overcome them. Have we not taken the lead in the last decades in tearing down barriers of gender and race, in the constantly renewed search for the perfect meritocracy? Even our movements of protest give us cause for pride. Where else are they so persistent, so diverse, so legitimate?

And in the one arena where, up to 1945, we tended to admit that we were not the avant-garde of the world, the arena of high culture, has that not now all changed? Is New York not today the world center of art, of theater, of music performance, of dance, of opera? Our cinema is so superior that the French government must resort to protectionist measures to keep French audiences from seeing still more of it.

We can put this all together in a phrase that Americans have not used much, at least until September 11, but which we largely think in our hearts: We are more civilized than the rest of the world, the Old World, as we used to say with a token of disdain. We represent the highest aspirations of everyone, not merely Americans. We are the leader of the free world, because we are the freest country in the world, and others look to us for leadership, for holding high the banner of freedom, of civilization.

I mean none of this ironically. I am deeply persuaded that this image of the lessness of the rest of the world is profoundly ingrained in the American psyche, however many there may be who will be embarrassed by my presentation, and insist that they are not part of such a consensus, that they are (shall we say?) more cosmopolitan in their views. And it is in this sense, first of all, that the Twin Towers are a perfect metaphor. They signaled unlimited aspirations; they signaled technological achievement; they signaled a beacon to the world.

II. ATTACK ON AMERICA

What the United States tastes today is a very small thing compared to what we have tasted for tens of years. Our nation has been tasting this humiliation and contempt for more than eighty years. . . . But if the sword falls on the United States, after eighty years, hypocrisy raises its ugly head lamenting the deaths of these killers who tampered with the blood, honor, and holy places of the Muslims. The least that one can describe these people is that they are morally depraved.

—OSAMA BIN LADEN, OCTOBER 7, 2001

Osama bin Laden does not think that America is beautiful. He thinks Americans are morally depraved. Now, of course, there are some Americans who also think that most Americans are morally depraved. We hear this theme from what might be called the cultural right in the United States. But whereas the critiques of the U.S. cultural right and those of Osama bin Laden overlap up to a point insofar as they deal with everyday mores, bin Laden's fundamental denunciation concerns what he calls U.S. hypocrisy in the world arena. And when it comes to America in the world arena, there are very few Americans who would agree with that characterization, and even those who might say something similar would want to nuance this view in ways that bin Laden would find irrelevant and unacceptable.

This was one of the two great shocks of September 11 for Americans. There were persons in the world who denied any good faith at all to American actions and motives in the world arena. How was it possible that persons who had less of everything worth having doubted that those who had more of everything had earned it by their merit? The moral effrontery of bin Laden amazed Americans and they found it galling.

To be sure, bin Laden was scarcely the first person to make this kind of verbal attack, but he is the first person who has been able to translate that verbal attack into a physical attack on U.S. soil, one that caught America by surprise and, momentarily at least, helpless. Until that happened, Americans could afford to ignore the verbal attacks so rampant in the world as the babblings of fools. But fools had now become villains. Furthermore, the villains had been initially successful, and this was the second great shock. We were supposed to be in a position to be able to ignore such criticisms because we were essentially invulnerable, and we have now discovered that we are not.

It has been frequently said that the world will never be the same again after September 11. I think this is silly hyperbole. But it is true that the American psyche may never be the same again. For once the unthinkable happens, it becomes thinkable. And a direct assault on mainland America by a scattered band of individuals had always been unthinkable. Now we have had to establish an Office of Homeland Security. Now we have the Pentagon discussing whether they should establish what they call an area command, a military structure hitherto limited to the areas outside the U.S. covering all the rest of the world, that would cover the United States itself.

Above all we now have "terrorists" in our vocabulary. In the 1950s, the term "Communists" received expansive employ. It covered not only persons who were members of Communist parties, not only those who thought of themselves or were thought of by others as "fellow travelers," but even those who lacked sufficient "enthusiasm" for the development of a hydrogen bomb. This was after all the specific charge that led the U.S. Atomic Energy Commission in 1953 to suspend the security clearance of J. Robert Oppenheimer, the very person who was known as, and had hitherto been honored as, the "father of the atomic bomb."

The term "terrorism" has now obtained the same expansive meaning. In November 2001 I watched the television program *Law and Order*. The plot for this particular episode revolved around the burning down of a building in the process of construction. The background to this was that the contractor had received the land from the city, land that had previously been a neighborhood garden, tended by the community. There was opposition to this construction in the community. A group of young persons identified as "environmental activists" decided to burn down the building in protest. The complication was that unbeknownst to them, by accident, someone was in the building and died in the fire. In the end, the arsonists are caught and convicted. The interesting point of this banal story is that throughout the program, the arsonists are repeatedly referred to as "terrorists." By any definition of terrorist, it is a stretch to use the term in this case. But no matter! It was so used, and it will continue to be so used.

We are the land of liberty, but today we hear voices—in the government, in the press, in the population at large—saying that we have accorded too much liberty, especially to noncitizens, and that "terrorists" have taken advantage of our liberty. Therefore it is said the privileges of liberty must give way to procedures that meet our requirements for security. For example, we apparently worry that if we catch "terrorists" and put them on trial, they may then have a public forum, they may not be convicted, or if convicted they may not receive the death penalty. So in order to ensure that none of these things happen, we are creating military courts to be convened by the president, with rules to be established by him alone. Originally the accused were to have no right of appeal to anyone, and the courts were to be operated in total secrecy. The courts will still be able to proceed rapidly to a conclusion—presumably to a death penalty. The degree to which normal defense rights will be ensured is still open. And in our land of liberty this is being widely applauded.

We consider, we have stated publicly, that the attack on America is an attack on our values and on civilization itself. We find such an attack unconscionable. We are determined to win the worldwide war against terrorism—against terrorists *and all those who give them shelter and support.* We are determined to show that, despite this attack, we are and remain the greatest country in the world. In order to prove this, we are not being adjured by our president to make individual sacrifices, not even the small sacrifice of paying more taxes, but rather to carry on our lives as normal. We are, however, expected to applaud without reservation whatever our government and our armed forces will do, even if this is not normal.

The extent of this requirement of "no reservations" may be seen in the widespread denunciation of those who try to "explain" why the events of September 11 occurred. Explanation is considered justification and virtual endorsement of terror. The American Council of Trustees and Alumni (ACTA), an organization whose founders are Lynne Cheney and Sen. Joseph Lieberman, issued a pamphlet in November 2001 entitled "Defending Civilization: How Our Universities Are Failing America and What Can Be Done About It."[2] It is a short pamphlet that makes its points with remarkable pithiness. It says that "college and university faculty are the weak link in America's response to the attack." It continues with this analysis: "Rarely did professors publicly mention heroism, rarely did they discuss the differences between good and evil, the nature of Western political order or the virtue of a free society. Their public messages were short on patriotism and long on self-flagellation. Indeed, the message of much of academe was: BLAME AMERICA FIRST!"

The pamphlet devotes most of its space to an appendix of 117 quotations that the authors feel illustrate their point. These quotations include statements not merely of such persons as Noam Chomsky and Jesse Jackson but of less usual targets of such denunciations—the dean of the Woodrow Wilson School at Princeton, a former deputy secretary of state. In short, the authors of the pamphlet were aiming wide.

It is clear at this point that even if the events of September 11 will not alter the basic geopolitical realities of the contemporary world, they may have a lasting impact on American political structures. How much of an impact remains to be seen. It does seem, however, that the puzzlement of Americans of which I spoke—why did this happen? and how could it happen?—is a puzzle to which we are not being encouraged to respond at least not yet.

The Twin Towers are also a metaphor for the attack on America. They were built with great engineering skill. They were supposed to be impervious to every conceivable kind of accidental or deliberate destruction. Yet, apparently, no one had ever considered that two planes filled with jet fuel might deliberately crash into the towers, and hit the buildings at precisely the point, 20 percent down from the top, that would maximize destruction. Nor had anyone anticipated that the buildings could collapse slowly, overwhelmingly, and in everyone's view, bringing down other buildings in their wake. No one ever expected that the fires such a collapse ignited would continue to burn for months afterward. The United States may be able to avenge the attack, but it cannot undo it. Technology turns out to be less than perfect as a protective shield.

III. AMERICA AND WORLD POWER

Anti-Catholicism, as it evolved [in Great Britain in the eighteenth century], usually served a dialectical function, drawing attention to the supposed despotism, superstition, military oppressiveness and material poverty of Catholic regimes so as to throw into greater relief supposed Anglo-British freedoms, naval supremacy, and agrarian and commercial prosperity, and consequently superior mode of empire.

—LINDA COLLEY, " MULTIPLE KINGDOMS"

I start with this quote from Linda Colley[3] to remind us that the United States is not the first hegemonic power in the history of the modern world-system, but rather the third, and that hegemony has its cultural rules as well as its vulnerabilities. One of the cultural rules is that the denigration of others is indispensable to sustaining the internal self-assurance that makes possible the effective exercise of world-power.

There is nothing so blinding as success. And the United States has had its fair share of success in the past two hundred years.

Success has the vicious consequence that it seems to breed almost inevitably the conviction that it will necessarily continue. Success is a poor guide to wise policy. Failure at least often leads to reflection; success seldom does.

Fifty years ago, U.S. hegemony in the world-system was based on a combination of productive efficiency that outstripped by far that of any rivals, a world-political agenda that was warmly endorsed by its allies in Europe and Asia, and military superiority. Today, the productive efficiency of U.S. enterprises faces very extensive competition, principally from the enterprises of its closest allies. As a result, the world-political agenda of the United States is no longer so warmly endorsed and is often clearly contested, even by its allies, especially given the disappearance of the Soviet Union. What remains for the moment is military superiority.

It is worth thinking about the objectives of U.S. foreign policy, as pursued for the last fifty years by successive U.S. governments. Obviously, the United States has been concerned with threats posed by governments it considered hostile or at least inimical to U.S. interests. There is nothing wrong or exceptional about this. This is true of the foreign policy of any state in the modern world-system, especially any powerful state. The question is how the United States has thought it could deal with such threats.

In the 1950s and 1960s, the U.S. seemed to be so strong that it could arrange, without too much difficulty and with a minimal use of force, that governments it did not like either could be neutralized (we called that containment) or, in the case of weaker governments, could be overthrown by internal forces supported covertly by the U.S. government, assisted occasionally by a little old-fashioned gunship diplomacy.

Neutralization was the tactic employed vis-à-vis the Communist world. The United States did not seek to overthrow the Soviet Union or any of its satellite regimes in eastern and central

Europe. Basically, it did not seek this because it was not in a military position to carry this out against the expected resistance by the government of the U.S.S.R. Instead, the U.S. government entered into a tacit accord with the U.S.S.R.—the Yalta agreement that it would not even try to do this, in return for a pledge by the Soviet Union that it would not try to expand its zone. The accord was not, however, intended to apply to East Asia where Soviet troops were absent, thanks primarily to the insistence of the Communist regimes in China and North Korea. So the U.S. did in fact try to overthrow these regimes, as well as that in Vietnam, but it did not, however, succeed. And these failed attempts left a serious scar on American public opinion.

The United States, was however, able to enforce its will in the rest of the world, and did so without compunction. Think of Iran in 1953, Guatemala in 1954, Lebanon in 1956, the Dominican Republic in 1965, and Chile in 1973. The coup in Chile by General Pinochet against the freely elected government of Salvador Allende, with the active support of the U.S. government, occurred on September 11. I do not know whether or not Osama bin Laden or his followers were aware of this coincidence of dates but it is nonetheless a symbolic coincidence that many, especially in Latin America, will notice. It also points to a further metaphor of the Twin Towers. The Twin Towers were a marvelous technological achievement. But technological achievements can and will be copied. The Malaysians have already copied the Twin Towers architecturally, and a bigger skyscraper is being built right now in Shanghai. Symbols too can be copied. Now we have two September 11 anniversaries on which victims mourn.

In the 1970s, U.S. foreign policy methods changed, had to change. Chile was the last major instance in which the United States was able so cavalierly to arrange other governments to its preferences. (I do not count the cases of either Grenada or

Panama, which were very small countries with no serious mode of military defense.) What had caused this change was the end of U.S. economic dominance of the world-economy, combined with the military defeat of the United States in Vietnam. Geopolitical reality had changed. The U.S. government could no longer concentrate on maintaining, even less on expanding, its power; instead its prime goal became preventing a too-rapid erosion of its power—both in the world-economy and in the military arena.

In the world-economy, the United States faced not only the hot breath of its competitors in western Europe and Japan but the seeming success of "developmentalist" policies in large parts of the rest of the world, policies that had been designed expressly to constrain the ability of countries in the core zone to accumulate capital at what was seen to be the expense of countries in the periphery. We should remember that the 1970s was declared by the United Nations the "decade of development." In the 1970s there was much talk of creating a "new international economic order," and in UNESCO of creating a "new international information order." The 1970s was the time of the two famous OPEC oil-price rises, which sent waves of panic into the American public.

The U.S. position on all these thrusts was either ambiguous discomfort or outright opposition. Globally, a counterthrust was launched. It involved the aggressive assertion of neoliberalism and the so-called Washington Consensus, the transformation of GATT (General Agreement on Tariffs and Trade) into the World Trade Organization, the Davos meetings, and the spreading of the concept of globalization with its corollary, TINA (there is no alternative). Essentially, all these efforts combined amounted to a dismantlement of the "developmentalist" policies throughout the world, and particularly in the peripheral zones of the world-economy. In the short run, that is, in the 1980s and

1990s, this counteroffensive led by the U.S. government seemed to succeed.

These policies on the front of the world-economy were matched by a persistent world-military policy that might be summarized as the "antiproliferation" policy. When the United States successfully made the first atomic bombs in 1945, it was determined to maintain a monopoly on such very powerful weapons. It was willing to share this monopoly with its faithful junior partner, Great Britain, but that was it. Of course, as we know, the other "great powers" simply ignored this claim. First the Soviet Union, then France, then China achieved nuclear capacity. So then did India and later Pakistan. So did South Africa, whose apartheid government however admitted this only as it was leaving power and was careful to dismantle this capacity before it turned over power to the successor, more democratic, government of the Black African majority. And so did Israel, although it has always denied this publicly. Then there are the "almost" nuclear powers, if indeed they are still in the "almost" category—North Korea, Iran, Iraq (whose facilities Israel bombed in the 1980s in order to keep it in the "almost" category), Libya, and maybe Argentina. And there are in addition the former Soviet countries that inherited nuclear capacity—Ukraine, Belorussia, and Kazakhstan. To this must be added the other lethal technologies, biological and chemical warfare. These are so much easier to create, store, and employ that we are not sure how many countries have some capacity, even a considerable capacity, in these fields.

The United States has had a simple straightforward policy. By hook or by crook, by force or by bribery, it wishes to deny everybody else access to these weapons. It has obviously not been successful, but its efforts over the past years have at least slowed down the process of proliferation. There is a further catch in U.S. policy. Insofar as it tries to employ international agreements to limit proliferation, it simultaneously tries not to be bound by such constraints itself, or to be minimally bound. The U.S. government has made it clear that it will renounce any such restraints whenever it deems it necessary to do so, while loudly condemning any other government that seeks to do the same.

As a policy, nonproliferation seems doomed to failure, not only in the long run but even in the middle run. The best that the United States will be able to do in the next twenty-five years is to slow the process down somewhat. But there is also a moral and political question here. The United States trusts itself, but trusts no one else. The U.S. government wishes to inspect North Korean locations to see if it is violating these norms. It has not offered the United Nations or anyone else the right to inspect U.S. locations. The United States trusts itself to use such weapons wisely and in the defense of liberty (a concept seemingly identical with U.S. national interests). It assumes that anyone else might intend to use such weapons against liberty (a concept seemingly identical here, too, with U.S. national interests).

Personally, I do not trust any government to use such weapons wisely. I would be happy to see them all banned, but I do not believe this is truly enforceable in the contemporary interstate system. So personally I abstain from moralizing on this issue. Moralizing opens one to the charge of hypocrisy. And where a cynical neorealist (a category that probably includes me) would say that all governments are hypocritical, moralizing jars badly if one wishes to attract support in other countries on the basis of one's comparative virtue.

IV. AMERICA: IDEALS VERSUS PRIVILEGE

To suggest that the universal civilization is in place already
is to be willfully blind to the present reality and, even

worse, to trivialize the goal and hinder the materialization
of a genuine universality in the future.

—CHINUA ACHEBE[4]

The opposition between globalization and local traditions
is false: globalization directly resuscitates local traditions, it
literally thrives on them, which is why the opposite of
globalization is not local traditions, but *universality*.

—SLAVOJ ZIZEK[5]

The story of U.S. and world power can be resumed quite simply at this moment. I do not believe that America and Americans are the cause of all the world's miseries and injustices. I do believe they are their prime beneficiaries. And this is the fundamental problem of the United States as a nation located in a world of nations.

Americans, especially American politicians and publicists, like to speak about our ideals. An advertisement for the "bestselling" book of the television host Chris Matthews, *Now, Let Me Tell You What I Really Think,* offers this excerpt: "When you think about it, we Americans are different. That word 'freedom' isn't just in our documents; it's in our cowboy souls."[6] "Cowboy souls"—I could not have said it better. Our ideals are perhaps special. But the same people who remind us of that do not like to talk about our privileges, which are also perhaps special. Indeed, they denounce those who do talk of them. But the ideals and the privileges go together. They may seem to be in conflict, but they presuppose each other.

I am not someone who denigrates American ideals. I find them quite wonderful, even refreshing. I cherish them, I invoke them, I further them. Take, for example, the First Amendment to the U.S. Constitution—something correctly remembered at all the appropriate ceremonies as incarnating American ideals. Let us, however, recall two things about the First Amendment. It wasn't in the original Constitution, which means it wasn't considered a founding principle. And public opinion polls have often shown that a majority of the American public would change, diminish, or even eliminate these guarantees, in whole or in part, even in so-called ordinary times. When we are in a "war" such as the "war on terrorism," then neither the U.S. government nor the U.S. public can be counted on to defend these ideals, and not even the Supreme Court can be relied upon to hold fast to them in an "emergency." Such defense is left largely to an often timid organization with at best minority support in public opinion, the American Civil Liberties Union, membership in which by a candidate in a general election is often cited as a reason not to vote for that candidate. So, I am in favor of freedom of speech and freedom of religion and all the other freedoms, but sometimes I must wonder if America is.

The reason is not that a Voltairean streak is lacking in the American public, but that sometimes we fear that our privileges are in danger of being eroded or disappearing. In such cases, most people place privilege ahead of ideals. Once again, Americans are not unusual in this regard. They simply are more powerful and have more privileges. Americans are freer to have the ideals because they are freer to ignore them. They have the power to override their cowboy souls.

The question before Americans is really the following: If American hegemony is in slow decline, and I believe it unquestionably is, will we lose the ideals because we will have less power to override them? Will our cowboy souls erect barbed wire around our national ranch in order to guard our privileges in danger of decline, as though they could not escape through the barbed wire? Let me suggest here another metaphor that comes from the Twin Towers. Towers that are destroyed can be rebuilt.

But will we rebuild them in the same way—with the same assurance that we are reaching for the stars and doing it right, with the same certainty that they will be seen as a beacon to the world? Or will we rebuild in other ways, after careful reflection about what we really need and what is really possible for us, and really desirable for us?

And who is "us"? If one follows the statements of Attorney-General John Ashcroft, seconded by many others in the U.S. government, in the press, and among the public in general, the "us" is no longer everyone in the United States, not even everyone legally resident in the U.S., but only U.S. citizens. And we may wonder whether "us" may not be further narrowed in the near future. As Slavoj Zizek points out, globalization is not the opposite of localism, it thrives on localism, especially the localism of the powerful. The "us" is by no stretch of the imagination *Homo sapiens sapiens*. Is *Homo* then so *sapiens*?

V. AMERICA: FROM CERTAINTY TO UNCERTAINTY

Darwin's revolution should be epitomized as the substitution of variation for essence as the central category of natural reality. . . . What can be more discombobulating than a full inversion, or "grand flip," in our concept of reality: in Plato's world, variation is accidental, while essences record a higher reality; in Darwin's reversal, we value variation as a defining (and concrete earthly) reality, while averages (our closest operational approach to "essences") become mental abstractions.

—Stephen J. Gould[7]

Nature is indeed related to the creation of unpredictable novelty, where the possible is richer than the real.

—Ilya Prigogine[8]

President Bush has been offering the American people certainty about their future. This is the one thing totally beyond his power to offer. The future of the United States, the future of the world, in the short run but even more in the medium run, is absolutely uncertain. Certainty may seem desirable if one reflects on one's privileges. It seems less desirable if one thinks that the privileges are doomed to decline, even disappear. And if it were certain that the Osama bin Ladens of this world in all camps were to prevail, who would cherish that certainty?

I return to the question I raised before as one of the puzzles that Americans are feeling right now: What must be done, what can be done, that an event like that of September 11 will not, could not happen again? The answer we are being offered is that the exercise of overwhelming force by the U.S. government, military force primarily, will guarantee this. Our leaders are prudent enough to remind us that this will take some time, but they do not hesitate to make medium-run assurances. For the moment, it seems that the American people are willing to test this hypothesis. If the U.S. government received criticism right after September 11, it came mostly from those who believe its expression of military power was far too timid. There are important groups who were pressing the U.S. government to go much further—to operate militarily against Iraq, and some would add Iran, Syria, Sudan, Palestine, North Korea. Why not Cuba next? There are some who are even saying that reluctant generals should be retired to make way for younger, more vigorous warriors. There are those who believe that it is their role to precipitate Armageddon.

There are two arguments one can make against this. One is that the United States could not win such a worldwide military conflagration. A second is that the United States would not wish to bear the moral consequences, first of all for itself, of trying to do so. Fortunately, one does not have to choose between realism and idealism. It is not belittling of our moral values that they are seconded by elementary common sense.

After the Civil War, the United States spent some eighty years pursuing its manifest destiny. It was not sure, all that time, whether it wished to be an isolationist or an imperial power. And when, in 1945, it had finally achieved hegemony in the world-system, when it had (in Shakespeare's choice) not only achieved greatness but had greatness thrust upon it, the American people were not fully prepared for the role they now had to play. We spent thirty years learning how to "assume our responsibilities" in the world. And just when we had learned this reasonably well, our hegemony passed its peak.

We have spent the last thirty years insisting very loudly that we are still hegemonic and that everyone needs to continue to acknowledge it. If one is truly hegemonic, one does not need to make such a request. We have wasted the past thirty years. What the United States needs to do now is to learn how to live with the new reality—that it no longer has the power to decide unilaterally what is good for everyone. It may not even be in a position to decide unilaterally what is good for itself. It has to come to terms with the world. It is not Osama bin Laden with whom we must conduct a dialogue. We must start with our near friends and allies—with Canada and Mexico, with Europe, with Japan. And once we have trained ourselves to hear them and to believe that they too have ideals and interests, that they too have ideas and hopes and aspirations, then and perhaps only then shall we be ready to dialogue with the rest of the world, that is, with the majority of the world.

This dialogue, once we begin to enter into it, will not be easy, and may not even be pleasant. For they shall ask us to renounce some privileges. They will ask us to fulfill our ideals. They will ask us to learn. Fifty years ago, the great African poet and politician Léopold-Sédar Senghor called on the world to come to the "rendez-vous du donner et du recevoir." Americans know what they have to give in such a rendezvous. But are they aware of something they wish to receive?

We are being called upon these days to return to spiritual values, as though we had ever observed these values. But what are these values? Let me remind you. In the Christian tradition (Matthew 19:24), it is said: "It is easier for a camel to pass through the eye of a needle than for a rich man to enter the kingdom of God." And in the Jewish tradition, Hillel tells us: "Do unto others as you would have them do unto you." And in the Muslim tradition, the Koran (52.36) tells us: "Or did they create the heavens and the earth? Nay! They have no certainty." Are these our values?

There is no single American tradition nor single American set of values. There are, and always have been, many Americas. We each of us remember and appeal to the Americas we prefer. The America of slavery and racism is a deep American tradition, and is still very much with us. The America of frontier individualism and gunslinging desperados is an American tradition, and is still very much with us. The America of robber barons and their philanthropic children is an American tradition, and is still very much with us. And the America of the Wobblies and the Haymarket riots, an event celebrated throughout the world except in America, is an American tradition, and is still very much with us.

Sojourner Truth, telling the National Women's Congress in 1851, "Ain't I a woman?" is an American tradition. But so were those late-nineteenth-century suffragists who argued for the vote for women on the ground that it would counterbalance the votes of Blacks and immigrants. The America that welcomes immigrants and the America that rejects them are both American traditions. The America that unites in patriotic resolve and the America that resists militarist engagements are both American traditions. The America of equality and of inequality are both American traditions. There is no essence there. There is no there there. As Gould reminds us, it is variation, not essence, that is the core of reality. And the question is whether the variation amongst us will diminish, increase, or remain the same. It seems to me exceptionally high at the moment.

Osama bin Laden will soon be forgotten, but the kind of political violence we call terrorism will remain very much with us in the thirty to fifty years to come. Terrorism is to be sure a very ineffective way to change the world. It is counterproductive and leads to counterforce, which can often wipe out the immediate set of actors. But it will nonetheless continue to occur. An America that continues to relate to the world by a unilateral assertion that it represents civilization, whether it does so in the form of isolationist withdrawal or of active interventionism, cannot live in peace with the world, and therefore will not live in peace with itself. What we do to the world, we do to ourselves. Can the land of liberty and privilege, even in amidst its decline, learn to be a land that treats everyone everywhere as equals? And can we deal as equal to equal in the world-system if we do not deal as equal to equal within our own frontiers?

What shall we choose to do now? I can have my preferences but I cannot, you cannot, predict what we shall do. Indeed, it is our good fortune that we cannot be certain of any of these projected futures. That reserves for us moral choice. That reserves for us the possible that is richer than the real. That reserves for us unpredictable novelty. We have entered a terrible era, an era of conflicts and evils we find it difficult to imagine but, sadly, one to which we can rapidly become accustomed. It is easy to allow our sensitivities to be hardened in the struggle to survive. It is far harder to save our cowboy souls. But at the end of the process lies the possibility, which is far from a certainty, of a more substantively rational world, of a more egalitarian world, of a more democratic world—of a universality that results from giving and receiving, a universality that is the opposite of globalization.

The last metaphor that is attached to the Twin Towers is that these structures were, are, and will be a choice. We chose to build them. We are deciding whether or not to rebuild them. The factors that enter into these choices were and are and will be very, very many. We are rebuilding America. The world is rebuilding the world. The factors that enter into these choices are and will be very, very many. Can we maintain our moral bearing amidst the uncertainty that the world we have made heretofore is only one of thousands of alternative worlds we might have created, and the world that we shall be making in the thirty to fifty years to come may or may not be better, may or may not reduce the contradiction between our ideals and our privileges?

In-sha 'allah.

NOTES

1. Published in *Theory and Society* 21, no. 1 (February 1992): 1–28.
2. The authors are Jerry L. Martin and Anne Neal.
3. "Multiple Kingdoms," *London Review of Books,* 19 July 2001, 23.
4. Chinua Achebe, *Home and Exile* (New York: Anchor Books, 2000), 91.
5. Slavoj Zizek, *On Belief* (New York: Routledge, 2001), 152.
6. *New York Times,* 28 November 2001, E8.
7. *Full House: The Spread of Excellence from Plato to Darwin* (New York: Three Rivers Press, 1996), 41.
8. Ilya Prigogine, *The End of Certainty: Time, Chaos, and the New Laws of Nature* (New York: Free Press, 1997), 72.

PART THREE

WHERE ARE WE HEADING?

CHAPTER TEN

The Left, I: Theory and Praxis Once Again

There is said to be a Yugoslav aphorism that goes like this: "The only absolutely certain thing is the future, since the past is constantly changing."[1] The world left is living today with two pasts that have almost totally disappeared, and rather suddenly at that. This is very unsettling. The first past that has disappeared is the trajectory of the French Revolution. The second past that has disappeared is the trajectory of the Russian Revolution. They both disappeared more or less simultaneously, and jointly, in the 1980s. Let me carefully explain what I mean by this.

The French Revolution is of course a symbol. It symbolizes a theory of history that has been very widely shared for two centuries, and shared far beyond the confines of the world left. Most of the world's liberal center also shared this theory of history, and today even part of the world's right. It could be said to have been the dominant view within the world-system throughout most of the nineteenth and twentieth centuries. Its premise was the belief in progress and the essential rationality of humanity. The theory was that history could be seen as linear upward process. The world was en route to the good society, and the French Revolution constituted and symbolized a major leap forward in this process.

There were many variants on this theory. Some persons, especially in the United States, wished to substitute the American for the French Revolution in this story. Others, especially in Great Britain, were in favor of substituting the English Revolution. Some persons wished to eliminate all political revolutions from the story, and make this theory of history the story of the steady commercialization of the world's economic processes, or the steady expansion of its electoral processes, or the fulfillment of a purported historic mission of the State (with a capital S). But whatever the details, all these variants shared the sense of the inevitability and the irreversibility of the historical process.

This was a hopeful theory of history, since it offered a happy ending. No matter how terrible the present (as for example when the fortunes of Nazi Germany seemed to be riding high, or when racist colonialism seemed at its most oppressive), believers (and most of us were believers) took solace in the knowledge we claimed to have, that "history was on our side." It was an encouraging theory, even for those who were privileged in the present, since it offered the expectation that eventually everyone else would share the privileges (without the present beneficiaries losing any) and that therefore the oppressed would cease annoying the oppressors with their complaints.

The only problem with this theory of history is that it did not seem to survive the test of empirical experience very well. This is where the Russian Revolution came in. It was a sort of codicil to the French Revolution. Its message was that the theory of history symbolized by the French Revolution was incomplete because it held true only insofar as the proletariat (or the popular masses) were energized under the aegis of a dedicated group of cadres organized as a party or party/state. This codicil we came to call Leninism.

Leninism was a theory of history espoused only by the world left, and in fact by only a part of it, at most. Still, it would be fatuous to deny that Leninism came to have a hold on a significant portion of the world's populations, especially in the years 1945 to 1970. The Leninist version of history was, if anything, more resolutely optimistic than the standard French Revolution model. This was because Leninism insisted that there was a simple piece of material evidence one could locate if one wanted to verify that history was evolving as planned. Leninists insisted that wherever a Leninist party was in undisputed power in a state, that state was self-evidently on the road to historical progress and, furthermore, could never turn back. The problem is that Leninist parties tended to be in power only in economically less well-off zones of the world, and conditions were not always brilliant in such countries. Still, the belief in Leninism was a powerful antidote to any anxieties caused by the fact that immediate conditions or events within a country governed by a Leninist party were dismaying.

I do not need to rehearse for you the degree to which all theories of progress have become suspect in the last two decades, and the Leninist variant in particular. I do not say that there are no believers left, since that would be untrue, but they no longer represent a substantial percentage of the world's populations. This constitutes a geocultural shift of no small proportion and, as I have said, has been particularly unsettling for the world left, which had placed most of its chips (if not all of them) on the correctness of at least the French Revolution version of this theory of history.

Why did this shift occur? There are many explanations that we are hearing today. From the world's center and right, the explanation comes that the world left misread this theory of history, and that it is still somehow true, but only if we define the good society as the one characterized by the predominance of an unfettered free flow of the factors of production, all in non-governmental hands, and most especially the free flow of capital. This utopia is called neoliberalism, and is quite popular today with politicians and many so-called public intellectuals. It is, however, a mirage as well as a deliberate delusion, one whose acme of influence is already past, and one that is worth a lot less discussion than it has been getting. By 2010, I warrant, we will scarcely remember this momentary mad fantasy.

A second explanation, coming from parts of the world left, is that the original theory remains correct, but that the world left has suffered some temporary setbacks, which will soon be reversed. All we have to do is to reiterate forcefully the theory (and the praxis). Given the degree to which such a massive "temporary setback" was nowhere predicted in the theory, and absent a more detailed explanation, this explanation seems to me to be a case of wishful thinking by some ostriches. I cannot see how Leninism, as an ideological stance and an organizational reality, can be resurrected, even should one want to do so. And the French Revolution arouses passion today only among a restricted group of scholars.

A third explanation for the collapse of this theory of history is that the collapse is in fact both a cause and a consequence of the crisis of the capitalist world-system. This is an explanation I have myself been expounding in various recent works.[2] I argue that the very theory of history widely espoused by the world left—that is, by what I call the antisystemic movements in their three historic variants, Communism, social democracy, and the national liberation movements—was itself a product of the capitalist world-system. As a result, although these movements did of course mobilize large masses of people to struggle against the system, they also paradoxically served historically as cultural undergirding for the system's relative political stability. The very belief in the inevitability of progress was substantively depoliticizing, and was particularly depoliticizing once an antisystemic movement came to state power. I believe further that the discrepancy between what was promised by these movements and what was realizable within the framework of the existing world-system once they were in state power inevitably became too great. As a consequence, the popular base eventually became disillusioned with the movements, which led to their ejection from power in a large number of states.

The decisive moment was the world revolution of 1968, during which the so-called Old Left (that is, the historic antisystemic movements) became an object of challenge by the participants in the various local expressions of this world revolution. One of the principal lasting results of 1968 was the rejection of the theory of inevitable and irreversible progress that had been preached by the movements. Thereupon, the world's populations began to turn away from the historic antisystemic movements themselves, and then began to delegitimize the state structures that the movements had been sustaining as essential mechanisms of progressive change. But this popular shift to antistatism, hailed though it was by the celebrants of the capitalist system, did not really serve the interests of the latter. For in actuality the antistatism has been delegitimizing *all* state structures, not merely particular regimes. It has thus undermined, rather than reinforced, the political stability of the world-system, and thereby has been making more acute its systemic crisis, which of course has had many other contributing causes as well.

In my view, the situation of the world left at present is the following: (1) After five hundred years of existence, the world capitalist system is, *for the first time,* in true systemic crisis, and we find ourselves in an age of transition. (2) The outcome is intrinsically uncertain, but nonetheless, and also for the first time in these five hundred years, there is a real perspective of, fundamental change, which *might* be progressive but will not necessarily be so. (3) The principal problem for the world left at this juncture is that the strategy for the transformation of the world that it evolved in the nineteenth century is in tatters, and it is consequently acting thus far with uncertainty and weakness and is in a generalized mild state of depression. Allow me to elaborate on each of these three points.

SYSTEMIC CRISIS

One of the unhappy results of the disarray of the world left is the suspicion that today surrounds any argument concerning a crisis of capitalism. Once burned, twice shy—and we have been burned so many, many times. The basic problem, if I may say so, is that most of the major figures of the world left of the past two centuries had not read Braudel on the multiplicity of social times, and were constantly confounding cyclical ups and downs with structural crises. This is easy to do, and especially within a geoculture like that of the modern world-system, one that gives pride of place to "newness" because of its total faith in the upward linearity of history. The left was particularly reluctant to embrace any argument that invoked cyclical processes because it incorrectly identified all such arguments with the subset that asserted what I would call the "eternal cyclicity of history." The latter theory had indeed been pervasively utilized by conservative thinkers as an argument against any and all transformational movements. But the concept of cycles within structures (to which I am referring) is not only different from the concept of eternal cyclicity; it is virtually its opposite, since structures are not at all eternal, only long-lasting, and the cycles within the structures are what guarantees that a structure can never be eternal. There are thus no eternal cycles, for there really is an arrow of time, even if it is not linear.

What seems to me therefore methodologically essential in the analysis of any historical social system (and the capitalist world-economy is a historical social system) is to distinguish carefully between, on the one hand, the cyclical rhythms that define its *systemic* character and that enable it to maintain certain equilibria, at least for the duration of the system, and on the other hand the secular trends that grow out of these cyclical rhythms defining its *historical* character and which mean that, sooner or later, a given system will no longer be able to contain its internal contradictions and that thus this system will enter into systemic crisis. In such a methodology, any historical system can be said to have three moments in time: its genesis (which needs to be explained, but which normally occurs as the result of the collapse of some other historical system), the relatively long period of what might be called the "quasi-normal" functioning of a historical system (the rules and constraints of which need to be described and analyzed), and its period of terminal crisis (which needs to be seen as a moment of historic choice whose outcome is always undetermined).

I believe that a number of trends have today at last reached points where they threaten the basic functioning of the system. I shall summarize briefly here what I have expounded at length elsewhere.[3] Capitalism as a historical system is defined by the fact that it makes structurally central and primary the endless accumulation of capital. This means that the institutions which constitute its framework reward those who pursue the endless accumulation of capital and penalize those who don't.

But how does one accumulate capital? The crucial *prerequisite* is obtaining profit from economic operations, the more the better. And profit is a function of the differential between real costs and possible prices. I say possible prices because of course no seller can infinitely increase the price demanded for a commodity and expect to sell it. There are always limits. Economists call this the elasticity of demand. Within the limits of the rate of elasticity, the actual profit depends upon three costs: the cost of labor, the cost of inputs and infrastructure, and the cost of taxation.

Now suppose we were to measure these costs globally as percentages of total sales prices and arrive hypothetically at average levels. This is an operation no one has ever done, and it is perhaps not doable. But it is possible to conceive of it, and to approximate the results. I would suggest to you that over five hundred years and across the capitalist world-economy as a whole, the three costs have all been steadily rising as a percentage of total value produced. And the net result is that we are in, and ever more coming into, a global profit squeeze that is threatening the ability of capitalists to accumulate capital.

This is actually something capitalists discuss all the time, but they use other terminology. They discuss "efficiency of production," by which they mean essentially lowering costs as a percentage of total value. In effect, they are talking about using fewer people to produce the same amount of goods, or of obtaining cheaper inputs (which often includes fewer people to produce the input). It is the case that in intercapitalist competition, the producer who is more efficient is likely to gain more profit than his competitor. But my question is different: Is production, considered globally and in all sectors taken together, more "efficient" today than it was one hundred, two hundred, or three hundred years ago?

Not only am I skeptical that global production is more "efficient" from the point of view of the producer, but I am contending that the curve has been steadily downward. All the so-called triumphs of efficient production are simply attempts to slow down the pace of the downward curve. One can regard the entire neoliberal offensive of the last two decades as one gigantic attempt to slow down the increasing costs of production—primarily by lowering the cost of wages and taxation and secondarily by lowering the costs of inputs via technological advance. I believe, further, that the overall degree of success has been quite limited, however painful it has been for those who have borne the brunt of the attack, and that even the limited gains are about to be reversed.

What else is the issue in all the constant screaming about the threat of inflation, so often invoked by Alan Greenspan and his cronies in Germany and Great Britain? If you read what they say, the potential cause of this terrible monster called inflation is that workers might actually get higher wages or that governments might spend even more (and therefore tax even more). They at least seem to have no illusion about the source of the threat to capital accumulation. Mild inflation, after all, is the normal condition of the capitalist world-economy when it is functioning smoothly, and has been going on for a long, long time. But normal inflation is indeed the consequence of rising wage and taxation levels, and therefore is precisely the phenomenon to which I am pointing.

Why are these three prices steadily if slowly rising over time, despite the best efforts of capitalists to attempt to slow them down? Let me briefly outline the reasons for each of the rising costs. Wages rise because workers organize. This is an ancient truism, but it is nonetheless accurate. The modes of organizing are multiple. Whenever workers' syndical action becomes too expensive for capitalists, and particularly in Kondratieff B-phases, when global competition is more acute, capitalists have sought to "run away"—from the city to the countryside, from loci where workers have been well organized to other loci where they have been less well organized.

If one regards the process over five hundred years, one sees that it has taken the form of transferring productive processes regularly (but not at all continuously) to zones newly incorporated into the capitalist world-economy. The reason has been simple. In such zones one can locate a workforce in rural areas that are less well commercialized who can be persuaded to engage in wage work at wage levels below the world standard. They can be so persuaded because, for them at that moment, such wages represent a real increase in total income. The hitch is that once these now displaced workers have been in the new work zone (usually an urban one) for some time (say twenty-five to fifty years), they shift their standards of comparison, learn the ways of the new work world, and begin in turn to organize and demand higher wage levels.

The poor capitalist is reduced to running away once again. The problem today is that, after five hundred years, there are few places left to run to. The process of rising wages has become extremely difficult to slow down. Today, even in the miserable barrios of the large urban centers of the countries of the South, the real alternatives for income of a potential wage worker is far higher than that of his rural grandparents; and therefore, if one wants his or her services in the so-called formal economy, one has to pay more for it.

The same process of exhaustion of low-cost zones has been occurring in the area of inputs. The main mechanism that capitalists have used to keep down the cost of inputs has been not to pay for some of them, but instead to obtain them at the expense of the collectivity. This is called externalization of costs. A producer externalizes costs primarily in three ways: he disposes of unprocessed waste outside of his property without paying anyone to process it; he purchases inputs at the cost of their being made available to him but without paying for the cost of their being replenished; he utilizes infrastructure built at collective expense. These three usages are no small part of reducing the cost of production and thereby increasing the rate of profit.

The first two of these three ways have depended on finding new areas to dump waste and new sources of raw materials whose previous sources are being exhausted. With the steady expansion of the areas included within the capitalist world-economy and the steady increase of the rate of their utilization, the globe is running out of replacement locales. This is the problem addressed by the ecology movement, who have pointed as well to the fact that inexpensive modes of disposal by producers and by the collectivity have wreaked major damage to the ecosystem, which is in urgent need of expensive repair. The third form of externalizing costs, using infrastructure built at collective expense, requires a steady increase in taxation, to which issue we are coming. The only real long-term solution to these problems is the internalization of costs, which, given the limits of the elasticity of demand, means a long-term profit squeeze.

Finally, taxes have been going up, as we are constantly reminded by all and sundry. It matters not that taxes are unevenly distributed. They have been going up for just about everyone, and this includes all producers. They have been going up for one simple reason, which political scientists refer to as the democratization of the world and whose consequence has been the expansion of the welfare state. People have been demanding higher state outputs on education, health, and guarantees of lifetime income. Furthermore, the threshold of demands has been steadily rising and spreading geographically to include more and more parts of the world. This has been the price of relative political stability, and there is no indication that the pressure from the bottom is letting up in any way.

One final point. It is not as though all these rising pressures on the rate of profit were only the result of the demands of persons other than the producers. Capitalists have been themselves partially responsible for this rise in costs. They (or at least some of them) have favored some rise in wage levels as a means of creating effective demand. They (or at least some of them) have favored internalization of some costs, as a mode of guaranteeing future production possibilities. They (or at least some of them) have wanted the welfare state as a way of appeasing the working classes. And they have favored other kinds of state expenditures (and therefore of taxation) as a way of repressing the working classes. And finally they (or at least some of them) have favored all of these measures as a way of creating financial pressures on their weaker competitors.

The net result of all of this, however, has been a massive rise in costs, which is leading to a worldwide squeeze on profits. The very madness of our current speculative mania, most acute in the stronghold of the system, the United States, is not disproof of this hypothesis but further evidence for it. I cannot, however, argue this thesis further here if I am to discuss the prospects for fundamental change and the strategy of the world left.

SYSTEMIC TRANSITION

What does it mean to say that a system enters into systemic crisis? It means that the secular trends are reaching asymptotes that they cannot cross. It means that the mechanisms that have been used up to that point to return the system to relative equilibria no longer can function because they require moving the system too near to the asymptote. It means, in Hegelian language, that the contradictions of the system can no longer be contained. It means, in the language of the sciences of complexity, that the system has moved far from equilibrium, that it is entering into a period of chaos, that its vectors will bifurcate, and eventually a new system or systems will be created. It means that the "noise" in the system, far from being an element that can be ignored, will come to the forefront. It means that the outcome is intrinsically uncertain, and is creative.

This description of crises in systems applies to any and all systems, from that of the entire universe to that of subatomic worlds, from physical to biological to historical social systems. It

applies most fully and with greatest complexity to historical social systems, since they are the most complex of all systems other
than that of the cosmos itself. Using such a model is not reducing
social phenomena to physical phenomena. It is exactly the reverse. It is interpreting physical phenomena as though they were
social phenomena, with agents, imagination, self-organization,
and creative activity.

I have always found it curious that this description has been
thought to be mechanistic and, even more strange, pessimistic. It
is a form of analysis that directly denies the validity of what we
have termed "mechanical" in the social thought of the last few
centuries. And it is not at all pessimistic because it is necessarily
neutral in its prediction of outcome. Neither good nor bad
outcomes are predicted. No outcomes can be predicted, since
alternative outcomes depend on an infinity of unknown and
unknowable choices.

The way we might think about a chaotic period of systemic
transition is that it is one in which "free will" more or less reigns
supreme, unfettered (as it normally is) by the straightjacket of
custom and structural constraints. The French Revolution and
the Russian Revolution were both incredible efforts to transform
the world, engaging the mobilized energies of many, many people in many parts of the world, and over a long period of time,
and yet they changed so much less than they were intended to
change. And to the extent that they thought they were implementing changes, many of these changes were later reversed or
subverted. By the yardstick of their hopes and their proclama-
tions, they cannot be said to have been notable successes, despite
the fact that they left indelible marks on everything that has occurred since their time.

The politics of the transition are different from those of the
quasi-normal period. It is the politics of grabbing advantage and
position at a moment in time when politically anything is possi-

ble and when most actors find it extremely difficult to formulate middle-range strategies. Ideological and analytic confusion becomes a structural reality rather than an accidental variable. The economics of everyday life is subject to wilder swings than those to which we have been accustomed and for which we have easy explanations. Above all, the social fabric seems less reliable and the institutions on which we rely to guarantee our immediate security seem to be faltering. Thus, antisocial crime seems widespread and this perception creates fear and the reflex of the expansion of privatized security measures and forces. If this sounds familiar, it is because it is happening, in varying degrees throughout the world-system.

One has to ask what are the likely reactions of different political forces in such a situation. The easiest to predict is the reaction of the upper strata of the world-system. They are of course a complex mix and do not constitute an organized caucus. But they probably can be divided into two main groups. The majority will share in the general confusion and will resort to their traditional short-run politics, perhaps with a higher dose of repressiveness insofar as the politics of concessions will not be seen as achieving the short-run calm it is supposed to produce.

And then there is the small minority among the upper strata who are sufficiently insightful and intelligent to perceive the fact that the present system is collapsing and who wish to ensure that any new system be one that preserves their privileged position. The only strategy for such a group is the di Lampedusa strategy—to change everything in order that nothing change. This group will have firm resolve and a great deal of resources at their command. They can hire intelligence and skill, more or less as they wish. They will do so. They may already have been doing so.

I do not know what this group will come up with, or by what means its members will seek to implement the form of transition they favor. I do know that whatever it is, it will seem attractive and will be deceptive. The most deceptive aspect is that such proposals may be clothed as radical, progressive change. It will require constantly applied analytic criticism to bring to the surface what the real consequences would be, and to distinguish and weigh the positive and negative elements. This has already been happening for a long list of relatively minor proposals concerning various specific types of problems, such as ecology or genetic engineering, and the list could go on.

On the other side of the virtual battlefield will be all those who would seek to reconstruct the world such that it would be more democratic and more egalitarian. I use these two criteria as a minimal but in fact crucial definition of the world left. Were the disparate groups who share this objective to get their act together, this is a moment of great possibility to achieve a significant transformation in the direction of their hopes. But, as I have said previously, their present state is that they are acting with uncertainty, weakness, and in a generalized state of depression. Uncertainty I can understand, though it is possible to overcome this. But there is no inherent need for the world left to be either weak or depressed, even if I can appreciate how the shocks of the last thirty years have induced such reactions.

We do not know who will prevail in this struggle to resolve the systemic bifurcation between those who wish to move in the direction of a new historical social system that shares with the present one the crucial characteristic of hierarchical privilege and those who wish to move in the direction of a relatively democratic, relatively egalitarian system. We do not know and cannot know it. If we act, we must act within the framework of an uncertain outcome. There is no bandwagon to climb aboard. There is only a harsh struggle in which we must try to make prevail the primacy of substantive rationality. It is to the possible routes of action that I now turn.

A STRATEGY FOR THE WORLD LEFT

What is wrong with the strategy the world left evolved in the course of the nineteenth century? There must be many things, since the strategy has not been successful. The centerpiece of the overall strategy was the concept of "two steps": first obtain state power, then transform the world. This sequence made sense insofar as control of the state machinery seemed the only way to overcome the accumulated economic and cultural power of the privileged strata and the only way to ensure that new kinds of institutions could be constructed—and maintained against counterattack. Any other route to social transformation seemed utopian (in the pejorative sense of being a pipe dream), and this view seemed to be confirmed by the fact that various other routes to transformation, whenever tried, met with aggressive counterattack and ultimately suppression.

So the two-step strategy seemed to be the only one that would work. And yet it failed. We know in retrospect what happened. The two-step strategy failed because once the first step was achieved—and it was indeed achieved in a very large number of countries—the new regimes did not seem to be able to achieve the second step. This is precisely the source of disillusionment with the Old Left. But why did the movements falter at the second step? For a long time it was argued that, if a given regime did not transform the world as it had promised, it was because the leadership had in some sense "betrayed" the cause and had "sold out." The idea that leaders sell out, just like the idea that the masses are falsely conscious, seems to me analytically sterile and politically disabling. To be sure, some leaders do place personal ambition above their proclaimed principles, just as some ordinary people do seem not to believe in the same principles that many (even most) of their fellows do. The question, however, is, why do such people prevail?

The basic problem is not ethical or psychological but structural. The states within a capitalist world-system have a lot of power, but they simply are not all-powerful. Those in power cannot do just anything they wish to do and still remain in power. Those in power are in fact rather severely constrained by all kinds of institutions, and in particular by the interstate system. This is a structural reality that, one after the other, these movements that have come to power have confronted. Like trees in a storm, such regimes have either bent or been broken. None has ever stayed straight, or could have stayed straight. And in many ways, it was dangerously naive to expect them to do so.

It is not that no one on the left ever warned of the dangers of the two-step strategy. It is that those who argued its dangers could never convince the majority that there was any efficacious alternative route. The fact that the powerful of the world controlled the weapons (via state armies and state police forces) seemed to make it impossible that any truly fundamental changes could be made before the movements obtained state power. And the majority on the left was probably right about this. There was indeed no alternative way, as long as they were operating within the ambit of the capitalist world-system that was still basically stable.

But there is more to it than this. The left analysis involved multiple biases that pushed it towards this state orientation. The first bias was that homogeneity was somehow better than heterogeneity, and that therefore centralization was somehow better than decentralization. This derived from the false assumption that equality means identity. To be sure, many thinkers had pointed out the fallacy of this equation, including Marx, who distinguished equity from equality. But for revolutionaries in a hurry, the centralizing, homogenizing path seemed easiest and fastest. It required no difficult calculation of how to balance complex sets of choices. They were arguing in effect that one cannot add apples and oranges. The only problem is that the real world is made up of precisely apples and oranges. If you can't do such fuzzy arithmetic, you can't make real political choices.

The second bias was virtually the opposite. Whereas the preference for unification of effort and result should have pushed logically toward the creation of a single world movement and the advocacy of a world state, the de facto reality of a multistate system, in which some states were visibly more powerful and privileged than other states, pushed the movements toward seeing the state as a mechanism of defense of collective interests within the world-system, an instrument more relevant for the large majority within each state than for the privileged few. Once again, many thinkers had pointed to the fallacy of believing that any state within the modern world-system would or could serve collective interests rather than those of the privileged few, but weak majorities in weak states could see no other weapon at hand in their struggles against marginalization and oppression than a state structure they thought (or rather they hoped) they might be able to control themselves.

The third bias was the most curious of all. The French Revolution had proclaimed as its slogan the trinity "Liberty, Equality, Fraternity." What has in practice happened ever since is that most people have tacitly dropped the "fraternity" part of the slogan, on the grounds that it was mere sentimentality. And the liberal center has insisted that "liberty" had to take priority over "equality." In fact, what the liberals really meant is that "liberty" (defined in purely political terms) was the only thing that mattered and that "equality" represented a danger for "liberty" and had to be downplayed or dropped altogether.

There was flimflam in this analysis, and the world left fell for it. The world left, and in particular its Leninist variant, responded to this centrist liberal discourse by inverting it, and insisting that (economic) equality had to take precedence over (political) liberty. This was entirely the wrong answer. The correct answer is that there is no way whatsoever to separate liberty from equality. No one can be "free" to choose, if his or her choices are constrained by an unequal position. And no one can be "equal" if he or she does not have the degree of freedom that others have, that is, does not enjoy the same political rights and the same degree of participation in real decisions.

Still, this is all water under the bridge. The left made its case, and it has had to live with it. Today, as a result and as we are very well aware, the world left is in great difficulty. I am arguing, however, that this should not be seen in isolation. The errors of the left, the failed strategy, were an almost inevitable outcome of the operations of the capitalist system against which the left was struggling. And the widespread recognition of this historic failure of the left is part and parcel of the disarray caused by the general crisis of the capitalist world-system.

The failure of the left yesterday and its recognition today is precisely what will make it possible for the world left tomorrow to achieve its objectives. *Possible, but not at all certain!* A new kind of historical system will be constructed in the next half century. The worldwide battle has already begun over what it will look like. So what can we do?

I think the first thing we on the left can do is analyze. I say this not because I am addressing social scientists, that is, persons who presumably engage in social analysis as their life work, but because one of the problems of the world, and in particular of the world left, is that our previous analyses have not been all that good and seem to have been part of the cause of why we are in the dilemmas we are in today. Here I can only repeat a number of themes I have been plugging for a while now. The first is the importance of the choice of the unit of analysis. I think the relevant unit of analysis is the modern world-system, which is a capitalist world-economy. The second thing we can do is analyze this system in the *longue durée,* which is, however, distinctly *not* eternal. What this does mean is that for any given historical system, such as, for example, the capitalist world-economy, we need to distinguish cyclical rhythms from secular trends, and use that to distinguish the periods of genesis, of quasi-normal operation, and of structural crisis of the system as a whole.

The third thing we can do is understand systemic processes in terms of their complexity, that is, their long-run tendency to move far from equilibrium and arrive at moments of bifurcation with indeterminate outcome. The fourth is to place particular emphasis on the institutional role within the capitalist world-economy of (a) the antisystemic movements and (b) the structures of knowledge. And the fifth is to place all this analysis within the context of unthinking (which is different from rethinking) the categories bequeathed to us largely in the nineteenth century so we can meet the needs and reflect the geoculture of the present world-system.

Analysis is of course always a necessary component of praxis. But it is particularly urgent and central when we are confronting a structural crisis because it is just then that accepted categories of thought provide the greatest hindrance to useful action. However analysis by itself is never action. Action requires organization. The world left has believed for the last two hundred years that this meant highly coordinated action, preferably within a single hierarchical structure, believing it to be the most, perhaps the only, efficacious form of action.

I think that this assumption has been proved wrong. The social components that potentially make up the world left are too diverse, face too many different immediate problems, originate in too many diverse cultural loci for a system of democratic centralism, even one that were genuinely democratic, to work. This has been recognized in recent years by the emergence of two slogans that point in another direction. One is the U.S. slogan of the "rainbow coalition," a phrase that has been copied in other parts of the world. It was generated by the sense that, for very many people, their politics are rooted in, or deeply affected by, their social position and their identities. The other phrase is the one launched in the last few years in France, "plural left." This phrase too is being copied. It refers less to the reality of different identities than to that of the multiplicity of political traditions and priorities.

However we appreciate the actual attempts heretofore to create a new style of left coalition, the core of the idea seems to me to be absolutely correct and indeed essential if we are to make any significant political progress. We are strengthened collectively, not weakened, insofar as people organize in forms and structures meaningful to them, provided only that the groups they form are ready to talk to each other, and to operate meaningful coalitions. This is far more than a matter of parliamentary politics. It can and should operate at all levels from the global to the local. But most of all, it cannot be merely a matter of political logrolling but one rather of constant debate and collegial analysis by these movements in concert one with the other. It is a question of creating and reinforcing a particular culture of collegial as opposed to hierarchical political action. It will not be easy.

What is it, however, that such coalitions should push? I think there are three major lines of theory and praxis to emphasize. The first is what I call "forcing liberals to be liberals." The Achilles heel of centrist liberals is that they don't want to implement their own rhetoric. One centerpiece of their rhetoric is individual choice. Yet at many elementary levels, liberals oppose individual choice. One of the most obvious and the most important is the right to choose where to live. Immigration controls are antiliberal. Making choice—say choice of doctor or school— dependent on possession of wealth is antiliberal. Patents are antiliberal. One could go on. The fact is that the capitalist world-economy survives on the basis of the nonfulfillment of liberal rhetoric. The world left should be systematically, regularly, and continuously calling the bluff.

But of course, calling the rhetorical bluff is only the beginning of reconstruction. We need to have a positive program of our own. There has been a veritable sea change in the programs of left parties and movements around the world between 1960 and 1999. In 1960, their programs emphasized economic structures. They advocated one form or another, one degree or another, of the socialization, usually the nationalization, of the means of production. They said little, if anything, about inequalities that were not defined as class-based. Today, almost all of these same parties and movements, or their successors, put forward proposals to deal with inequalities of gender, race, and ethnicity. Many of the programs are terribly inadequate, but at least they feel it necessary to say something. On the other hand, there is virtually no party or movement today that considers itself on the left and that advocates further socialization or nationalization of the means of production, and a number are actually proposing moving in the other direction. It is a breathtaking turnabout. Some hail it, some denounce it. Most just accept it.

There is one enormous plus in this cataclysmic shift of emphasis. The world left had never addressed with sufficient seriousness the biggest problem of all for almost everyone, which is the day-by-day reality of worldwide multiple inequalities. Equality means very little if it is equality only among the wealthy. The capitalist world-system has resulted in the greatest geographic polarization of wealth and privilege the planet has ever known. And the top priority of the world left must be to decrease the gap radically and as rapidly as possible. But this is not the only gap that needs to be addressed. There are all the ones we have talked about for a long, long time: class, race, ethnicity, gender, generation. In short, we have to take the issue of equality as one about which something can indeed be done.

But what? Decreeing equality as an objective is not achieving it. For even with goodwill all around—and this of course cannot be assumed; indeed quite the contrary—it is not easy to find equitable solutions. Here is where I think we need to reintroduce, indeed revive, Weber's concept of substantive rationality. We should note here incidentally a problem of translation. The term Weber used in German was "*Rationalität materiel*"—"material" as opposed to "formal." The accepted English translation, "substantive rationality," only conveys "*materiel*" if we associate it with "substance" and not with "substantial" in our minds. What Weber was talking about was that which is rational in terms of collective, widely applicable value systems as opposed to that which is rational in terms of particular, narrowly described sets of objectives an individual or an organization might set itself. Weber himself was ambivalent about the attitude to take vis-à-vis "substantive rationality." He sometimes described it in ways that made it seem his priority and sometimes in ways that underlined his fears that ideological organizations (read, the German Social-Democratic Party) might impose their views on everyone else.[4] Most of Weber's post-1945 acolytes have only noticed the latter sentiments and ignored the former. But we can make our own use of this important concept and the insights it gives us.

What it seems to me that Weber was pointing to is that, in a world of multiple actors and multiple sets of values, there can be resolutions of the debates that are more than the result of simple arithmetic (counting the votes) and more than a free-for-all in which everyone pursues his own fancy. There can exist substantively rational ways of making social decisions. To know what they are requires a long period of clear, active, and open debate and a collective effort to balance priorities over the short run and the long run.

Take a very obvious issue, the problem of generational priorities. There is at any given time a given social surplus, which can be divided among four generational groups: children, working-age adults, the elderly, and the as-yet-unborn. What is the right proportion to allocate in terms of collective expenditures? There surely is no easy or self-evident answer. But it is a question that needs some measured decisions, arrived at democratically (that is, involving the real participation of everyone, at least everyone living, in some meaningful way). At the present time, in the present system, we have no real process by which this can be done, not even within a single state, not to be speak of doing it globally. Can we construct such a process? We must. If we cannot, we renounce forever the traditional objective of the world left, a relatively democratic, relatively egalitarian world. I am not ready to renounce this objective. Thus, I am in principle optimistic that humanity can construct such procedures. But remember, not only is it difficult, but there are many, many powerful persons who do not wish to see such procedures established.

What we can say about these issues of multiple inequalities and the ways they might be overcome is that at least, and at last, they are the subject of serious debate today. They are on the agenda of the world left. And if we have not come up with very good answers up to now, we do seem to be working at it, and with far less internal backbiting than one might have feared and than seemed to be happening twenty to thirty years ago.

But the great plus on the issue of the multiple inequalities has gone along with a great minus on the side of reconstructing our basic economic institutions. If capitalism collapses, do we still have an alternative that fulfils the traditional socialist objective—a socially rational system that maximizes collective utility and fair distribution? If the world left today is putting forth such proposals, I haven't heard of them. Between those at one end of the left spectrum who are proclaiming "new" ideas that are simply watered-down versions of centrist administration of the capitalist system and those at the other end who are nostalgic for the nostrums of yesterday, there seems to be a real poverty of serious ideas.

The world left needs to face up to the most systematic and effective critique of historical socialist rhetoric, the charge that nonprivate ownership of the means of production leads to waste, disinterest in technological efficiency, and corruption. This critique has not been untrue of what we today call "real-existing socialism." This has been recognized by such of these regimes as still survive (or at least most of them), but their response has been to create a large place for private ownership within their regimes and label this "market socialism." This may seem to solve some short-run economic difficulties but in fact it fails utterly to address the underlying issues that the world socialist movement sought to address in the first place—gross inequality and gross social waste.

I suggest there may be another route, one that has in fact been tried partially and is rather promising. I think one might be able to get most of the advantages of private ownership yet eliminate most of the negatives by ensconcing productive activities within medium-size, decentralized, competitive nonprofit structures. The key is that they would be nonprofit, that is, no one would receive "dividends" or "profit distributions" and any surplus either would go back to the organization or would be taxed by the collectivity for reinvestment elsewhere.

How might such structures work? Well, actually we know how, in the sense that there are parallels. Most major universities and hospitals in the United States have worked on such principles for two centuries now. Whatever we can say of their functioning, it is not the case that they have been "inefficient" or "technologically backward" by comparison with the few for-profit institutions that have existed. Quite the contrary. I'm aware that there is currently a move to try to transform such structures into for-profit institutions, but insofar as this has occurred in hospital structures the results have not been very good and the move to profit-oriented institutions has not yet been seriously tried in universities. Of course, in most countries, hospital and university structures are state-financed but traditionally they have usually been allowed enough autonomy for us to consider them examples of decentralization. These state-financed nonprofit structures have not in any case been notably less efficient than the private nonprofit ones.

So why wouldn't this work for steel firms, for computer technology giants, for manufacturers of aircraft and biotechnology? No doubt there would be a lot of details to argue about, especially the degree to which such nonprofit corporations should be taxed, but per se it seems to me viable, and promising, and an alternative road that would not be out of sync with the commitment to a worldwide higher standard of living for everyone. At the very least, it would seem to me to be something we should be seriously discussing and an idea we should be elaborating.

What I think we should keep in the forefront of our minds is that the basic issue is not ownership or even control of economic resources. The basic issue is the decommodification of the world's economic processes. Decommodification, it should be underlined, does not mean demonetization, but the elimination of the category of profit. Capitalism has been a program for the commodification of everything. The capitalists have not yet fulfilled it entirely, but they have gone a long way in that direction, with all the negative consequences we know. Socialism ought to be a program for the decommodification of everything. Five hundred years from now, if we start down that path, we may not have fulfilled it entirely, but we can have gone a long way in that direction.

In any case, we need to be debating the possible structures of the historical social system we want to construct as the present system collapses. And we ought to be trying to construct the alternative structures now, and in the next half-century, during the period of transition. We need to pursue this issue forcefully, if not dogmatically. We need to try out alternatives, as mental experiments and as real experiments. What we cannot do is ignore this issue. For if we do, the world right will come up itself with new noncapitalist alternatives that will involve us in a new, hierarchical, inegalitarian world order. And then it will be too late, for a long while thereafter, to change things.

Allow me to say one last word that is obvious, but needs to be said. Social scientists are specialists. Of course, we are not the only brand of specialists. In a sense, the world is constituted of an endless series of specialists, some of whom have had longer periods of training than others. How do specialists relate to nonspecialists? How should they? The world left has tended to define this as the issue of how middle-class left-oriented intellectuals should relate to the working classes. And we have tended to favor the theory that they must be "organic intellectuals," by which we have meant that they must be involved in social movements, working with them, for them, and ultimately under them. The collapse of the movements has left a bad taste in the minds of erstwhile and putative organic intellectuals about the whole idea.

There is however another way to look at the issue. Consider how a client relates to a lawyer or a physician. As we know, it is basically a matter of class. The working-class client may feel ignorant and helpless vis-à-vis the professional, and accept the judgment of the professional, sometimes gratefully, sometimes with great resentment, but usually accepting it nonetheless. A wealthy or otherwise powerful person may treat the lawyer or the physician as a subordinate, whose primary function it is to give technical advice to a superior.

Is there some way in which the specialist can relate to the nonspecialist as an equal? Obviously, the specialist has some specialized knowledge. That is the whole point of multiple, differential training programs. And obviously again, the specialist knows many things that are relevant to solving particular kinds of problems of which the nonspecialist is unaware. That is why the nonspecialist consults the specialist, to get the benefit of the expertise the specialist has. But it is also obvious that the nonspecialist knows many other things—about his needs and preferences, about other problems he or she is facing—of which the specialist is unaware, or if aware, on which the specialist has no specialized knowledge.

Somewhere along the line, a total judgment has to be made as to whether or not a particular line of action the specialist recommends is substantively rational. I am of course assuming that it is formally rational, that is, that it will achieve the narrowly defined objective the specialist has taken into consideration. But who will make this decision? And how? If one transposes this issue from the realm of an individual encountering a specialist to resolve a personal problem to that of a collectivity encountering a group of specialists to resolve a collective problem, we see immediately that once again there is no simple answer. But I think once again this is a conundrum not impossible to overcome, merely difficult. Neither of two extremes is acceptable: that the specialists impose their solution on the collectivity; that the political decision-making bodies ignore the knowledge and the recommendations of the specialists. We need somehow systematically to intrude public debate on the issues, and the balancing of multiple needs and interests. We are thus back to the issue of substantive rationality.

This whole program for the left would be hard enough were we to face it among only ourselves and in all tranquillity. But we face these issues while under constant attack by those who wish to prevent our basic objectives from being achieved, and who have powerful resources at their command. Furthermore, we shall not be doing it in times of tranquillity but in times of chaos. It is the transitional chaos that offers us our opportunity, but at the same time this chaotic ambiance confuses us and presses us to turn away from the long-run reconstruction of a historical social system to the short-turn solution of urgent problems.

Finally, those of us in the United States find ourselves before one further obstacle, which C. Wright Mills saw clearly in 1959, and which has not fundamentally changed since then: "[I]ntellectuals of [our] sort, living in America and in Britain, face some disheartening problems. As socialists of one sort or another, we are a very small minority in an intellectual community that is itself a minority. The most immediate problem we face is the nationalist smugness and political complacency among the dominant intellectual circles of our own countries. We confront a truly deep apathy about politics in general and about the larger problems of the world today."[5]

In short, and I say this for the last time, it will not be easy. But the game is surely worth the candle.

NOTES

1. I found this as the epigraph of an article by E. M. Simonds-Duke, "Was the Peasant Uprising a Revolution? The Meanings of a Struggle over the Past," *Eastern European Politics and Societies* 1, no. 2 (Spring 1987): 187.
2. See *After Liberalism* (New York: New Press, 1995), *Utopistics* (New York: New Press, 1998), and *The End of the World As We Know It: Social Science for the Twenty-first Century* (Minneapolis: University of Minnesota Press, 1999).

3. See chapter 3.
4. I have discussed this in "Social Science and Contemporary Society: The Vanishing Guarantees of Rationality," in *The End of the World as We Know It,* 137–56.
5. C. Wright Mills, *Letters and Autobiographical Writings,* edited by Kathryn Mills with Pamela Mills (Berkeley: University of California Press, 2000), 232.

Chapter Eleven

The Left, II:
An Age of Transition

I n 1999 I gave a talk at the Caucus for a New Political Science on left politics today.[1] In that talk, I summarized the contemporary situation of the world left in the following way:

(1) After five hundred years of existence, the world capitalist system is, for the first time, in true systemic crisis, and we find ourselves in an age of transition. (2) The outcome is intrinsically uncertain, but nonetheless, and also for the first time in these five hundred years, there is a real perspective of fundamental change, which might be progressive but will not necessarily be so. (3) The principal problem for the world left at this juncture is that the strategy for the transformation of the world which it had evolved in the nineteenth century is in tatters, and it is consequently acting thus far with uncertainty and weakness, and in a generalized mild state of depression.

I would like to take these three points as assumptions and ask what these assumptions imply for a left strategy over the next ten to twenty years.

The first thing it implies is that we have in no way been defeated globally. The collapse of the Soviet Union was not a disaster for the world left. I am not sure I would even call it a setback. It not only liberated us collectively from the albatross of a no longer useful Leninist strategy and rhetoric, but it also imposed an enormous burden on the world liberal center, removing the structural support it in fact received from the Leninist movements, which had held in check popular radicalism for a long time by their guarantees of "shining tomorrows" via faith in a Leninist developmentalist present.[2]

Nor do I think the global offensive of neoliberalism and so-called globalization has strangled our possibilities. For one thing, a lot of it is hype that will not survive the coming deflation. For another thing, it will breed, it has bred, its countertoxin. For a third thing, world capitalism is actually in bad shape structurally, rather than enjoying a "new economy."

Here again, let me summarize my position without arguing it. In addition to the political difficulties caused by the collapse of Leninism and the end of the Cold War, capital is running into three structural asymptotes which are cramping irremediably its ability to accumulate capital: (1) the deruralization of the world, ending capitalism's ability to check the rising share of expenditure on labor power as a percentage of world total value created; (2) the ecological limits of toxification and nonrenewal of resources, limiting the ability of capital to reduce costs of inputs by continued externalization of these costs; (3) the spreading democratization of the world, evidenced by ever-expanding popular pressures for expenditures on health, education, and lifetime income guarantees, which have created a steady upward pressure of taxes as a share of world value created.

To be sure, capital seeks to reduce these structural pressures all the time. This is what the neoliberal offensive of the last twenty years has been about. But the long-term curve looks like an upward ratchet. They succeed regularly in reducing these pressures but always to a lesser degree than the next upward bump augments them. In order to fight against this, they preach TINA (there is no alternative), in the attempt to reduce counterpolitical will. This is also nothing new. Gareth Stedman Jones, seeking to explain relative political stability in late-nineteenth-century Great Britain, attributed it to the "apparent inevitability of capitalism" and its "apparent invulnerability."[3] The First World War undid such sentiments, at least for a long while. They are being resuscitated now, or at least the right is attempting to resuscitate them.

If we are to look at a left strategy for the twenty-first century, we must first remind ourselves what the left strategy has been. The left strategy that was developed in the second half of the nineteenth century and was more or less rejected in the last third of the twentieth century (symbolically 1848 to 1968) was a very clear one. It was the so-called strategy of two steps: first, gain state power; second, transform the world. Three things should be noted about this strategy. (1) It was probably the only one possible at the time, since movements with any other kind of strategy could be simply crushed by the use of state power. (2) It was adopted by *all* the major movements: both branches of the world socialist movement, the social democrats and the Communists, as well as the national liberation movements. (3) The strategy failed because it succeeded. All three kinds of movements came to power almost everywhere in the period 1945 to 1970, and none of them was able to change the world, which led to the profound disillusionment that presently exists with this strategy, and the serious antistatism that has been its sociopsychological result.[4]

In the period since 1968, there has been an enormous amount of testing of alternative strategies by different movements old and new, and there has been in addition a rather healthy shift in the relations of antisystemic movements to each other in the sense that the murderous mutual denunciations and vicious struggles of yesteryear have considerably abated, a positive development we have been underestimating. I would like to suggest some lines along which we could develop further the idea of an alternative strategy.

1. Expand the spirit of Porto Alegre.

What is this spirit? I would define it as follows. It is the coming together in a nonhierarchical fashion of the world family of anti-systemic movements to push for (a) intellectual clarity, (b) militant actions based on popular mobilization that can be seen as immediately useful in people's lives, (c) attempts to argue for longer-run, more fundamental changes.

There are three crucial elements to the spirit of Porto Alegre. It is a loose structure, more or less approximating what was called by Jesse Jackson "the rainbow coalition." It is a structure that has brought together on a world scale movements from the South and the North, and on more than a merely token basis. It is militant, both intellectually (it is not in search of a global consensus with the spirit of Davos) and politically (in the sense that the movements of 1968 were militant). Of course, we shall have to see whether a loosely structured world movement can hold together in any meaningful sense, and by what means it can develop the tactics of the struggle. But its very looseness makes it difficult to suppress and encourages the hesitant neutrality of centrist forces.

2. Use defensive electoral tactics.

If the world left engages in loosely structured, extraparliamentary militant tactics, this immediately raises the question of our attitude toward electoral processes. Scylla and Charybdis are on the one hand thinking they're crucial and on the other thinking they're irrelevant. Electoral victories will not transform the world, but they cannot be neglected. They are an essential mechanism of protecting the immediate needs of the world's populations against incursions to achieved benefits. They must be fought in order to minimize the damage that can be inflicted by the world right via control of the world's governments.

This makes, however, electoral tactics a purely pragmatic matter. Once we cease thinking of obtaining state power as a mode of transforming the world, elections are always a matter of the lesser evil, and the decision of what is the lesser evil has to be made case by case and moment by moment. They depend in part on the particular electoral system. A winner-takes-all system must be manipulated differently than a system with two rounds or a system with proportional representation. But the general guiding rule has to be the rainbow coalition, a "plural left," a slogan coined in France, which in Latin America has been called the *frente amplio*. There are many different party and subparty traditions among the world left. Most of these traditions are relics of another era, but many people still vote according to them. Since state elections are a pragmatic matter, it is crucial to create alliances that respect these traditions, aiming for the 51 percent that counts pragmatically. But no dancing in the streets when we win! Victory is merely a defensive tactic.

3. Push democratization unceasingly.
The most popular demand on the states everywhere is "more"— more education, more health, more guaranteed lifetime income. This is not only popular; it is immediately useful in people's lives. And it tightens the squeeze on the possibilities of the endless accumulation of capital. These demands should be pushed loudly, continuously, and everywhere. There cannot be too much.

To be sure, expanding all these "welfare state" functions always raises questions of efficiency of expenditures, of corruption, of creating overpowerful and unresponsive bureaucracies. These are all questions we should be ready to address, but they should never lessen the basic demand of more, much more.

Popular movements should not spare the left-of-center governments they have elected from these demands. Just because it is a friendlier government than an outright right government does not mean that we should pull our punches. Pressing friendly governments pushes right-wing opposition forces to the center-left. Not pushing them pushes center-left governments to the center-right. Although there may be occasional special circumstances that obviate such actions, the general rule on democratization is "More, much more."

4. Make the liberal center fulfill its theoretical preferences.
This is otherwise known as forcing the pace of liberalism. The liberal center notably seldom means what it says, or practices what it preaches. Take some obvious themes, say, liberty. The liberal center used to denounce the U.S.S.R. regularly because it didn't permit free emigration. But of course the other side of free emigration is free immigration. There's no value in being allowed to leave a country unless you can get in somewhere else. We should push for open frontiers.

The liberal center regularly calls for freer trade, freer enterprise, keeping the government out of decision making by entrepreneurs. The other side of that is that entrepreneurs who fail in the market should not be salvaged. They take the profits when they succeed; they should take the losses when they fail. It is often argued that saving the companies is saving jobs. But there are far cheaper ways of saving jobs—pay for unemployment insurance, retraining, and even starting job opportunities. But none of this need involve salvaging the debts of the failing entrepreneur.

The liberal center regularly insists that monopoly is a bad thing. But the other side of that is abolishing or grossly limiting patents. The other side of that is not involving the government in protecting industries against foreign competition. Will this hurt the working classes in the core zones? Well, not if money and energy is spent on trying to achieve greater convergence of world wage rates.

The details of the proposition are complex and need to be discussed. The point, however, is not to let the liberal center get away with its rhetoric and with reaping the rewards of that, while not paying the costs of its proposals. Furthermore, the true political mode of neutralizing centrist opinion is to appeal to its ideals, not its interests, and calling the claims on the rhetoric is a way of appealing to the ideals rather than the interests of the centrist elements.

Finally, we should always bear in mind that a good deal of the benefits of democratization are not available to the poorest strata, or not available to the same degree, because of the difficulties they have in navigating the bureaucratic hurdles. Here I return to the thirty-year-old proposition of Richard Cloward and Frances Fox Piven that one should "explode the rolls," that is, mobilize in the poorest communities so that they take full advantage of their legal rights.[5]

5. Make antiracism the defining measure of democracy.
Democracy is about treating all people equally—in terms of power, in terms of distribution, in terms of opportunity for personal fulfillment. Racism is the primary mode of distinguishing between those who have rights (or more rights) and the others, who have no rights or less rights. Racism both defines the groups and simultaneously offers a specious justification for the practice. Racism is not a secondary issue, either on a national or a world scale. It is the mode by which the liberal center's promise of universalistic criteria is systematically, deliberately, and constantly undermined.

Racism is pervasive throughout the existing world-system. No corner of the globe is without it, and without it as a central feature of local, national, and world politics. In her speech to the Mexican National Assembly on March 29, Commandant Esther of the EZLN said: "The Whites [*ladinos*] and the rich people make fun of us indigenous women for our clothing, for our speech, for our language, for our way of praying and healing, and for our color, which is the color of the earth that we work."[6]

She went on to plead in favor of the law that would guarantee autonomy to the indigenous peoples, saying: "When the rights and the culture of the indigenous peoples are recognized, . . . the law will begin to bring together its hour and the hour of the indigenous peoples. . . . And if today we are indigenous women, tomorrow we will be the others, men and women, who are dead, persecuted, or imprisoned because of their difference."

6. Move toward decommodification.

The crucial thing wrong with the capitalist system is not private ownership, which is simply a means, but commodification, which is the essential element in the accumulation of capital. Even today, the capitalist world-system is not entirely commodified, although there are efforts to make it so. But we could in fact move in the other direction. Instead of turning universities and hospitals (whether state-owned or private) into profit-making institutions, we should be thinking of how we can transform steel factories into nonprofit institutions, that is, self-sustaining structures that pay dividends to no one. This is the face of a more hopeful future, and in fact could start now.

7. Remember always that we are living in the era of transition from our existing world-system to something different.

This means several things. We should not be taken in by the rhetoric of globalization or the implication of TINA (there is no alternative). Not only do alternatives exist, but the only alternative that doesn't exist is continuing with our present structures.

There will be immense struggle over the successor system, which will continue for twenty, thirty, fifty years, and whose outcome is intrinsically uncertain. History is on no one's side. It depends on what we do. On the other hand, this offers a great opportunity for creative action. During the normal life of a historical system, even great efforts at transformation (so-called revolutions) have limited consequences since the system creates great pressures to return it to its equilibrium. But in the chaotic ambiance of a structural transition, fluctuations become wild, and even small pushes can have great consequences in favoring one branch or the other of the bifurcation. If ever agency operates, this is the moment.

The key problem is not organization, however important that be. The key problem is lucidity. The forces who wish to change the system so that nothing changes, so that we have a different system that is equally or more hierarchical and polarizing, have money, energy, and intelligence at their disposal. They will dress up the fake changes in attractive clothing. And only careful analysis will keep us from falling into their many traps.

They will use slogans we cannot disagree with—say, human rights. But they will give it content which includes a few elements that are highly desirable with many others that perpetuate the "civilizing mission" of the powerful and privileged over the noncivilized others. We must carefully dissect their proposals and call their bluffs. If an international judicial procedure against genocide is desirable, then it is only desirable if it is applicable to everyone, not merely the weak. If nuclear armaments, or biological warfare, is dangerous, even barbaric, then there are no safe possessors of such weapons.

In the inherent uncertainty of the world, at its moments of historic transformation, the only plausible strategy for the world left is one of intelligent, militant pursuit of its basic objective—the achievement of a relatively democratic, relatively egalitarian world. Such a world is possible. It is by no means certain that it will come into being. But then it is by no means impossible.

NOTES

1. See chapter 10.
2. I argue this in detail in *After Liberalism* (New York: New Press, 1995).
3. *Languages of Class* (Cambridge, England: Cambridge University Press, 1982), 74.
4. See this analysis in greater detail in Giovanni Arrighi, Terence K. Hopkins, and Immanuel Wallerstein, *Antisystemic Movements* (London: Verso, 1989), plus the essay by the same authors, "1989: A Continuation of 1968," *Review* 15, no. 2 (Spring 1992): 221–42.
5. Frances Fox Piven and Richard A. Cloward conclude their book on public welfare thus: "In the absence of fundamental economic reforms, therefore, *we take the position that the explosion of the rolls is the true relief reform,* that it should be defended, and expanded. Even now, hundreds and thousands of impoverished families remain who are elegible for assistance but who receive no aid at all" (*Regulating the Poor: The Functions of Public Welfare* [New York, Pantheon, 1971], 348 [italics in original]).
6. <http://www.ezln.org/marcha/20010320.htm>

CHAPTER TWELVE

The Movements: What Does It Mean to Be an Antisystemic Movement Today?

I coined the term "antisystemic movement" in the 1970s in order to have a formulation that would group together what had, historically and analytically, been two distinct and in many ways rival kinds of popular movement—those that went under the name "social" and those that were "national." Social movements were conceived primarily as socialist parties and trade unions; they sought to further the class struggle within each state against the bourgeoisie or the employers. National movements were those that fought for the creation of a national state, either by combining separate political units that were considered to be part of one nation—as, for example, in Italy—or by seceding from states considered imperial and oppressive by the nationality in question—colonies in Asia or Africa, for instance.

Both types of movement emerged as significant bureaucratic structures in the second half of the nineteenth century and grew stronger over time. Both tended to accord their objectives priority over any other kind of political goal—specifically, over the goals of their national or social rival. This frequently resulted in severe mutual denunciations. The two types seldom cooperated politically and, if they did so, tended to see such cooperation as a temporary tactic, not a basic alliance. Nonetheless, the history of these movements between 1850 and 1970 reveals a series of shared features.

Most socialist and nationalist movements repeatedly proclaimed themselves to be "revolutionary," that is, to stand for fundamental transformations in social relations. It is true that both types usually had a wing, sometimes located in a separate organization, that argued for a more gradualist approach and therefore eschewed revolutionary rhetoric. But generally speaking, initially—and often for many decades—those in power regarded all these movements, even the milder versions, as threats to their stability, or even to the very survival of their political structures.

Second, at the outset, both variants were politically quite weak and had to fight an uphill battle merely to exist. They were repressed or outlawed by their governments, their leaders were arrested, and their members often subjected to systematic violence by the state or by private forces. Many early versions of these movements were totally destroyed.

Third, over the last three decades of the nineteenth century both types of movement went through a parallel series of great debates over strategy that ranged those whose perspectives were "state-oriented" against those who saw the state as an intrinsic enemy and pushed instead for an emphasis on individual transformation. For the social movements, this was the debate between the Marxists and the anarchists; for the national movements, that between political and cultural nationalists.

What happened historically in these debates—and this is the fourth similarity—was that those holding the "state-oriented" position won out. The decisive argument in each case was that the immediate source of real power was located in the state apparatus and that any attempt to ignore its political centrality was doomed to failure, since the state would successfully suppress any thrust toward anarchism or cultural nationalism. In the late nineteenth century, these groups enunciated a so-called two-step strategy: first gain power within the state structure; then transform the world. This was as true for the social as for the national movements.

The fifth common feature is less obvious, but no less real. Socialist movements often included nationalist rhetoric in their arguments, and nationalist discourse often had a social component. The result was a greater blurring of the two positions than their proponents ever acknowledged. It has frequently been remarked that socialist movements in Europe often functioned more effectively as a force for national integration than either conservatives or the state itself; while the Communist parties that came to power in China, Vietnam, and Cuba were clearly serving as movements of national liberation. There were two reasons for this. First, the process of mobilization forced both groups to try to draw increasingly broad sectors of the population into their camps, and widening the scope of their rhetoric was helpful in this regard. But secondly, the leaders of both movements often recognized subconsciously that they had a shared enemy in the existing system—and that they therefore had more in common with each other than their public pronouncements allowed.

The processes of popular mobilization deployed by the two kinds of movement were basically quite similar. In most countries, both types started out as small groups, often composed of a handful of intellectuals plus a few militants drawn from other strata. Those that succeeded did so because they were able, by dint of long campaigns of education and organization, to secure popular bases in concentric circles of militants, sympathizers, and passive supporters. When the outer circle of supporters grew large enough for the militants to operate, in Mao Zedong's phrase, like fish swimming in water, the movements became serious contenders for political power. We should, of course, note too that groups calling themselves "social democratic" tended to be strong primarily in states located in the core zones of the world-economy, whereas those that described themselves as movements of national liberation generally flourished in the semiperipheral and peripheral zones. The latter was largely true of Communist parties as well. The reason seems obvious. Those in weaker zones saw that the struggle for equality hinged on their ability to wrest control of the state structures from imperial powers, whether these exercised direct or indirect rule. Those in the core zones were already in strong states. To make progress in their struggle for equality, they needed to wrest power from their own dominant strata. But precisely because these states were strong and wealthy, insurrection was an implausible tactic, and these parties used the electoral route.

The seventh common feature is that both these movements struggled with the tension between "revolution" and "reform" as prime modes of transformation. Endless discourse has revolved around this debate in both movements—but for both, in the end, it turned out to be based on a misreading of reality. Revolutionaries were not in practice very revolutionary, and reformists not always reformist. Certainly, the difference between the two approaches became more and more unclear as the movements pursued their political trajectories. Revolutionaries had to make many concessions in order to survive. Reformists learned that hypothetical legal paths to change were often firmly blocked in practice and that it required force, or at least the threat of force, to break through the barriers. So-called revolutionary movements usually came to power as a consequence of the wartime destruction of the existing authorities rather than through their own insurrectionary capacities. As the Bolsheviks were reported to have said in Russia, in 1917, "Power was lying about in the streets." Once installed, the movements sought to stay in power, regardless of how they had got there; this often required sacrificing militancy, as well as solidarity with their counterparts in other countries. The popular support for these movements was initially just as great whether they won by the bullet or by the ballot—the same dancing in the streets greeted their accession to power after a long period of struggle.

Finally, both movements had the problem of implementing the two-step strategy. Once stage one was completed, and they had come to power, their followers expected them to fulfill the promise of stage two: transforming the world. What they discovered, if they did not know it before, was that state power was more limited than they had thought. Each state was constrained by being part of an interstate system in which no one nation's sovereignty was absolute. The longer they stayed in office, the more they seemed to postpone the realization of their promises; the cadres of a militant mobilizing movement became the functionaries of a party in power. Their social positions were transformed and so, inevitably, were their individual psychologies. What was known in the Soviet Union as the *Nomenklatura* seemed to emerge in some form in every state in which a movement took control—that is, a privileged caste of higher officials with more power and more real wealth than the rest of the population. At the same time, the ordinary workers were enjoined to toil even harder and sacrifice ever more in the name of national development. The militant, syndicalist tactics that had been the daily bread of the social movement became "counterrevolutionary," highly discouraged and usually repressed, once it was in office.

Analysis of the world situation in the 1960s reveals these two kinds of movements looking more alike than ever. In most countries they had completed stage one of the two-step strategy, having come to power practically everywhere. Communist parties ruled over a third of the world, from the Elbe to the Yalu; national liberation movements were in power in Asia and Africa, populist movements in Latin America, and social democratic movements, or their cousins, in most of the pan-European world, at least on an alternating basis. They had not, however, transformed the world.

It was the combination of these factors that underlay a principal feature of the world revolution of 1968. The revolutionaries had different local demands but shared two fundamental arguments almost everywhere. First of all, they opposed both the hegemony of the United States *and* the collusion in this hegemony by the Soviet Union. Second, they condemned the Old Left as being "not part of the solution but part of the problem." This second common feature arose out of the massive disillusionment of the popular supporters of the traditional antisystemic movements with the movements' actual performance in power. The countries in which they operated did see a certain number of reforms—usually there was an increase in educational and health facilities and guarantees of employment. But considerable inequalities remained. Alienating wage labor had not disappeared; on the contrary, it had increased as a percentage of work activity. There was little or no expansion of real democratic participation, either at the governmental level or in the workplace; often it was the reverse. On the international scale, these countries tended to play a very similar role in the world-system to that which they had played before. Thus, Cuba had been a sugar-exporting economy before the revolution and remained one after it, at least until the demise of the Soviet Union. In short, not enough had changed. The grievances might have altered slightly but they were as real and, generally, as extensive. The populations of these countries were adjured by the movements in power to be patient, for history was on their side. But their patience had worn thin.

The conclusion that the world's populations drew from the performance of the classical antisystemic movements in power was negative. They ceased to believe that these parties would bring about a glorious future or a more egalitarian world and no longer gave them their legitimation; and having lost confidence in the movements, they also withdrew their faith in the state as a mechanism of transformation. This did not mean that large sections of the population would no longer vote for such parties in elections; but it had become a defensive vote, for lesser evils, not an affirmation of ideology or expectations.

Since 1968 there has nonetheless been a lingering search for a better kind of antisystemic movement—one that would actually lead to a more democratic, egalitarian world. There have been four different sorts of attempt at this, some of which still continue. The first was the efflorescence of the multiple Maoisms. From the 1960s until around the mid-1970s there emerged a large number of different, competing movements, usually small but sometimes impressively large, claiming to be Maoist, by which they meant that they were somehow inspired by the example of the Cultural Revolution in China. Essentially, they argued that the Old Left had failed because it was not preaching the pure doctrine of revolution, which they now proposed. But these movements all fizzled out, for two reasons. First, they quarrelled bitterly among themselves as to what the pure doctrine was, and therefore rapidly became tiny, insulated sectarian groups, or if they were very large, as in India, they evolved into newer versions of the Old Left movements. Second, and more fundamentally, with the death of Mao Zedong Maoism disintegrated in China, and the fount of their inspiration disappeared. Today, no such movements of any significance exist.

A second, more lasting variety of claimant to antisystemic status was the new social movements—the Greens and other environmentalists, feminists, the campaigns of racial or ethnic "minorities," such as the Blacks in the United States or the Beurs in France. These movements claimed a long history, but in fact they either became prominent for the first time in the 1970s or else reemerged then, in renewed and more militant form. They were also stronger in the pan-European world than in other parts of the world-system. Their common features were, first, their vigorous rejection of the Old Left's two-step strategy, its internal hierarchies and its priorities—the idea that the needs of women, "minorities," and the environment were secondary and should be addressed "after the revolution." And second, they were deeply suspicious of the state and of state-oriented action.

By the 1980s, all these new movements had become divided internally between what the German Greens called the *Fundis* and the *Realos*. This turned out to be a replay of the "revolutionary versus reformist" debates of the beginning of the twentieth century. The outcome was that the *Fundis* lost out in every case, and more or less disappeared. The victorious *Realos* increasingly took on the appearance of a species of social democratic party, not too different from the classic variety, although with more rhetoric about ecology, sexism, and racism, or all three. Today, these movements continue to be significant in certain countries, but they seem little more antisystemic than those of the Old Left—especially since the one lesson the Old Left movements drew from 1968 was that they, too, needed to incorporate concerns about ecology, gender, sexual choice, and racism into their programmatic statements.

The third type of claimant to antisystemic status has been the human-rights organizations. Of course some, like Amnesty International, existed prior to 1968, but in general these became a major political force only in the 1980s, aided by President Carter's adoption of human-rights terminology in dealing with

Central America, and the signing of the 1975 Helsinki Accords regarding the Communist states of eastern and central Europe. Both gave Establishment legitimacy to the numerous organizations that were now addressing civil rights. In the 1990s, the media focus on ethnic cleansing, notably in Rwanda and the Balkans, led to considerable public discussion of these issues.

The human-rights organizations claimed to speak in the name of "civil society." The term itself indicates the strategy: civil society is by definition *not* the state. The concept draws upon a nineteenth-century distinction between *le pays légal* and *le pays réel*—between those in power and those who represent popular sentiment—which leads to the question: How can civil society close the gap between itself and the state? How can it come to control the state, or make the state reflect its values? The distinction seems to assume that the state is currently controlled by small privileged groups, whereas "civil society" consists of the enlightened population at large.

These organizations have had an impact in getting some states—perhaps all—to inflect their policies in the direction of human-rights concerns; but in the process they have come to be more like the adjuncts of states than their opponents and, on the whole, scarcely seem very antisystemic. They have become NGOs, located largely in core zones yet seeking to implement their policies in the periphery, where they have often been regarded as the agents of their home state rather than its critics. In any case, these organizations have seldom mobilized mass support, counting rather on their ability to utilize the power and position of their elite militants in the core.

The fourth and most recent claimant to antisystemic status has been the so-called antiglobalization movements—a designation applied not so much by these movements themselves as by their opponents. The use of the term by the media scarcely predates its reporting of the protests at the Seattle World Trade Organization (WTO) meetings in 1999. "Globalization" as the rhetoric of neoliberal advocates of free trade in goods and capital had of course become a strong force during the 1990s. Its media focus was the Davos World Economic Forum, and its institutional implementation was brought about via the Washington Consensus, the policies of the IMF (International Monetary Fund), and the strengthening of the WTO. Seattle was intended as a key moment in expanding the role of the WTO, and the significant protests, which actually disrupted its proceedings, took many by surprise. The demonstrators included a large North American contingent, drawn from the Old Left, trade unions, New Left movements, and anarchist groups. Indeed, the very fact that the AFL-CIO was ready to be on the same side as environmentalist groups in so militant an action was something new, especially for the United States.

Following Seattle, the continuing series of demonstrations around the world against intergovernmental meetings inspired by the neoliberal agenda led in turn to the construction of the World Social Forum, whose initial meetings have been held in Porto Alegre; the second, in 2002, drew over 50,000 delegates from over a thousand organizations. Since then, there have been a number of regional meetings in preparation for the 2003 WSF in Porto Alegre, which had almost 100,000 participants.

The characteristics of this new claimant for the role of anti-systemic movement are rather different from those of earlier claimants. First of all, notably, the WSF seeks to bring together all the previous types—Old Left, new movements, human-rights bodies, and others not easily falling into these categories—and includes groups organized in a strictly local, regional, national, and transnational fashion. The basis of participation is a common objective, struggle against the social ills consequent on neoliberalism, and a common respect for each other's immediate priorities. Importantly, the WSF seeks to bring together movements from the North and the South within a single framework. The only slogan as yet is "Another world is possible." Even more strange, the WSF seeks to do this without creating an overall superstructure. At the moment it has only an international coordinating committee, some hundred-strong, representing a variety of movements and geographic locations.

Though there has been some grumbling from Old Left movements that the WSF is a reformist façade, thus far the complaints have been quite minimal. The grumblers question; they do not yet denounce. It is, of course, widely recognized that this degree of success has been based on a negative, on the rejection of neoliberalism as ideology and as institutional practice. Many have argued that it is essential for the WSF to move toward advocating a clearer, more positive program. Whether it can do so and still maintain the level of unity and absence of an overall (inevitably hierarchical) structure is the big question of the next decade.

If, as I have argued elsewhere, the modern world-system is in structural crisis and we have entered an "age of transition"—a period of bifurcation and chaos—then it is clear that the issues confronting antisystemic movements pose themselves in a very different fashion than those of the nineteenth and most of the twentieth centuries. The two-step, state-oriented strategy has become irrelevant, which explains the discomfort of most existing descendants of erstwhile antisystemic organizations in putting forward either long-term or immediate sets of political objectives. Those few who try meet with skepticism from their hoped-for followers or, worse, with indifference.

Such a period of transition has two characteristics that dominate the very idea of an antisystemic strategy. The first is that those in power will no longer be trying to preserve the existing system (doomed as it is to self-destruction); rather, they will try to ensure that the transition leads to the construction of a new system that will replicate the worst features of the existing one—its hierarchy, privilege, and inequalities. They may not yet be using language that reflects the demise of existing structures, but they are implementing a strategy based on such assumptions. Of course, their camp is not united, as is demonstrated by the conflict between the so-called center-right traditionalists and the ultraright, militarist hawks. But they are working hard to build backing for changes that will not be changes, a new system as bad as—or worse than—the present one. The second fundamental characteristic is that a period of systemic transition is one of deep uncertainty, in which it is impossible to know what the outcome will be. History is on no one's side. Each of us can affect the future, but we do not and cannot know how others will act to affect it, too. The basic framework of the WSF reflects this dilemma, and underlines it.

A strategy for the period of transition ought therefore to include four components—all of them easier said than done. The first is a process of constant, open debate about the transition and the outcome we hope for. This has never been easy, and the historic antisystemic movements were never very good at it. But the atmosphere is more favorable today than it has ever been, and the task remains urgent and indispensable—underlining the role of intellectuals in this conjuncture. The structure of the WSF has lent itself to encouraging this debate; we shall see if it is able to maintain this openness.

The second component should be self-evident: an antisystemic movement cannot neglect short-term defensive action, including electoral action. The world's populations live in the present, and their immediate needs have to be addressed. Any movement that neglects them is bound to lose the widespread passive support that is essential for its long-term success. But the motive and justification for defensive action should not be that of remedying a failing system but rather of preventing its negative effects from getting worse in the short run. These two motives are quite different psychologically and politically.

The third component has to be the establishment of interim, middle-range goals that seem to move in the right direction. I would suggest that one of the most useful—substantively, politically, psychologically—is the attempt to move toward selective, but ever-widening, decommodification. We are subject today to a barrage of neoliberal attempts to commodify what was previously seldom or never appropriated for private sale—the human body, water, hospitals. We must not only oppose this but move in the other direction. Industries, especially failing industries, should be decommodified. This does not mean they should be "nationalized"—for the most part, simply another version of commodification. It means we should create structures, operating in the market, whose objective is performance and survival rather than profit. This can be done, as we know, from the history of universities or hospitals—not all, but the best. Why is such a logic impossible for steel factories threatened with delocalization?

Finally, we need to develop the substantive meaning of our long-term emphases, which I take to be a world that is relatively democratic and relatively egalitarian. I say "relatively" because that is realistic. There will always be gaps—but there is no reason why they should be wide, encrusted, or hereditary. Is this what used to be called socialism, or even communism? Perhaps, but perhaps not. That brings us back to the issue of debate. We need to stop assuming what the better (not the perfect) society will be like. We need to discuss it, outline it, experiment with alternative structures to realize it; and we need to do this at the same time as we carry out the first three parts of our program for a chaotic world in systemic transition. And if this program is insufficient, and it probably is, then this very insufficiency ought to be part of the debate which is point one of the program.

CHAPTER THIRTEEN

Geopolitical Cleavages of the Twenty-First Century: What Future for the World?

I n this first decade of the twenty-first century, and probably for several decades to come, the world is beset by three quite different geopolitical cleavages, which interact with each other but have separate dynamics. Most analysts of the contemporary world situation err precisely by failing to discern the distinctiveness of the three cleavages, sometimes seeming to argue that only one of these cleavages exists or at least that only one really matters. These three cleavages are: (1) the struggle among the so-called Triad—the United States, the European Union, and Japan—in their search to be the primary locus of capital accumulation in the coming decades; (2) the struggle between North and South, or between core zones and other zones of the world-economy, given the continuing polarization—economic, social, and demographic—of the world-system; (3) the struggle between the spirit of Davos and the spirit of Porto Alegre about the kind of world-system we collectively intend to build.

The first two conflicts are locatable geographically, and involve interstate relations per se, although not exclusively. The third conflict is *not* an interstate conflict, but between two groups/movements/strata, each located across the world. In order to evaluate the question "What future for the world?" one has to take each of the three conflicts and spell out its processes and likely developments over the next twenty-five to fifty years, and then see how they interact with other.

THE TRIADIC CLEAVAGE

The concept of the Triad first became popular in the 1970s.[1] It had its first institutional expression in the Trilateral Commission.[2] The commission itself came into existence as a consequence of two economic realities: the improved economic performance of western Europe and Japan, allowing them to "catch up" to the United States during the 1960s; and the economic difficulties in the world-economy of the 1970s, signaled by but not caused by the radical rise in oil prices as a result of OPEC decisions. The first new economic reality meant that western Europe and Japan could no longer be treated so cavalierly by the United States, since they were no longer in any significant sense dependent economically on decisions of the U.S. government. The second economic reality meant that there was a reduction in profit rates worldwide, and that there was therefore now acute competition among the three members of the Triad, each seeking to minimize its losses (inevitably at the expense of the others).[3]

The Trilateral Commission was a political attempt to reduce the emerging tensions between the three partners of the Triad. It was at best partially successful.[4] The period 1940/45 to 1967/73, which has been described as the *"trente glorieuses,"* was a Kondratieff A-period. It was a period of overall expansion of the world-economy, indeed the most remarkable such expansion in the history of the capitalist world-economy, and exemplified the motto "A rising tide raises all ships." But the thirty years since then have been a Kondratieff B-period, one in which profits from productive activities have been lower than in the preceding A period, leading to relocation of industries, a shift to speculative activities as a source of profit, increased unemployment worldwide, and a sharp acceleration of economic polarization both globally and within states.

In this B-period, the three major loci of accumulation expressed their competition with each other by an effort to "export unemployment" to each other in order to maximize the maintenance and increase of national wealth.[5] It was a situation in which all three could not do well simultaneously. A crude summary of the situation is that Europe did best relatively in the 1970s, Japan in the 1980s, and the United States in the 1990s. None of them saw a significant drop in their standard of living (something that did happen in other parts of the world-economy), but the differences between the members of the Triad were quite important in each decade. The media seemed to think that in the 1970s the oil states plus Germany were unbeatable. In the 1980s Japan was acclaimed as world champion, to be replaced in the 1990s by the United States. This was essentially media hype, even though many policy-makers believed the hype and adjusted their policies in the light of this hype.

The fact is that all three loci have been for some time approximately equal in fundamental strength. They all have the technical competence (so-called human capital) and the financial underpinnings (essentially accumulated wealth) to engage in productive activity in those arenas which at the moment are the most likely to produce high levels of profits. They also all have commercial networks across the world to ensure their ability to purchase and to sell on the world market. They are all seeking to secure advantages by promoting appropriate research and development activities, and each has the scientific community with which to do this successfully. I don't mean to suggest that their resources are absolutely identical, but I do mean to suggest that any differences that are to be found are neither determinative nor impervious to being overcome in relatively short order by the countries of the Triad that are momentarily behind.

On the assumption that this long Kondratieff B-period will come to an end (even if there may still occur a further dramatic drop in the economic arena), what will then determine which of these three arenas will come out ahead in the struggle to be the dominant locus of accumulation in the next thirty years? I do not think that we will find the answer in that elusive category, productivity, so favored by the pundits. Advantage in productivity (even if it is measured accurately, which is very difficult) is too often a passing phenomenon. Nor do I think the answer is to be found in entrepreneurial culture, since I believe that, for capitalists, the drive to accumulate has marvelous ways of overcoming cultural obstacles. And, finally, I do not believe it has much to do with the strength of trade unions. For one thing, I think the differences between the three loci in this regard are exaggerated. And for a second thing, I do not think that trade-union strength primarily accounts for differences in the cost of personnel in productive activities.

What then are the differences that count in the Triadic competition? It seems to me that there are two crucial ones: first, the priorities of the states concerning research and development, and therefore investments in innovations; and second, the ability of the upper strata (broadly defined) to command access to consumable wealth. In these two arenas, there are indeed striking differences between the United States on the one hand and the European Union and Japan on the other hand. These differences are not to be measured by annual variations on the many economic indices that are produced for us. They constitute underlying, medium-term, politico-cultural realities that constrain what goes on in the sphere of production and finance.

The United States thinks of itself as the sole superpower of the world-system in the twenty-first century. This self-image is based primarily on its overwhelming military strength, which far exceeds that of any other country or even of many other countries combined. That this self-image masks what I believe is the constantly declining real political power of the United States in the world-system is not the issue here.[6] What the United States—and especially what the elites who decide policy in the United States—believe about the United States explains, indeed determines, the priorities assigned by its government in the economic arena. And, of course, despite the official line to the contrary, governments have a good deal to say about what is emphasized in terms of economic development, directly by their power as consumers and indirectly by their taxation and regulation policies.

A superpower whose only important claim to superiority in the world arena is military must (and will) emphasize continuing investment in military hardware. From the point of view of long-term economic development, military hardware is a side path. To be sure, there are always spillover possibilities of applying what one has learned or invented in this arena to other arenas. But however real the side benefits, they are less than the benefits of using the same money to create more long-term productive enterprises.

One of the ways in which the United States seeks to maintain its military superiority is to discourage all others from engaging in similar activities, especially in terms of cutting-edge technology. This applies not least of all to western Europe and Japan. To be sure, neither western Europe nor Japan shows much interest in competing seriously with the United States in this arena. Or, rather, they are willing to devote a much smaller percentage of their national budgets to the military arena, now and in the decades to come. The combination of U.S. pressure and the inclinations of western Europe and Japan mean that in fact the latter are not competitive militarily with the United States, nor are they about to become so. But the other side of that medallion is that they do intend to compete vigorously in all kinds of strictly economic innovations. The fact that nonmilitary development is given a far higher priority by western Europe and Japan is likely to pay off handsomely over the next twenty to thirty years.

This advantage of western Europe and Japan over the United States is compounded by the issue of costs of production. Usually, what is compared when we talk of the cost of labor is how much is paid to ordinary workers (whether skilled or unskilled), adding that which is paid directly in wages to that which is paid indirectly via so-called social wages. If one adds to this amount what is paid via government redistribution (in education, health care, and lifetime income guarantees), the differences between the members of the Triad are not very great, as anyone who travels to these countries and observes the real standard of living of these workers can see quite clearly.

But there is a second group who receive payments for their services—the upper strata and the cadres, both those who work directly for various productive enterprises and those who operate in the nonprofit sector or are so-called free professionals. Whatever name we give to the sums of money these persons receive, from the point of view of investors in an enterprise, they represent wages paid out of the returns from sales and thereby reduce the level of profits. Here the differences are enormous, and are largely explicable by the cultural difference between an erstwhile hegemonic power and contenders for future hegemonic power. In the United States, the real pay of CEOs, the real pay of the cadres, and the real income of those in the nonprofit sector or who are free professionals is simply much, much higher than what is realized in western Europe or Japan. This is not only because individually the returns are higher but also because the percentage of such persons in the overall workforce is much larger.

The recent well-publicized scandals in U.S. corporate enterprises are but the tip of a very large iceberg, whose effects over time cannot but be felt in a more serious decline in the profit rates of U.S.-based enterprises than in that of their long-term competitors. The only way that the United States can reduce this gap is by reducing the outflow to the top 10 to 20 percent of the population or increase the outflow in western Europe and Japan. It seems politically virtually impossible in the short run to reduce seriously the outflow within the United States. A government that moved in this direction would promptly lose the support of essential supporters.

So, the real alternative for the United States is to try to increase outflow in western Europe and Japan. When the United States government preaches to Japan or to Germany about the need to "reform" their outmoded governmental policies, what is being urged is that these countries emulate the United States in the distribution of wages to the upper strata, and thus eliminate their long-term advantage in this respect. This, more than mysterious cultural variables, best explains why these countries have been so resistant to this advice. Unlike countries in the South (even relatively strong countries like Brazil), western Europe and Japan cannot be coerced by IMF action to "reform" their economic structures. For one thing, even when their governments raise the debt level to deal with recessionary problems, their debts are largely internal and thus not exposed to international pressure—as, for example, that of Argentina.[7] The governments of western Europe and Japan, unlike that of the

United States, reduce the pain of unemployment by more generous welfare payments and by allowing deflation to pursue its course.[8]

We do not have today an integrated world-economy. We have essentially a Triadic world-economy, with three main zones.[9] And this Triadic division will probably grow stronger in the coming decades.[10] What we have therefore is a geopolitical Triadic cleavage in which the United States is likely to do least well over the next twenty to thirty years. American military clout will be less and less useful in reversing this underlying economic shift. In such a situation, the real competition will be between western Europe and Japan, and each will seek to have the United States on its side. I continue to believe that a U.S.-Japan economic alliance is more probable than a U.S.-Europe alliance.[11] But in either case, the U.S. is not likely to be the leading partner, hard as it may be for Americans (and perhaps others) to envisage such a scenario today.

THE NORTH-SOUTH CLEAVAGE

How the Triadic conflict unfolds will depend very much on what form the other two geopolitical cleavages take. In the North-South conflict, the three members of the Triad constitute the North. They therefore share geopolitical interests in this conflict, but of course they have followed somewhat different policies with regard to them, and have different "special" relationships with various parts of the South. In North-South conflicts, at the present time the United States takes the lead as protagonist of the North, by virtue both of its military strength and of its high degree of influence in the IMF and the World Bank.

As the North is not always a unified bloc, so neither is the South. The South is politically divided in two ways. There are regimes in power in the South that are essentially client regimes of the North, virtually paid agents of the North, and others that are not. But regardless of the particular regimes, there are also objective differences between relatively strong semiperipheral zones and what is sometimes referred to as the Fourth World (that is, the weakest, poorest, smallest states). Indeed, in the South there are some very large states that have actual or potential real geopolitical power—Russia, China, India, Brazil, Indonesia, Korea, and the list could continue.

Nonetheless, the North-South cleavage is real and is part of the fundamental structure of the capitalist world-economy. Economically, there is a continuing polarization, which although it occasionally slows down, on the whole expands geometrically. The North maintains this structure by its monopolization of advanced productive processes, its control of world financial institutions, its dominance of world scholarship and world media, and, most important, by its military strength. If the conflicts among the Triad usually seem restrained, that is only because of the strengths of each vis-à-vis the others. North-South conflicts are seldom similarly restrained. The North uses an iron fist, if once in a while enclosed in a velvet glove.

How does the South deal with this reality—an increasing socio-economic gap combined with the iron fist of the North? In the period from 1945 to 1970, the major tactic of the South was developmentalism. The theory that informed the actions of the movements and regimes located in the South was that "national development" was possible and was essentially a function of two steps: (1) establishing a national regime dedicated to national development; (2) then employing the correct policies.

To be sure, there was considerable disagreement about how to implement either step. This debate went on very largely within the framework of what we call the national liberation movements.

But the debate in the end was largely irrelevant. In the first place, there existed a geocultural consensus that development was possible, not only in the South but in the North. There were two versions of the story—a liberal version peddled largely by the United States and Europe and a so-called socialist version peddled primarily by the Soviet Union. But both versions insisted that a "modernizing" government (the Soviet Union called it a "socialist" government) could establish the necessary social framework to permit so-called economic development, with the assistance of appropriate governmental actions and external aid. Both versions offered the reversal of polarization in the world-system as the eventual outcome of such "developmentalist" programs. Both versions failed globally, and country by country they seemed to work at best in a few countries. The reason why a few countries developed when most did not had little to do with the particular policies followed by particular states. Rather, developmentalist policies aided a few countries, but not most, for two reasons. Only a small minority of states can ever at any given time improve their relative position in the rankings of the capitalist world-economy, given the ways in which it functions. Those states which succeeded (such as Korea or Taiwan) did so more in function of their geopolitical location (in terms of Cold War posturings) than because of any other single factor.

The period after 1970 was a period of disillusionment with "developmentalism"—both on the part of the core zones, which began to preach neoliberalism instead, and on the part of the South, which began to seek alternative paths to reducing the growing polarization. Basically, the South evolved three strategies in the post-1970 period as mechanisms to struggle with the North: (1) the assertion of radical alterity, using rhetoric that was foreign to the modern world-system; (2) direct confrontation, using tools and rhetoric deriving from the existing world-system; (3) population transfer.

Radical alterity meant the rejection of the basic values of the West in the modern world-system, that is, essentially those of the Enlightenment with its theory of inevitable progress based on the spread of secularism and education. To be sure, there had always been persons throughout the world who rejected these values. But such persons and groups had for a long time been fighting essentially rear-guard actions—dragging their feet, resisting the pressures—and were largely unsuccessful. What was new and particularly important in the post-1970 era was the emergence of what might be called "modernist" movements of radical alterity. Sometimes these are called fundamentalist or integrist movements, especially when they claim to incarnate religious faiths. But we should notice several things about such movements.

First, their original and primary target was less the "West" in general and more the historic antisystemic movements in their own countries, which had espoused the developmentalist ideal. The basic argument put forward by the movements of radical alterity was that the national liberation movements had failed to deliver on their promises of transforming the social world and overcoming the polarization of the world-system. The movements of radical alterity ascribed this failure to the fact that the national liberation movements, despite their claim to being antisystemic, were in fact preaching the values of the dominant geoculture, hence were inevitably tied to the world power structure, and were therefore incapable of delivering on their promised transformations.

Second, the movements of radical alterity offered themselves as agents of the civil society against the failed states of the South. They stepped in wherever and whenever these states were unable to provide basic assistance to the needy in their state, which was almost all the time. The movements of radical alterity offered material as well as spiritual comfort to those that were in pain, while the movements of national liberation coasted on the glories of past nationalist struggles and quite often padded the pockets of the new *Nomenklatura*.

Third, the movements of radical alterity were deeply involved in the technological advances of the modern world, utilizing—and effectively—all the modern infrastructure of communications, technology, and warfare. It has often been noted that such movements of radical alterity have been able to recruit strongly among university students in engineering and the hard sciences.

Finally, these movements of radical alterity invented a theology that was seldom traditional, if by that is meant one that was preached and practiced centuries ago. They utilized the texts to reinterpret them, to render them most able to create political structures in the modern world that could survive and thrive. But of course in order to demonstrate their unswering alterity, these movements had to assert their absolute opposition, at a theoretical and personal level, to whatever incarnated the West.

The most spectacular such movement of radical alterity was that led by Ayatollah Khomeini in Iran. It dethroned a leading ally of the North, in a wealthy, large state. It denounced the United States as the Great Satan, and the Soviet Union as Satan No. 2. It defied international law by seizing the United States embassy, and it survived. For a while it raised hysterical hackles in the United States, and the U.S. consequently encouraged the Arab world in general, and Saddam Hussein in Iraq in particular, to seek to contain, eventually to overthrow, the Iranian regime. That this movement was unable to spread far beyond its borders is primarily a function of the fact that it based its claims on a particular religious tradition which has adherents in only a few other countries.

It did, however, let us see that a movement of radical alterity can resonate deeply in the South and demonstrate great political strength. It became, in formal terms, a model for other such movements. It is not that movements like Aum Shinrikyo in Japan or Al Qaeda are consciously modeled on Khomeini's movement. It is that they are utilizing some of the same techniques of social organization and some of the same kinds of rhetoric. There are today many such movements, some strong, some minor, most in the South but many in the North as well. What they represent is a continuing (and largely unpredictable) pressure against the kind of stability on which the North relies to maintain its position of privilege. It is a force whose impact should grow greater, not less, in the next twenty-five to fifty years, given the chaotic struggles of a world-system in structural crisis. Such movements are one expression of the political chaos, and will not disappear until the transition from our existing world-system to its successor world-system is completed. In the meantime, they represent a continuing military headache for the North.

The second tool of the South, strategy of direct confrontation, is quite different from the strategy of radical alterity. One might think that confrontation is the most normal aspect of interstate relations. But in point of fact the weaker nations of the South have usually avoided confrontation with the North, precisely because they were weaker. Many of the confrontations were provoked by the North, which wished to impose something or prevent something that was being done by a state in the South. What I am speaking of now is the possibility of direct confrontations provoked by the South.

The model example is Saddam Hussein and the Iraqi occupation of Kuwait. It seems to me that the way to understand this best is neither to assume that Hussein was somehow mad or that he was simply a vicious conqueror of a neighbor. I think Hussein's calculation was Bismarckian—bold chess moves that would expose the weaknesses of the North, strengthen the South (specifically in this case the Arab world) militarily, and prepare for future shifts in the balance of world power.

When Iraq invaded Kuwait on August 2, 1990, there were, I believe, in Saddam Hussein's mind, two possibilities. The world (that is, the North plus Saudi Arabia) would not react and he would win the gambit. Or the world would react, and he would end up with a truce at the line of departure. He did not think that he would lose the war, lose power, and see Western troops occupy Iraq. Of course, as we know, it was the second outcome that occurred—a truce at the line of departure. To be sure, Iraq was saddled with inspections and injunctions to destroy weapons of mass destruction. We know that these U.N. actions were partially successful but partially unsuccessful.

We must ask why the U.S.-led forces did not march on Baghdad in 1991. There was a series of reasons that seemed to persuade the U.S. government that this would not be a wise option. (1) It would be costly, in military terms, and probably lead to considerable loss of life, which in turn would be unacceptable to the American public, and would revive the so-called Vietnam syndrome. (2) It might be impossible to install a replacement regime in power that could stabilize the situation and hold the country together. And neither Turkey nor Saudi Arabia wanted Iraq to fall apart because of the consequences each would suffer were there a Kurdish state in the north and a Shiite state in the south. (3) A prolonged war would probably be immediately destabilizing for a large number of regimes in the whole Middle East. (4) A replacement regime might only be able to survive with an interim occupation army of U.S.-led troops, which might cause significant internal U.S. problems. What all these considerations added up to is that the United States simply was not strong enough to march on Baghdad.

The analysis of the hawks that has driven U.S. world policy since September 11 and perhaps will do so for several years to come is that all these considerations were essentially invalid, and that acting on the basis of them permitted a political victory for Saddam Hussein. That is why the United States is now engaged in marching on Baghdad. We shall soon see whose predictions are most valid. Should things turn out as both Saddam Hussein and the first Bush administration expected they would, the march on Baghdad will lead to a major political defeat for the United States. It will then encourage other states in the South to follow the example of Saddam Hussein in his cautiously bold Bismarckian strategy. In any case, we may be sure that the drive to acquire nuclear weapons is fundamental to the tactics of the stronger states in the South. They know that they cannot compete with U.S. nuclear capacity. But they intend to obtain weapons that can incur enough damage so that they act as a deterrent. The U.S. attempt to contain proliferation is at the very most a delaying mechanism, and cannot succeed. It didn't work when the U.S. was far more powerful than it is today, and we may expect to see another dozen nuclear powers within the next decade.

The last element in the cupboard of strategic tools for the South is one that is not played consciously but may well be the most telling of the three. The socio-economic polarization of the world-system is matched by a demographic polarization, which has become acute only in the last fifty years. The simple fact is that the states in the North are not reproducing their populations in sufficient number to fill their employment needs and to maintain a sufficiently large working-age population to sustain the programs of economic transfers (social security and medical care primarily) to the ever-growing percentage of the population over sixty-five. The North needs immigrants, and needs them badly.

At the same time, the South is filled with persons of some training and education and with some money who are unable to find appropriate employment and income in their home countries, and are thus willing and anxious to emigrate to the North.

However, although the North needs these immigrants, they are politically unpopular among large segments of the population of the North, who believe that the immigrants threaten jobs and wage levels and engage in antisocial practices in these countries. This conflicting pressure means that the governments of the North are repeatedly ambiguous on the issue of welcoming immigrants. They blow hot and cold. From the point of view of potential immigrants, this encourages the use of illegal channels to immigrate.

The result of this situation, which will become worse in the decades to come, is that there is a large wave of South-to-North immigration, much of which is illegal. Though legal barriers exist and are constantly being strengthened, they are unable to stanch the flow. However, once the illegal immigrants arrive and become part of the ongoing social networks, there is pressure both for and against legalizing their status. What this means over time is that the North is creating a large stratum of persons resident in the country who have less than full political, economic, or social rights. How much less varies according to particular states of the North, but the stratum exists everywhere and will grow. We can expect this to be a great source of political tension internal to the North, one that will affect not only the stability of countries in the North but their ability to pursue their interests in the North-South struggle.

THE DAVOS—PORTO ALEGRE CLEAVAGE

The World Economic Forum was founded in 1971, and is commonly referred to as Davos, because it has met there every year (except 2002). It describes itself as "an independent organization committed to improving the state of the world . . . by creating partnerships between and among business, political, intellectual and other leaders of society to define, discuss and advance key issues on the global agenda." The World Social Forum has been meeting annually only since 2001, and is commonly referred to as Porto Alegre, the Brazilian city where it has held its initial meetings. It describes itself as "an open meeting place where groups and movements of civil society opposed to neo-liberalism and a world dominated by capital or by any form of imperialism, but engaged in building a planetary society centred on the human person, come together to pursue their thinking, to debate ideas democratically, in order to formulate proposals, share their experiences freely and network for effective action." Davos boasts of having as members over one thousand of foremost global companies." Porto Alegre boasts of bringing together over one thousand of "the widest range of social movements." The difference in social base is patent.

The spirit of Davos and the spirit of Porto Alegre are in direct counterposition one to the other. Davos came into existence to be a meeting ground of the powerful and would-be powerful of the world seeking to coordinate in some sense their actions and to establish a normative worldwide program, a gospel to be spread. Porto Alegre came into existence to challenge Davos—its underlying philosophy, its specific programs, its vision of the future. The slogan of Porto Alegre is "Another world is possible." Other than which? Obviously, the world envisaged and implemented by Davos.

Of course, both these structures are forums. They are public arenas hoping to be observed publicly and to persuade publicly. But Davos is also a locale where the conflicts of the Triad can be displayed, debated, and perhaps attenuated. It is a locale in which the North can pursue its objectives, hopefully with the concurrence of some political, economic, and intellectual leaders located in the South. Porto Alegre, on the other hand, has sought

to bring together movements of all kinds—transnational, regional, national, and local, but, most important, from both South
and North. It seeks to restructure the world-system. It seeks to
be generally on the side of the South in North-South issues. But
it is also deeply concerned with the internal life of the North. It
has no position on the conflicts among the Triad, and has thus far
largely ignored them.

Both the spirit of Davos and the spirit of Porto Alegre are
movements of transformation. Davos is no more for the status
quo than is Porto Alegre. They both are built on the premise that
major structural changes are possible, imminent, and desirable.
But their vision of what these should be or can be is substantially
different, even diametrically opposed. In my language, though
not always explicitly in theirs, they represent reactions to a
world-system in structural crisis, a world-system therefore undergoing chaotic bifurcation, a world-system in which there are
real political and moral choices to be made, one in which such
choices have a realistic possibility of affecting the outcome.

WHAT FUTURE FOR THE WORLD?

The cleavage between the spirit of Davos and the spirit of Porto
Alegre knows no geographical localization. It is clearly the most
fundamental cleavage of the three, because it is the one that is
concerned with the future of the world not over the next twenty-
five to fifty years but over the next five hundred years. But the actual trajectory of this cleavage is enormously constrained by, and
will be deeply affected by, the evolution of the two other cleavages in the next few decades—that among the Triad, and that of
North versus South.

Because the future is intrinsically indeterminate, the most one
can do is signal the most likely loci of acute, sudden change in the
next decade:

- It is quite possible that, as a result of the second Iraq war, nuclear weapons will be used and become banalized as a mode of warfare. If this happens, we may expect a rapid acceleration of proliferation.
- The ability of the dollar to remain the world's only real reserve currency may come to a sudden end. It is currently based on faith in greater economic stability in the United States than in other members of the Triad. It has permitted the U.S. to have a major economic advantage. But given the enormity of the U.S. debt, any collapse of this faith could result in a rapid withdrawal of non-U.S. money from U.S. investments and create in one fell swoop a tri-monetary reserve system.
- Although the euro is going strong and it is likely that the holdouts (Great Britain, Sweden, and Denmark) will soon join it, Europe has two interlocked problems that are not easily solved. It needs to create a responsible political structure of some kind, and it is being besieged by applicants. The two pressures do not necessarily go in the same direction. If Europe cannot establish a viable political structure, it will be quite weakened in the inter-Triadic struggle. Europe's interests in permitting the entry of eastern and central European states and its interests in closer relations with Russia do not necessarily go in the same direction. Failure to come to terms with Russia will also weaken Europe in the inter-Triadic struggle.
- Both Russia and China are giant powers, weaker than they could be or want to be. Both of them have the problem of remaining unified states, expanding the base of their productive enterprises, and strengthening their armed forces. If they succeed in these three areas, the geopolitics of the world will be transformed quite sud-

denly. If they fail, the chaotic consequences would reverberate across the globe.

- The drive toward Korean unification is as strong as was the drive for German unification. The two situations are not identical, and the Korean case is informed by the Koreans' observations of what happened in Germany. But new generations are arriving in power, and Korean unification is definitely on the agenda, in one form or another. A reunited Korea would be a powerful actor in East Asia, and might make more possible an East Asian trinity of China-Korea-Japan, if only because the presence of Korea would cushion the inevitable tensions between China and Japan. A reunited Korea would reduce radically the military role of the United States in East Asia.

- Saudi Arabia and Pakistan have been in many ways pillars of the present structures of the Middle East. Each has been able historically to balance the needs of a modernizing, pro-Western elite with a very Islamist population. They have done this by maintaining an ambiguous relationship with the United States. Bin Laden's actions are clearly aimed at destroying these regimes, and bin Laden seems to have enlisted George Bush on his side by getting Bush to push the two regimes to end their ambiguities. The collapse of either regime, a fortiori of both, would have a rolling impact throughout the Islamic world from Morocco to Indonesia, from Uzbekistan to the Sudan.

- There has been a quiet rumble of rebellion throughout Latin America in the last few years—in Argentina, Ecuador, Brazil, to name only the most obvious sites. The taming of Latin America by the United States, the grand project of the 1980s and 1990s, may suddenly collapse too, in the backyard of the United States, and possibly to the rapid advantage of Europe and Japan.

- Many of these changes would strengthen the hands of the proponents of the spirit of Porto Alegre. But this movement is beset by a very loose structure and a lack of specificity concerning their positive program. It too could fall apart. But if it does not, it might find itself in a very strong position circa 2010.

That is as far as one can go in discerning the geopolitical cleavages of the twenty-first century. What future for the world? The answer is uncertain. But it is quite certain than we can all, individually and collectively, affect that future more than we think, precisely because we live in an era of transition, of chaotic bifurcations, of choice.

NOTES

1. See Kenichi Ohmae, *Triad Power: The Coming Shape of Global Competition* (New York: Free Press, 1985).
2. For early documents, see *The Trilateral Countries in the International Economy of the 1980s* (New York: Trilateral Commission, 1982).
3. On the 1970s as a period of "decelerated growth, intensified structural change, and heightened political instability," see Folker Fröbel, "The Current Development of the World-Economy: Reproduction of Labor and Accumulation of Capital on a World Scale," *Review* 5, no. 4 (Spring 1982): 507–55.
4. See my "Friends as Foes," *Foreign Policy,* no. 40 (Fall 1980): 119–31.
5. Despite all the public blather about the virtues of free trade, all three members of the Triad have been recurrently and seriously protectionistic. Stanley Fischer, deputy managing director of the IMF in the 1990s, called these protectionist policies "scandalous" ("Rich Nations Are Criticized for Enforcing Trade Barriers," *New York Times,* September 30, 2002).
6. See chapter 1.
7. "An estimated 95% of Japan's debt is domestically owned. Japan does not

need to default but can simply crank the printing presses" ("World Report—Japan," *Financial Times,* September 30, 2002, 1).

8. Reporting on the economic situation in Japan "since the bubble burst," the *Financial Times* ("Japan 2000," September 30 2002) noted that "Japan remains in profound economic shock. But from the point of view of most individuals, at least those who have not joined the increasing ranks of the unemployed, times have rarely been better."

9. Tietung Su ("Myth and Mystery of Globalization," *Review* 25, no. 4 [2002]) has made a careful study of world trade networks in 1928, 1938, 1960, and 1999. He finds that the pattern of 1999 is far closer to that of 1938 than to that of 1928 or 1960, that is, that it is more segmented despite the expansion of trade volume. "As for now, globalization, at least trade globalization, is as real as the stars we see in the night, illusions of the reality from the past, or maybe the future."

10. See John Ravenhill, "A Three Bloc World? The New East Asian Regionalism" (*International Relations of the Asia-Pacific* 2, no. 2 [2002]: 167–95) for a balanced discussion of the degree to which eastern Asia is moving toward a regional structure, more slowly than Europe, but steadily.

11. Su ("Myth and Mystery of Globalization") finds that, already in 1999, there is large "overlap" between the U.S. and Japan blocs in terms of trade relations, but little of either with the German and French blocs.

AFTERWORDS

1. The Righteous War

February 15, 2003

George Bush has led the valiant troops into battle in a righteous war against the despotic tyrant. He will not turn back, no matter what pusillanimous or venal European politicians, major religious figures around the world, retired generals, and other erstwhile friends of liberty and the United States may think or do. Never has a war been the subject of so much prior discussion and had so little backing from world public opinion. No matter! The decision for war, based on a calculus of American power, was made in the White House a long time ago.

We have to ask ourselves why. To begin with, we have to lay to rest two major theories about the motivations of the U.S. government that have been insistently put forth. The first is advanced by those who favor the war. They argue that Saddam Hussein is a vicious tyrant who presents an imminent danger to world peace, and the earlier he is confronted, the more likely he can be stopped from doing the damage he intends to do. The second theory is put forward primarily by opponents of the war. They argue that the United States is interested in controlling world oil. Iraq is a key element in the edifice. Overthrowing Hussein would put the United States in the driver's seat.

Neither thesis holds much water. Virtually everyone around the world agrees that Saddam Hussein is a vicious tyrant, but very few are persuaded that he is an imminent danger to world peace. Most people regard him as a careful player of the geopolitical game. He is accumulating so-called weapons of mass destruction, to be sure. But it is doubtful he would use them against anyone now, for fear of the reprisals. He is certainly less likely, not more likely, to use them than North Korea. He is in a tight political corner, and, were absolutely nothing done, he would probably be unable to move out of it. As for his links with Al Qaeda, the whole affair lacks credibility. He may play tactically and marginally with Al Qaeda, but not one tenth as intensively as the U.S. government did for a long time. In any case, should Al Qaeda grow stronger, he is near the top of their list for liquidation as an apostate. These charges of the U.S. government are propaganda, not explanations. The motives must be sought elsewhere.

What about the alternative view, that it's all about oil? No doubt oil is a crucial element in the operation of the world-economy. And no doubt the United States, like all the other major powers, would like to control the oil situation as much as it can. And no doubt, were Saddam Hussein to be overthrown, there might be some reshuffling of the world's oil cards. But is the game worth the candle? There are three things about oil that are important: participating in the profits of the oil industry; regulating the world price of oil (which has such a great impact on all other kinds of production); and access of supply (and potential denial of access to others). In all three matters, the United States is doing quite well right now. American oil firms have the lion's share of the world profits at the present time. The price of oil has been regulated to U.S. preferences for most of the period since

1945, via the efforts of the government of Saudi Arabia. And the United States has a fairly good hold on the strategic control of world oil supply. In each of these three domains, perhaps the U.S. position could be improved. But can this slight improvement possibly be worth the financial, economic, and political cost of the war? Precisely because Bush and Cheney have been in the oil business, they must surely be aware of how small the advantage to be gained would be. Oil can be at most a collateral benefit of an enterprise undertaken for other motives.

So why, then? We start with the reasoning of the hawks. They believe that the world position of the United States has been steadily declining since at least the Vietnam War. They believe that the basic explanation for this decline is the fact that U.S. governments have been weak and vacillating in their world policies. (They believe this is true even of the Reagan administration, although they do not dare to say this aloud.) They see a remedy, a simple remedy. The United States must assert itself forcefully, to demonstrate its iron will and its overwhelming military superiority. Once that is done, the rest of the world will recognize and accept American primacy in everything. The Europeans will fall into line. The potential nuclear powers will abandon their projects. The U.S. dollar will once again rise supreme. The Islamic fundamentalists will fade away or be crushed. And we shall enter into a new era of prosperity and high profits.

We need to understand that the hawks really believe all of this, and with a great sense of certitude and determination. That is why all the public debate worldwide about the wisdom of launching a war has been falling on deaf ears. They are deaf because they are absolutely sure that everyone else is wrong and, furthermore, that shortly everyone else will realize that they have been wrong. It is important to note one further element in the self-confidence of the hawks. They believe that a swift and relatively easy military victory is at hand—a war of weeks, not of months, and certainly not longer. They simply ignore the fact that virtually all the prominent retired generals in the United States and the United Kingdom have publicly stated their doubts on this military assessment. The hawks (almost all of them civilians) do not even bother to rebut their arguments

The full-speed-ahead, damn-the-torpedoes attitude of the Bush administration has already had four major negative effects on the world position of the United States. Anyone with the most elementary knowledge of geopolitics would know that, after 1945, the one coalition the United States had to fear was that of France, Germany, and Russia. American foreign policy has been geared to rendering this impossible. Every time there was the slightest hint of such a coalition, the United States mobilized to break away at least one of the three. This was true when de Gaulle made his early gestures to Moscow in 1945–46, and when Willy Brandt announced the *Ostpolitik*. There are all sorts of reasons why it has been quite difficult for such an alliance to come together. George Bush has overcome the obstacles and achieved the realization of this nightmare for the United States. For the first time since 1945, these three powers have lined up publicly against the U.S. on a major issue. Official American reaction to this public stand is having the effect of cementing the alliance further. If Donald Rumsfeld thinks that waving the support of Albania and Macedonia, or even Poland and Hungary, in French, German, and Russian faces sends shivers up the spines of the new trio, he must be very naive indeed.

The logical riposte to a Paris-Berlin-Moscow axis would be for the United States to enter into a geopolitical alliance with China, Korea, and Japan. The U.S. hawks are making sure that such a coalition will not be easily achieved, however. They have goaded North Korea into displaying its teeth of steel, offended South Korea by not taking its concerns seriously, made China more suspicious than before, and led Japan to think about becoming a nuclear power. Bravo!

Then there's oil. Controlling the world price of oil is the most important of the three oil issues mentioned earlier. Saudi Arabia has been the key. Saudi Arabia has done the work for the U.S. for fifty years for a simple reason: The dynasty needed the military protection of the Americans. The U.S. rush to war, its obvious ricochet effect on the Muslim world, the open disdain of the U.S. hawks for the Saudis, and the Bush administration's overwhelming support for Prime Minister Ariel Sharon have led the Saudis to wonder, out loud, whether U.S. support is not an albatross rather than a mode of sustaining them. For the first time, the faction in the royal house that favors loosening its links with the U.S. seems to be gaining the upper hand. The United States is not easily going to find a substitute for the Saudis. Remember that the Saudis have always been more important to American geopolitical interests than Israel. The United States supports Israel for internal political reasons. It has supported the Saudi regime because it has needed them. The United States can survive without Israel. Can it survive the political turmoil in the Muslim world without Saudi support?

Finally, American administrations have been valiantly trying to stop nuclear proliferation for fifty years. The Bush administration has managed in two short years to get North Korea, and now Iran, to speed up their programs, and not to be afraid to indicate this publicly. If the United States uses nuclear devices in Iraq, as it has hinted it may, it will not merely break the taboo, but it will ensure a speedy race of a dozen more countries to acquire these devices.

If the Iraq war goes splendidly for the U.S., perhaps it can recuperate a little from these four geopolitical setbacks. If the war goes badly, each negative will be immediately reinforced. I have been reading recently about the Crimean War, in which Great

Britain and France went to war against the Russian tyrant in the name of civilization, Christianity, and the struggle for liberty. A British historian wrote in 1923 of these motives: "What Englishmen condemn is almost always worthy of condemnation, if only it has happened." *The Times* of London was in 1853 one of the strongest supporters of the war. In 1859, the editors wrote their regret: "Never was so great an effort made for so worthless an object. It is with no small reluctance that we admit a gigantic effort and an infinite sacrifice to have been made in vain." When George Bush leaves office, he will be leaving the United States significantly weaker than when he assumed office. He will have turned a slow decline into a much speedier one. Will the *New York Times* write a similar editorial in 2005?

2. *"Shock and Awe"?*

April 2003

The U.S hawks promised that their preemptive strike on Iraq would inspire "shock and awe." Have they accomplished this? They think so. But whom were they supposed to shock and awe? Most immediately, the Iraqi regime and its internal supporters. The United States did win the war militarily quite rapidly, and those of us (many military figures, but also me) who had predicted that a long difficult war was the greater possibility were proven wrong. When the top Iraqi command disappeared, the military structure collapsed. The relatively quick victory does, however, be it said, undo the official U.S. justification that the Iraqi regime had posed an immediate serious military threat to its neighbors or the United States.

Does it follow that those of us who thought the war a folly were wrong on everything else? I don't think so. In chapter 1 of this book (written in mid 2002), I opened with the following sentences: "The United States in decline? Few people today would believe the assertion. The only ones who do are the U.S. hawks, who argue vociferously for policies to reverse the decline." The hawks now think they have succeeded in doing this. They are awash with inflated self-confidence. They seem to have adopted

Napoleon's motto, "L'audace, l'audace, toujours l'audace." It worked for Napoleon—for a while.

The hawks didn't even wait for the end of the fighting to begin a campaign against Syria. Syria was chosen in part because it has a foreign policy that is not considered friendly by the U.S., plays a key role in the Middle East, and is militarily virtually helpless. Not having found weapons of mass destruction in Iraq (at least to date), the U.S. government is now suggesting that they are to be found in Syria. Secretary of Defense Donald Rumsfeld has designated it a "rogue state." President Bush has some simple advice to the Syrians: They should cooperate with the United States.

The United States has moved on from Afghanistan to Iraq without accomplishing much more there than the overthrow of the previous regime and the turnover of power to a series of local warlords—in short, the U.S. has brought into being what is elsewhere often called a "failed state." Will the U.S. now do the same in Iraq, moving on from there to elsewhere? Quite possibly. And if Syria is next, what comes after Syria? Palestine and Saudi Arabia, or North Korea and Iran? No doubt fierce debates about priorities are going on right now in the inner councils of the U.S. regime. But that the U.S. will now move on to further military threats seems not to be in question. The hawks seem to be sure that they have (and ought to have) the world's future in their hands, and they have exhibited not the least sign of humility about the wisdom of their course of action. After all, how many troops does the pope have, as Stalin famously said?

Still, one should look at the priorities the hawks seem to have established. Number one seems to be reconfiguring the Middle East. This includes three key elements: eliminating regimes hostile to the United States, undermining the power (and perhaps the territorial integrity) of Saudi Arabia, and imposing a solution on the Palestinians by getting them to accept a Bantustan type of solution. This is why the hawks have immediately raised the issue of Syria as a new "threat" to the security of the United States.

While this Middle Eastern reorganization is going on, the U.S. would, I believe, prefer to freeze the situation in northeast Asia. Immediate military action is risky, and the hawks hope to use China to persuade the North Koreans not to go further in their nuclear quest. One might think of this as a temporary truce. Such a truce would allow the hawks time to deal with other matters first and North Korea later, when their hands would be freer. For they have no intention of allowing the North Korean regime to survive.

My guess is that priority number two is the home front. The hawks want to shape the U.S. government budget so that it has no room for anything but military expenditures. And they will move on all fronts to cut other expenses—by reducing federal taxes and privatizing as much of Social Security and Medicare as they can. They also want to limit the expression of opposition at home—to give themselves a freer hand to deal with the rest of the world, and to ensure their perpetual hold on power. The immediate issue is to make permanent the so-called Patriot Act, which has a clause that causes it to expire in three years. Thus far, the Patriot Act has been used primarily against persons of Arab or Moslem identity, but federal authorities can be expected steadily to expand its reach. On both these fronts, the 2004 elections will be crucial.

Europe is probably priority number three. It seems to the hawks harder to break the back of Europe than that of the Middle East or of the U.S. opposition. So they will probably wait a bit, counting on spreading enough shock and awe so as to weaken fatally the will of the Europeans. In their spare time, the hawks may ask that troops be sent to Colombia, that the United States consider a new invasion of Cuba and otherwise flex its muscles around the globe.

One must say, the U.S. hawks think big. "L'audace, l'audace, toujours l'audace." In chapter 1, I also said that the United States is "a lone superpower that lacks true power, a world leader nobody follows and few respect, and a nation drifting dangerously amidst a global chaos it cannot control." I reaffirm that assessment today, specifically in the light of the U.S. military conquest of Iraq. My view is based on my belief that U.S. decline in the world-system is structural, and is not the result merely of errors in policy committed by previous U.S. governments. It cannot be reversed. To be sure, it can be managed intelligently, but that is precisely what is not happening now.

The structural decline has two essential components. One is economic, and one is political-cultural. The economic component is really quite simple. In terms of basic capabilities—available capital, human skills, research and development capacity—western Europe and Japan/East Asia are at a competitive level with the United States. The U.S. monetary advantage—resting on the dollar's use as a reserve currency—is receding and will probably disappear entirely soon. The U.S. advantage in the military sphere translates into a long-term disadvantage in the economic sphere, since it diverts capital and innovation away from productive enterprises. When the world-economy begins to revive from its now quite long-term stagnation, it is most likely that both western European and Japanese/East Asian enterprises will do better than U.S.-based enterprises.

For thirty years, the U.S. has slowed down this creeping economic decline relative to its major competitors by political-cutural means. It based its claims to do this on residual legitimacy (as the leader of the free world) and the continuing existence of the Soviet Union. The collapse of the Soviet Union undermined these claims severely and unleashed the growing anarchy of the world-system—"ethnic" wars in the former Soviet Union and Yugoslavia, civil wars in multiple African states, the two Gulf wars, the expanding cancer of the Colombian civil war, and the severe economic recessions in a number of Third World states.

Under Ronald Reagan, George Bush father, and Bill Clinton, the United States continued to negotiate with western Europe and Japan-East Asia to keep them more or less on the same our side in what have been essentially North-South struggles. The hawks under George Bush son have thrown aside this strategy and substituted one of unilateral machismo. The backs of everyone else have gone up everywhere, and the U.S. victory over Saddam will get them further up. This is not despite but precisely because of the fact that the rest of the world is so terrified.

On legitimacy, note two things. In March, the United States had to withdraw a resolution from the U.N. Security Council, which it introduced in hopes of getting a vote in support for the attack on Iraq. This was an issue that was really important to the U.S., one in which it invested all its efforts, including repeated telephone calls by George Bush to leaders around the world. It was the first time in 50 years that the United States was unable to get a simple nine-vote majority on the Security Council. It was a humiliation.

Second, notice the use of the word "imperial." Up to two years ago, to speak of imperialism was the reserve of the world left. All of a sudden, the hawks started to use the term with a positive connotation. And then, western Europeans who were not at all on the left began to use the term to express their worry that the United States was behaving like an imperial power. And since the collapse of Saddam Hussein, suddenly the word is found in almost every news story. Imperial(ism) is a delegitimating term, even if hawks think it is clever to affirm it.

In the history of the world, military power never has been sufficient to maintain supremacy. Legitimacy is essential, at least legitimacy recognized by a significant part of the world. With their preemptive war, the American hawks have undermined very fundamentally the U.S. claim to legitimacy. And thus they have weakened the United States irremediably in the geopolitical arena.

PERMISSIONS

I am grateful to the original publishers for their kind cooperation in granting permission for republication here.

ch. 1: "The Eagle Has Crash Landed," *Foreign Policy,* July–August 2002.

ch. 2: "The Twentieth Century: Darkness at Noon," in R. Grosfoguel and A. M. Cervantes-Rodriguez, eds., *The Modern/Colonial/Capitalist World-System in the Twentieth Century,* Westport, CT: Greenwood Press, 2002. Reproduced with permission of Greenwood Publishing Group, Westport, CT.

ch. 3: "Globalization or the Age of Transition? A Long-Term Trajectory of the World-System," *International Sociology,* XV, 2, June 2000.

ch. 4: copyright Immanuel Wallerstein.

ch. 5: "Islam, the West, and the World," *Journal of Islamic Studies,* X, 2, May 1999.

ch. 6: copyright Immanuel Wallerstein.

ch. 7: "Democracy, Capitalism, and Transformation," in O. Enwezor et al., eds., *Democracy Unrealized,* Ostfildem-Ruit, Hatje Kantz, 2002.

ch. 8: "Intellectuals in an Age of Transition," in W. Dunaway, ed., *Emerging Issues in the Twenty-first Century World-System,* Westport, CT: Greenwood Press, 2003. Reproduced with permission of Greenwood Publishing Group, Westport, CT.

ch. 9: "America and the World: The Twin Towers as Metaphor," in C. Calhoun et al., eds., *Understanding September 11.* New York: New Press, 2002.

ch. 10: "A Left Politics for the Twenty-first Century, Or, Theory and Praxis Once Again," *New Political Science,* XXII, 2, June 2000.

ch. 11: "Left Politics in an Age of Transition," *Monthly Review,* LIII, 8, Jan. 2002.

ch. 12: "New Revolts Against the System," *New Left Review,* No. 188, Nov.– Dec. 2002.

ch. 13: copyright Immanuel Wallerstein.

INDEX